1

Foreword

I had the great pleasure of meeting Diane, when she and Dan came on holiday to Gozo, prior to them actually moving here to live in September 2019. We first met at Jacks bar, also my local, run by her sister in law, I immediately really liked her, there was a special energy she radiated.

Some time ago she made me aware of the charity CatchU, that she was planning to start and the book she was writing that explains her reasons why. Having worked in the print and binding industry for 20 years prior to my retirement and also having published a book myself, I offered to proofread her book and she accepted. We met up weekly and spent many happy hours over a glass of wine, discussing the book and the charity.

This unique and amazing book, 'Daughter of a Murderer' is a true account of Diane's life story from the age of ten to the present day. What an emotional rollercoaster of a book, over 40 years of her life, shaped not only by her fathers actions and the loss of her mother, but also by both sides of her family and their responses to the tragic event.

I'm an avid reader of a wide genre of books, but I strongly resonate with a true life account and believe me, this book has it all.

I laughed, I cried, I empathised, it even changed some of my preconceived beliefs and I couldn't wait to get to the next chapter. Diane's book is a, 'no holds barred' - 'gritty'- 'tell it as it is' account of her life, she bares her soul for all to see. The content, really does deserve the right to become a best seller.

I salute her candid honesty and bravery in writing this book and will be there to support her with her CatchU charity.

We, as a society have come a long way in helping humanity to survive trauma, however what is available to help now, can and must be improved and expanded upon. What a tragedy that this was not available for Diane and her brother in their hour of need all those years ago.

Kay Treglown, Reiki Master and Hypnotherapist

A Message From Holly

You know when you skim a stone, it bounces several times off the water, and when it sinks it creates a circling ripple effect, well that's what trauma is! It hits you several times and there is a constant rippling tide of emotions. I was raised in this ripple, having a Mom who was always there....but there was a cloud there too.

Beaming to hand over my handmade Mother's Day gifts....to be greeted with a broken smile and teary eyes. I never went round to my Nan's for Sunday dinner, there was always an empty seat at performances that she should have been sat at.

The paths my mother took over the years are a representation of a system letting a child down. If she was given the correct help from a young age she would have learned that she's not alone and she would have learned how to cope and deal with the emotions moving forward.

The idea of CatchU is to help children deal with the trauma that has been thrusted upon them. My mother is an advocate for these children as she has lived through the hurdles.

This book will show you the effects that this type of trauma brings, it's a rollercoaster, I cried and laughed.

Well done Mom, I am so grateful I have you.

It's a circle, we're all connected.

I love you x

Contents

Introduction

Mother's are like buttons, they hold things together. When you lose a button, things fall apart. Across the globe there are children walking around with a button missing, some have a safety pin and profess to be ok, some remove all their buttons and hope no one notices, some spend their life looking for the one that's missing. All of these children know the man that ripped the button from their shirt. He is called Dad.

I'm Diane and my Dad killed my Mom. I wonder will you read on, you have all you need to know about me, after all. Many might be aroused and want to know more about the chronicle tribulations of a childhood trauma. Some will steer clear, it's deep, it's heavy and so depressing, they won't even go there. To be honest, I don't want to talk about it either, it's painful, personal and pointless, dwelling on an irreversible past. Our backgrounds are our backgrounds. We cannot go back and change them, we cannot do anything about them either. I'm not that special, there are over 5000 people just like me in the UK alone. However, protectionism forces us into a silent world of noise, which causes more harm. I guess, this is the humility needed to pave the road to trust and integrity.

'Daughter of a murderer' is about my loss and confusion, in a world of prejudice and exploitation, and the changes that are needed to support the rights of the child. I get knocked down and I get up again, more times than Floyd Patterson. It was a struggle that didn't kill me, it made me stronger. Of course, I had choices, I could have become an astronaut and flown to the moon, like everyone else. But my mission was more complex and required more preparation.

This book provides academic professionals and the general public, a glimpse into the real world of someone who has been there, someone who has worn the shirt, without the buttons. You need to read this from the beginning to the end, if you dip in here and there, you will not understand my journey and it won't make sense. It's a reflection of how I felt at the time. You may be alarmed by my tone, my remarks and my actions as I try to figure things out for myself. My opinions change over time as I study, work and live in this silent world of noise.

My desire is to end the shame, stigma and silence that surrounds children bereaved by domestic homicide or suicide as a result of domestic violence. My mission is to give these children a voice, so this book is dedicated to them, the silent ones. I want all children that are a victim of this crime to understand this is not their fault. Children have a right to feel safe, free from abuse and harm.

I wish to thank Barbara Parker and Richard Steeves for doing their long term effects of uxoricide study in Australia, it surpassed that of Harris-Hendricks, Kaplan and Black and made me realise I was pretty normal. I appreciate the years of academic research Dr. Bessel Van Der Kolk has completed on complex trauma, his work gave me the knowledge to appreciate the benefits of self care, feeling safe and socialising.

My gratitude goes to CatchU's Trustees; Claire Moore from Certain Curtain Company, my first trustee and a woman who understands the importance of acting for healing trauma and raising awareness of domestic abuse and healthy relationships; Kay Treglown, a hypnotherapist, reiki healer, for her wisdom, help and support and for proof reading this book; the wonderful Meeta Sahni for her direction, taking my trillion ideas to create a theory of change and develop a strategy; and the beautiful Arpu Kaur a devoted and dedicated human rights lawyer. And a special thank you to CatchU's first Patrons, Holly, Kay, Elanor, Gene, Zoe, Jayne and Sophie.

Finally, I would like to thank my family; my children, Holly and Nathan, for their love and support, despite sacrificing their own perfect childhoods because of intergenerational trauma and my wonderful husband Dan, for just letting me be me and providing unconditional love and laughter.

Chapter 1
Abandonment

On Saturday the 15th April 1978, Mom stood in the porch in her dressing gown, saying her goodbyes. She handed me my packed lunch and off I went to my first dance competition, aged 10, in Wales with the Gingham Girls. We met at the bus stop and excitedly boarded the coach. After a few hours travelling, we arrived and enthusiastically changed into our competition uniforms like contortionists from the confines of our seats. The older girls' sashes were covered in medals that jingled as they moved. As I tied the ribbon on my white plimsolls, I watched them in admiration, hoping one day I would wear a sash full of medals too.

We confidently competed as our music played in the massive resonating hall. Our timings were perfect, our lines were perfect, climbing onto our seniors shoulders, steady and proud. We watched the other troupes perform their routines, then we received our awards. I accepted my very first medal, beaming with pride. I was fascinated by the picture of a dance troupe in the centre and how the gold sparkled from the light that shined down on us. I felt overwhelmed with a sense of belonging which surpassed what I had felt about being a member of the school's, less successful netball team. Mr. Hooper, our coach, had trained us with military discipline for months and the hard work had paid off.

I was now part of a winning team, the bond between us was so strong, the Gingham Girls were like a second family. We sang songs on the coach journey home, celebrating together. It had been a wonderful but exhausting day. As the sunlight faded I drifted off to sleep. I woke up a few hours later with a sharp pain in my neck. We were nearly home. I took my medal out of my bag and held it in my hand. At 9pm we arrived back at the bus stop, in Cheslyn Hay and I hopped off the coach eager to show my parents what I had won. I looked around but couldn't see them amongst the other parents waiting to collect their children. I felt an uneasy sense of abandonment. Mom or Dad had always collected me from dance practice when it was dark. I knew something was wrong.

"It's OK, Diane, you can walk back with us" Lisa's mother said. She eased my anxiety. She presumed we would see Mom or Dad on the way. We walked on past Lisa's home and continued towards my street. As I turned the corner, I could see blue flashing lights outside my house. My pace quickened and my heart began to race. I sensed something dreadful had happened. I passed several police cars and an ambulance and raced up my drive, leaving my friend's mother to enquire what had happened with the crowd of concerned neighbours that were congregating in the street.

A young female police officer was guarding the house. She told me to get off the drive and said there was nothing to see, treating me like I was some random curious kid. I told her this was my house. She looked confused and didn't seem to understand what I was saying, so I repeated myself for a second time and proceeded towards the front porch. As I opened the door to my home, I was whisked up into the air and handed over the garden wall, to my Aunty Barbara next door. She quickly bundled me into her daughters' bedroom. Julie and Suzanne were playing with their Sindy dolls and had no idea what was happening round at my house.

The bedroom door opened after a few minutes, Barbara said for me not to worry and that my Uncle Malcolm was coming to get me. Julie put on her record player to cheer me up and played our favourite song; "Oh doctor I'm in trouble, oh goodness gracious me…..my heart goes boom baddy boom, baddy boom, baddy boom" I faked a smile.

I was relieved to see my uncle, having some expectation of getting clarification on what was going on. Like Barbara, he told me not to worry and reassured me everything was going to be alright. He refrained from telling me what had happened and just said he was taking me to my Nan. He was breathing heavily and his face looked serious, naturally I couldn't help but worry. He didn't know what to say to me so he didn't say anything, his silence frustrated me.

He pulled away heavy on the accelerator and drove like a racing driver, it seemed like we were flying. I rocked with every bend and holding my medal in one hand and my seat belt in the other, I somehow managed to remain seated. It didn't take us long to get to Nan and Gramp's house, in Wolverhampton. I was relieved to get out of the car. I cleaned my medal on my leg, wet by my sweaty palm and walked down the drive to their house.

Nan's house was always brightly lit and full of life but not on this night. The living room was unusually quiet and dim, the television was switched off and the only light came from a corner table lamp. I noticed Nan, Gramps and Aunt June each looked distraught and their eyes were red from crying. I noted the decanter and sherry glasses were on the coffee table, next to a box of opened tissues, I knew this was not a celebratory drink, they were drowning their sorrows. Sunny, their dog was pleased to see me. I stroked his head as Nan told me to go upstairs to her bedroom to sleep and they would talk to me in the morning. Sensing an unsettling atmosphere, I didn't ask any questions, I walked slowly up the stairs to my grandparent's bedroom, listening to them having a whispered conversation.

There cradled in my Nan's bed was my little brother, Ray, sound asleep. I was so pleased to see him. It was hard to wake him, I shook him frantically, convinced he would tell me what had happened. I was quickly disappointed by his response; he didn't know anything. As I stripped off to my pants and vest and folded my clothes onto the chair, he went on to tell me he was asleep in his bed and he remembered waking up to see strange faces, these people were all in his bedroom and he didn't know any of them. "Then Uncle Malcolm came and brought me here in my pyjamas" he laughed with confused embarrassment.

Nothing made any sense to me, where had my parents gone? Who were these strange people and what were they doing in our house? Had the police got them out? Why didn't Ray have a chance to get dressed? I got into my Gramps' bed and showed Ray the medal I had won. He seemed quite impressed and wondered if it was real gold. I wondered where my grandparents were going to sleep as he drifted back off to sleep.

Early the next morning, my brother and I sat uncomfortably on the sofa waiting to be told what had happened. Mom's family stood together in a united line in front of us. Aunty Linda, Aunty June, Nan and Gramps all showed concern in their eyes. Gramps had the duty of telling us and he didn't mince his words. "Your Mom is dead. Your Dad has killed her with a knife. He stabbed her in her heart. It happened in the back garden. Your Dad has been arrested by the police. Your Mom was having an affair. She was leaving home. It was a case of 'if I can't have her no-one will'."

I knew that this affair had something to do with a man called Benny but she hadn't told me she was leaving. The thought of my mother abandoning us was incomprehensible. The adults synchronised their cries like a pack of wolves and the heart-breaking sound triggered my emotions. I instinctively began to cry. Ray started to laugh and I instructively nudged him, it may have been a nervous reaction but I think this was the first time he didn't believe our wonderful, humorous, storytelling Gramps.

I initially thought about the logistics, where were we going to live and who would look after us? Then I quickly brushed aside my egocentric concerns, trivialised by the prominent and paramount needs of my maternal family. The family dynamics had instantaneously changed. I didn't think it was appropriate to share my concerns or seek their support when they, themselves, were suffering. "You're lucky, you're too young to understand" my heart broken Nan, ironically, said.

Cigarette smoke filled the air and sorrow suffocated their previously happy, settled lives. Solace was sought from the imperishable drink's cabinet. My grandparents, Elizabeth Barlow and Horace Barlow each had their own bottle of prescribed Valium tablets on the mantel piece, alongside a box of tissues and a newly framed photograph of my mother. Their eyes were open but their minds were adrift, tragedy struck and shell shocked. I observed their silent tears roll down their cheeks, deniably wiped away on auto pilot. I could hear their hearts breaking, as they drowned in their private grief upstairs. I had never experienced a death in the family before, I had to be strong when everything around me appeared to be broken.

Great uncles and aunts and distant family members would visit throughout the day, arriving with flowers, joining my grandparents in a traditional bereavement process which annoyingly prohibited sunlight and made everyone upset. They would talk about 'Pauline' the light of everyone's life, the soul of the party. It was interesting to hear their versions of my mother's life; as they shared their fond memories, I realised, I had nothing in common with them. I had only known her as my Mom and my relationship with her didn't seem to be as special as theirs.

Each visitor would talk about how difficult it must be for my grandparents and my Mom's sisters. They would leave flowers and cards "with sympathy" which gradually filled the room. It was like a florist, it smelt beautiful but the flowers didn't work. My grandparents had lost their much-loved daughter, their first-born child. My aunts had lost their precious big sister. It was dreadful to witness my family devastated by their loss. I didn't know what to do so I focussed on the practical things. I helped them out by doing the household chores. I gave them hugs, fetched the tissues and tried my best to make them all smile. I loved my family, I behaved well and did everything I could to support them.

However, despite my efforts, they were constantly whispering behind my back and this caused me such anxiety. I would sneak around the house like a secret agent, trying to work out what they were talking about. I would pretend to go upstairs and sit behind the banister and listen. I held a glass to the wall. I tip-toed into the kitchen and mastered how to slowly and silently open the kitchen hatch to listen. I knew they were plotting or hiding something from me. I felt like I was an insignificant outsider that couldn't be trusted with what they knew. I wondered if they were lying to me in some sort of sick minded cover up.

"Have you seen the front page of the Express and Star?" I heard Nan say to someone on the telephone. I wondered what it said and furtively rummaged through rubbish bags trying to find the newspaper reports but they weren't there. They didn't want me to know the truth. They deliberately turned the TV off during news reports but I could hear them whispering about what was reported to friends and family. Each time I lost the thread of the conversation. I didn't have a clue what was really going on.

Disbelief set in. I felt angry and betrayed that my mother had simply disappeared from my life without a trace. I was certain she would never have contemplated walking out on us. She had let me down, big style. I asked if I could see my mother. My request was frowned upon and conveniently rejected on the grounds that I was "too young to see her". It was also suspicious that my Uncle Malcolm, the only one to actually see her dead, still hadn't mentioned this to me. Had he been sworn to secrecy as he drove me to my Nan's? Additionally, I had overheard Uncle George say he was convinced he had seen 'Pauline' in town and she smiled and waved to him, he said he couldn't believe the news. I knew she had to be alive and she owed me an apology for her desertion.

I tried to analyse the situation. Yes, Mom was fed up with Dad, she might have left him. She detested him when he came home drunk and smothered her. He'd smile at me as he cuddled her and kissed her neck. He was so funny when he was drunk. I couldn't understand why Mom was always so miserable when he was at home. He tried his best to make her laugh by tickling her. "Leave me alone" she'd moan. He wouldn't let her go and he'd wrestle her to the floor. Prince, our dog would continuously growl and bark attempting to protect her. I'd be scared, thinking the dog would bite him but my Dad wasn't frightened of the dog. Mom would run off to the bedroom to get away. Dad would always reassure me they were just 'play fighting' surely he'd never kill her?

Mom would stay in her bedroom crying, while Dad would have me on his lap, tickling me to make me laugh. He'd whisper "You're Daddy's girl" in my ear and I would end up being on his side again. "Daddy is the strongest" we would shout out loud so Mom could hear us. Ray would run after her to check she was ok. He would come back and punch Dad as hard as he could in his beer belly but Dad would just laugh in hysterics. Ray wasn't sure whose side to be on. Sometimes he'd stay with us and join in the chanting. "Daddy is the strongest." She could never win, she was weak but she always got away from him eventually.

They didn't just 'play fight', they argued too. It was usually about money or cigarettes. Mom survived without either. Sometimes they completely ignored each other. I would relay messages to and fro. I knew it was an unproductive game to attain harmony in a dysfunctional relationship. I wanted them to be happy together but I have to admit my efforts in mediation were pretty pointless. In reality, they didn't like each other at all. The tension in the air only eased when we had visitors. I noticed how they put on a show and pretended to like each other when we had people round or when we went out visiting others.

They were two very different people. Dad was the boss, he was strong and clever, had lots of money and spent lots of time out with his friends playing darts, he always seemed jolly. He would take us swimming every Saturday and he would always help me with my homework. Mom was moody, she would slap me for talking like my father but that was because I knew she was 'thick', she couldn't read or spell, she had no money, worked in a factory, and spent most of her time cooking and cleaning until recently.

Things started to change when Aunty June, Mom's youngest sister was going through her divorce. Mom said she was feeling lonely so she started going out with her to cheer her up. I thought both Aunty June and Mom needed a cheer up, so I was happy for both of them. Having a happy mother meant the slapping stopped, so I was happier too. They had another friend called Michelle. They all got ready at our house and off they went for a girl's night out dancing. Aunty June would usually sleep over at ours. She was quite funny and I liked spending time with her. Mom didn't seem bothered about Dad and his ways anymore. She was earning good money at the factory and could afford to go out and enjoy herself. It seemed my parents were happy doing their own thing and my Mom certainly had a new lease of life.

Sometimes we went across the road to Nicola's house for a party. I would watch Mom dance with Benny, he was always gazing into her eyes, affectionately amused. From my seat I gained an eye level shot of their lust gyrating in a rhythmic pelvic thrust. I was revolted by the embarrassing situation as they were both visibly aroused. I looked at my drunk, oblivious father as he helped himself to another beer. I glanced over at Benny's ignorant wife, she continued to chat to her sister about the hard labours of motherhood. I saw it all and said nothing.

I caught my Mom secretly talking to Benny in the hall at one of our parties. "Let me introduce you to Benny" she officially said. I already knew who he was, he was Nicola's uncle. He looked like Benny from Abba, the hair, the stature, the beard and the clothes. He annoyingly ruffled my hair and said he'd heard a lot about me. I was a little confused by what he had heard and distanced myself from him. I was always sober so I noticed things. I peeked into Moms bedroom and found Dad and Aunty June were fast asleep in the bed. Strange, I thought but they were both ridiculously drunk and acting very stupid. I went off to bed at the end of the night. Mom was tidying up. Benny was the only adult that hadn't said goodbye. I assumed he was helping Mom or stopping over. The next morning, I noticed Benny had gone but Mom was lying on the sofa bed in the lounge, with a glint in her eye that said it all.

Despite my Moms newfound happiness, my parents were still arguing all the time. I was fed up hearing their rows, day after day. I would take Ray into the garden where we couldn't hear them. We enjoyed playing in the garden. We'd splash about in the paddling pool and push each other as high as we dare go on the swing. I'd hit the ground on the see-saw and he would fly into the air, leaving his seat in hysterics, hanging on for his life. I liked to see him laugh but he did worry about Mom and she worried about him. She fussed over him all the time. I wasn't jealous of their special relationship, he was the youngest in the family, he had always been her mommy's boy.

She wasn't much use to me anyway, she couldn't help me with my spellings because she was 'thick'. She said she didn't want me to pick up her bad habits. I felt disadvantaged having such a 'thick' mother and I told her so. She hit me for talking like my father. It was hard for me to do my homework and I was too embarrassed to tell the teachers. I didn't want them to know she was 'thick' but I guess she did encourage me to do well. One night, she gave me a loving kiss on my forehead and held my hand. "Promise me one thing Diane, you'll work hard at school, get a good career and not end up like me, scrimping and scraping, working your fingers to the bone in a factory". I reassured her that I would work hard. I told her that one day I would be a teacher. I knew I could be anything I wanted to be. I didn't take after my mother, I was clever, just like my Dad that's why I was 'Daddy's girl'.

I did, however, have a strange psychic bond with my mother. At school I had felt a stabbing pain in the lower right-hand side of my stomach. The head teacher was concerned and took me home in his car. Surprisingly, Nan opened the front door and told us that my mother has been rushed into hospital to have her appendix out. Whilst my mother was having her operation, the doctor came to see me and he diagnosed I had a rumbling appendicitis. It was a strange coincidence and Nan agreed.

When Mom came home, her stomach was sore and she struggled to walk. I told her how strange it was that I had a rumbling appendix whilst she had hers removed. "We must be connected" I said. She brushed aside my comments and being meticulously house-proud, complained to my Nan that the carpets weren't vacuumed. So of course, I would have known if she was really dead, waking up on the coach with a stiff neck didn't count. If he had stabbed her in the heart, I would have had a pain in my heart.

I had to speak to my Dad to find out what had really happened. I knew I wasn't getting all the facts from my secretive, whispering family. So on my request my dutiful Gramps, in silence, drove us to Cannock police station where Dad was being held. He waited for us whilst the police bundled us into a small dark room with wooden panelling. Dad came in wearing hand cuffs, accompanied by several police officers. I had never known "Daddy is the strongest" to cry but now he sobbed like a little baby. He was a pitiable emotional wreck and I felt instinctively sorry for him.

Restricted by the handcuffs, he tried unsuccessfully to put his arms around us. He crouched down and rubbed his wet bristled face all over mine. He was smothering me, like he smothered my mother and I really didn't like it. There was no room to manoeuvre and I felt quite claustrophobic. "I'm so sorry kids, I'm so, so sorry" he repeated the phrase over and over again. I felt traumatised by witnessing him in such a state. I couldn't cope seeing him that way. I was relieved to get out of the room. I left the police station without any further explanations. I was aware he had apologised for something and he was clearly suicidal.

My father's typical tough temperament had disappeared. Without his why's or how's, I was left to make up my own assumptions. My Dad didn't normally go around killing people. He had never killed anyone before so I believed it had to be a mistake or some kind of accident. And even with all the play fighting in the past he had only ever made Mom cry. I couldn't entertain the idea that he had deliberately murdered her. As a Christian, I had to forgive my suicidal father and I had to help my family get through their ordeal.

We were taken back to the car in silence and returned to my grandparent's home. We didn't discuss what had happened in that room. I sensed my grandparents really didn't care how my father was or if he was suicidal. How could my grandparents just stop loving him? With Dad locked away and Mom gone, I felt we were now a burden to my grandparents and I still worried about what was going to happen to us. With no support, I instinctively started to adapt to life, living in two very separate worlds, caught up in the middle, loved and simultaneously ostracised by both sides, I felt awkwardly alone and riddled with guilt.

You see, it was my fault my mother was dead because I wasn't at home to mediate. I could have stopped my father from killing her, had I been there. Yet undeservedly, I was ritualistically bestowed my mother's wedding ring and engagement ring. I noticed the thin gold had worn away on the back, broken beyond repair, like their marriage. I placed them on my finger in perplexed appreciation, they were far too big. What use were they to me? I couldn't wear them. Overseen by Aunt Linda, I placed them in my jewellery box for safe keeping. One day I would wear her rings, I would have to take her place.

It was my responsibility now to hold my family together. I felt I owed it to them, to help them through their trauma, to compensate them for their loss. My Dad couldn't help them, not in his state or whilst he was locked away in prison so I covered for him. I needed someone objectively to explain how I should tackle things, someone who didn't cry each time I asked them a question. I needed someone to give me advice but everyone around me was traumatised. I was no child psychologist but I knew my brother desperately needed help too.

I had Mom's rings but Ray was awarded my grandads war medals for being a brave soldier. I observed him locked in a repetitive world of play. He held two toy soldiers in his hands. The one soldier killed the other. The dying soldier cried out in pain and crashed to the floor. It wasn't normal for him to play like that but I didn't want to worry my grandparents, who had enough on their plate. They were happy to see him playing. He played at the top of the stairs, alone with his soldiers. It started to drive me mad listening to the noise of the dying soldier day after day.

At home, Ray had routinely played with his matchbox cars and the loop the loop track or he would build a house with Lego bricks. Soldiers and death were now a new obsession in his life. I didn't know if it was acquiring my grandads medals that had changed his behaviour, or if he was processing what he had witnessed. I knew he wouldn't have slept if he was worried about my mother. I tried to talk to him, to find out what he had seen but he said he just couldn't remember. I didn't believe him, he laughed as he spoke, he chose not to remember.

He had always got in my bed at bedtime for a story. Mom couldn't read so I was happy to do this as it got him ready for sleep time. He would go to the toilet and then to his own bed. Mom would need to change his sheets every morning, unless his bed was dry, then she made a big fuss and rewarded him with five pence. Ray moved into the box room at Nan's. I slept with Aunty June in a double bed and we'd talk about my mother for hours. These chats were more important to me than reading Ray a story. I wanted to know everything about the Pauline I had never known.

Ray still wet the bed and my Nan changed the sheets. He didn't complain there was no reward for dry beds. I knew he shouldn't be wetting the bed when he was eight years old but he couldn't help it. The speech therapy sessions he had resulted in better progress. Gramps would make fun of him as he couldn't pronounce his r's. "Are you all wight Waymond?" he'd joke. "Yes Gwamps, I'm all wight" he'd reply. He wasn't clever like me, but I loved him to bits and now with Mom gone, I knew I had to look after him. He needed mothering.

We were offered the choice of either staying with Nan and Gramps or going to live with Aunty Linda. I instantly chose Aunty Linda. I loved my Grandparents but they were set in their ways and with their loss, they were inconsolable and oblivious to my brothers' unhealthy mindset. We desperately needed some normality back in our lives and a break from their grieving. It wasn't easy living with them and it was obvious they weren't our real parents. I listened to them talking to strangers, whilst I played at the local park. They told them we were their grandchildren and they had to look after us. We were a burden to them and the talk of the town, the highlight of peculiar conversations. I was still me but these new people treated me differently. I noticed their looks of disgust, looks I had never experienced before. It was as though they were insinuating I was some sort of contaminated human being.

I had a special bond with my Aunty Linda, she was my Godmother, I was her only niece. She had taken me away on holiday with her, before she had her own children. Unlike my mother she had plenty of money and would spoil me with beautiful gifts. I was over the moon when she took me to have my ears pierced. She was a very important person in my life. I had always preferred being at her house than being at home with my parents arguing. I liked looking after my younger cousins, we had more fun. Aunty Linda used to be a nurse and was much braver than my mother. When Mom accidentally shut the front door on my finger it was Aunty Linda who took me to hospital and sat with me. Mom didn't like blood, she said she was tickled stomached and she couldn't drive, so it was Aunty Linda who came to my rescue. She loved me and knew how to cheer me up, the choice to live with her was easy.

Off we went house hunting with Aunty Linda and Uncle Malcolm. We were going to get a new home and all live together as one big happy family in Wolverhampton. I felt so excited when we looked at the first house. It was a lovely spacious home, full of light and happiness. I went upstairs to choose my bedroom. It looked like life was finally going to get better, my anxiety about being a burden to my grandparents drifted away with hope on the horizon for a bright future. Aunty Linda looked as delighted as me. We adored each other so to be moving in together was a perfect solution to our unplanned circumstances. But, all too quickly, after a talk, they changed their minds about buying the property.

I was her niece but I was also the daughter of her sister's murderer, that must have made things awkward. The commitment was too much to ask of them, they had three young children of their own and the expense of a bigger house, they said, made things impossible. Outwardly, I took what they said on the chin and showed my appreciation for their thoughtful offer, but inside, I was broken-hearted, I had been rejected by my closest relative. We were to remain a burden to my grandparents, in the community where I felt shunned, my anxiety returned.

We continued to stay with Nan and Gramps but their stiff drinks and the Valium didn't seem to help their darkened lives. I learned from them that the hardest thing for any parent to face was the death of their child. No parent should have to go to their own child's funeral. It's not the natural order of things. It's something that parents never come to terms with. They said there was nothing worse. My once happy family were converted into sad, heartbroken people and nothing, it seemed, would ever change the way they felt.

As my mother's replacement, I tried my hardest to put a smile back on their faces and light up their lives, like Pauline had. I tried to be the soul of the party and make them laugh. I worked hard around the house. I cleaned the cupboards out, washed the dishes, weeded the garden, polished and vacuumed the house. I attempted to make up for what my Dad had done to them. I tried so hard but when they looked at me all I could see was their never-ending sadness. And they continued to say how lucky I was that I was too young to understand.

As selfless as it may seem, it was them I felt sorry for. They had lost Pauline but my entire life had changed. My mother, my father, my home, my friends, my school, my dance club, and Prince were all gone from my life. I asked them where Prince was. My grandparents told me how they had bought Prince for my mother to cheer her up following the loss of her first baby, Julie. My older sister had given up her fight for life shortly after her birth. Julie would have been two years older than me. It would have been nice to have had an older sister. I had ended up with a disobedient black Labrador instead but I loved him.

I thought about the times Prince had played happily in the back garden with us. He would always escape if the gate was left open. He had fatally attacked Nicola's little dachshund dog whilst we were playing in the street with him. Prince raced over and bit into his neck. We stood there screaming, witnessing Prince dragging him to and fro, an action he had practiced daily indoors with the cushions from the sofa. I was powerless to stop my dogs rage, watching the blood splatter from the little dog's limp body and seeing my young friends traumatised by the death of their much-loved pet. We made sure the gate stayed locked after that day.

On the 15th of April, Prince had been found locked in the shed. I worried about him and what he had been through. I imagined him trying to protect my mother, witnessing her death. He loved my Mom. I wanted to cuddle him and check he was ok. I was told my father's friend was looking after him but he was constantly crying and refusing to eat. I asked Gramps if Prince could stay with us but having two dogs already, he said it wasn't practical.

Prince was put to sleep for being a sad and lonely dog. I felt the loss and sobbed my heart out, like my grandparents had done over my mother's death. I felt guilty for caring more for my dog than my mother but I didn't get to say goodbye to him. To them he didn't matter, he was just a dog. Prince had always been part of my family and I was sad not having him around. But like everything else he was gone and I had no choice but to accept the way things were.

The bedtime conversations with Aunty June were a great comfort to me. She told me all about their childhood growing up in Australia. She said Mom was such a happy person and she was always singing. They used to harmonise together and they sounded really good. I told her about a tape I had with my Mom singing happy birthday to me and how we could play it when I got my things. "I could play it every year on my birthday" I said. That idea made me feel warm inside.

Aunty June recalled the time they returned to England for their uncle's funeral. My Dad was there and my Mom had fallen in love with him because he was really good at football. He was only young but he had a promising career ahead of him, playing for West Bromwich Albion and back then West Bromwich Albion were one of the best teams in the country. I remembered his old scruffy suit case, with his football strip and boots, surplus to requirements, nostalgically stored above his wardrobe. Aunty June had liked my Dad but she hadn't wanted my Mom to stay in England and get married, in the end the family all stayed, they couldn't go back to Australia without her. That's how much they all loved her.

We talked about the factory, where she worked with my mother, making electric fires for Sun House Ltd. I learned that Mom had earned the highest wages on the production line because she was so quick fingered. June said she could never keep up with her. I realised that she wasn't as broke as she had been in her previous jobs. I told June how I had felt guilty about the night when we had gone to school together, discussing the plans for my school holiday to France. It was an expensive trip but my Mom was determined that I should go. I had never been away with the school before so I was very excited. I had read the list of the things I needed to take with me and Mom had made sure I had everything. The holiday she had worked so hard to pay for, wasn't going to happen and my old school had all that money for nothing.

We discussed Benny. I told her that I knew who he was, he was Nicola's uncle and he always turned up at parties. She told me how Mom used to dance with Benny when they went out and how happy they were together. Like me, Aunty June had kept the affair a secret but she thought Benny was just a Casanova and their relationship wouldn't have lasted long. "It wasn't serious" she laughed "your Mom just enjoyed the attention". I knew their relationship was actually more serious than Aunty June had realised. At least she had found happiness, I thought.

Aunty June reassured me that my mother really did love me, she hadn't wanted to abandon me, she was planning to get a home first. I was relieved to hear this after feeling betrayed. My mother was going to look after us after all. I could talk freely with Aunty June but it was always when I should have been sleeping. We'd both listen to what Nan and Gramps were saying when they lay in bed talking. It was Aunty June who showed me how to hold a glass to the wall to hear more clearly.

Like Prince, Gramps said it wasn't practical to have all of our belongings from our house because there just wasn't the room. We made a list of what we wanted the most. I thought carefully about what I should ask for, just my old treasured teddy and my most recent possession's. I reflected on my 10th birthday. Mom, yet again, had spelt my name wrong on the card. To "DaiNE" it had said. It didn't matter, what she lacked in her academic ability she had made up for in other ways. She wanted me to have a wonderful birthday and wanted me to look good so we went to the hairdressers first. I wanted my hair cut just like hers but with the fringe flicked to the right instead. Naively, I was striving for individuality but I become a mirror image of my mother. We walked back home hand in hand, both feeling glam and special.

She handed me my presents. I tore the paper in excitement to reveal a double Abba album complete with song lyrics. This was my first ever Album so it was pretty special. "Now you can read, you can learn all the words" she said. Mom already knew the lyrics; Abba was her favourite group and she loved to sing their songs. I liked reading the lyrics 'Cause you know I've got, So much that I wanna do. When I dream I'm alone with you, it's magic.You want me to leave it there. Afraid of a love affair, but I think you know. That I can't let go." That's probably why she was so attracted to Benny, he took a chance on her and it was magic.

The next present I opened was a tape recorder and Mom impatiently told me to press the play button. She had recorded "Happy birthday to you, happy birthday to you, happy birthday dear Diane, happy birthday to you." Her beautiful voice, made me feel special, it was a wonderful present. She held my hand and guided me into the hall for another surprise. It was a purple bicycle with a front shopping basket and a large saddle bag on the back. "Now this is for us to share Diane, I only need it to go shopping, now and then if that's alright with you?" I didn't mind sharing the beautiful bike with her.

My friends and family arrived for the party and Mom lit the candles on my cake. My Dad wasn't there, like most men, he didn't like kids parties. Everyone sang happy birthday and I felt quite overwhelmed being the centre of attention. I blew out the candles and made a wish. 'Please can I have my ears pierced?' It was a typical child's birthday party and everyone was happy. We played pass the parcel, musical statues and musical chairs. I noticed Mom stopped the music just at the right time so everyone won something. She was all about fairness. We all had a fantastic time. Mom and I held hands as we danced and sang like Dancing Queen's, it was a very special day.

I handed Gramps my list and asked if I could accompany him to help. He said it was best for me to stay with my Nan. I looked at her and she smiled, supporting his wishes. I couldn't argue with them. He set off to collect our belongings from our house. I sat there craving my material possessions, like I was getting some of my life back. He stormed back into the house a while later. I overheard him privately telling Nan "They were like vultures". My Dad's family had been taking things from our house. Our home was being emptied so it could be sold. I was disappointed to be told I hadn't got my growling bear. Gramps couldn't find it, even though it would have been easy to find, sitting proudly on my bed. I assumed he had carelessly forgotten it, he seemed very stressed so I didn't make a fuss. I didn't believe for one minute that someone would have stolen my teddybear.

I looked at my bike in the hallway, the saddle was raised up, Mom must have been shopping on the 15th of April, buying us something nice for Sunday dinner, I thought. No-one noticed me lowering the saddle on my bike for the last time, realising she would never use it again. I moved the bike into Gramp's shed out of their way. "I've got you all to myself now, no more sharing with Mom" I thought. I was trying to find a positive but it hurt so much. The rest of my things were placed on shelves in the verandah above where the dog slept.

The next day, I got my tape recorder and my tapes and took them up to the bedroom. I tried to find the one with Mom's beautiful voice singing happy birthday. Her voice had been purposefully wiped from the tape. It was just a tape but it was one I had preserved and now more than ever, I wanted to treasure it. I wanted to play it every year on my birthday. It was the only way I could keep her alive. She was gone forever. I took a deep breath and went back downstairs. I didn't say anything. I pretended it didn't bother me but I was furious and wondered who had done the deed. I didn't know who I could trust anymore.

On the day of 'Pauline's' funeral, I urged my Nan to open the curtains as it was a beautiful sunny day outside. They told me the curtains had to be drawn as a mark of respect. Everyone solemnly wore black clothing for the occasion. Ray and I were wearing our brightly coloured summer clothes. I told them Mom would have wanted them to be happy not sad. I pulled the curtain away from the window and let the sunlight flood the room. My Nan glared at me, horrified by my unruly behaviour and shut the sunlight out. They wanted everyone to be sad.

The reason people attend funerals is to say goodbye to someone who has died. I was still hesitantly contemplating reality, I wanted to see if she really was dead and that being the case, I too, wanted to say goodbye to her. However irrelevant I was, she was still my Mom. Gramps stated we couldn't go. "It's not a place for children" he said. He used the excuse, we were 'too young' again. I didn't think that was a valid reason. I knew he was lying. I was fuming inside, frustrated and confused. He didn't want me there, he reinforced my perception of being the outsider, the child of a murderer. I didn't cause a scene. I said nothing and accepted his decision. I knew it was a hard day for them. So my family went to say their goodbyes whilst the next-door neighbour babysat.

We didn't really know the lady next door and it was difficult to strike a conversation with her. She didn't really know what to say to us so she left us alone and kept herself busy making sandwiches in the kitchen. Ray and I went out into the back garden. Ray was playing army with the garden broom killing imaginary soldiers. I sat on a bench behind the shed and stared up at the sky. The clouds were a fluffy white and beyond them was a clear blue sky. I apologised to my mother that I couldn't attend her funeral. I promised her I would never go to anyone else's funeral because I couldn't go to hers.

The adults returned to the house and were all talking amongst themselves about 'Pauline' and what a wonderful, happy woman she was. The woman I had known had been miserable for years, but they didn't see that side of her. They didn't know how hard she slapped me, or that she cried in her bedroom after my Dad hurt her. They didn't see the look on her face when my Dad groped her or see how she struggled financially whilst my father went out drinking. Uncle George still believed it was her he had seen waving, he had waved back to her. Nan told everyone that she had seen the oranges in the fruit bowl juggling in mid-air. She believed it was my Mom making contact with her. I stood in the kitchen staring at the fruit bowl. She wasn't bothering to juggle the oranges for me.

I was feeling quite insignificant when Gramps handed me a gift from Mr. Hooper, my dance teacher. I wondered how he knew where I was. After all I had just vanished from Cheslyn Hay. It was nice that he had thought of me and bought me a scientific calculator. I wanted to thank him personally but Gramps said it wasn't necessary as he had thanked him on my behalf. Gramps informed me that it was an expensive piece of equipment and advised me to look after it.

I kept the calculator safe in the bureau in the front room. I had no real use for a calculator. No-one else made contact with me and I thought everyone had just forgotten about me. My grandparents' house was full of cards. I longed for a card from school or a letter from a friend but no-one seemed to care about what had happened in my life.

After the funeral Aunty Linda started to take me to Bushbury crematorium each week. It was full of people who had lost loved ones so I felt familiarly at home there, although I was always spooked by the howling wind that caught me just where my mother's ashes were laid to rest. I sensed this was my mother expressing her wish for me not to visit her, perhaps because I didn't go to her funeral or maybe because I felt sorry for my Dad.

I looked at the big ornate grave stones there. I would read them with intrigue, some said "beloved mother" and had angels surrounding them. I liked those head stones. I would polish a shine on Mom's tiny, insignificant slate, it said 'In Loving Memory, Pauline Ann Benton, nee Barlow, 1946 - 1978'. My mother wasn't a beloved mother, like the others but I still left her fresh flowers. We always had some left over so I would place a flower in the flower wells for each person around her. I wanted them all to feel loved, not forgotten.

Chapter 2
Two Worlds

I watched as Gramps cut my Fathers face from every photograph they had, even their wedding pictures. He stood outside burning them in a private ritual. He couldn't see me peeping through the window, hidden behind the net curtain. "What's Gramps doing Nan?" I asked. She claimed he was just burning some old rubbish. Perhaps she didn't want to upset me whilst my father was removed from the family album forever, burnt to a crisp. I went upstairs a few minutes later and found Gramps looking at the photographs he had carefully rearranged. He was crying his heart out.

How I wished I could have taken away his pain. I sat beside him and gave him a comforting hug and he smiled. We looked at the photographs together, it was a very special moment. I was relieved to see I was still in the album. Mom looked so happy in all of the photographs. I desperately wanted to have just one photograph but I didn't like to ask him. They had lost their daughter and I didn't want to take anything else from them. Photographs were all they had left.

Along with Mom's wedding rings, I had also been given Mom's old sewing box which was just a plastic Tupperware container. I remembered the job that she had before the factory, selling Tupperware products in people's homes. Off she would go with her suitcases full of goods to sell. We had lots of Tupperware containers in our kitchen cupboards but I don't think she ever made much money selling them. The sewing box signified her efforts to provide for her family so it was of some sentimental value. Inside were buttons she had collected for 'make and mend' moments, needles and cotton and safety pins 'to hold things together' these symbolised my newfound family role.

It was difficult to hold things together during the court case. We were sheltered from all the details. Gramps continued to hide the newspapers and turn off the TV each time they mentioned it on the news. I listened on the stairs, he was telling Nan how he had helped my Dad get off with murder. I didn't understand how he had helped him or what he had done to help. As usual, I lost the thread of the conversation to whispers. He was angry that Dad was only given three years for manslaughter. I was confused again. Three years was a long punishment for an accident, I thought. And as my grandad had helped him with the murder why could they not forgive him and I could?

Despite only being ten years old, I started thinking about my future and the day I would marry. "Will you not be at my wedding?" I asked them. I wanted the family to be united again and overcome this tragedy. I cried, pointlessly pleading with them to forgive him. I felt so guilty because I couldn't see things from their perspective. "You must forgive him, it was an accident" I said. Knowing I was a Christian, Nan explained she had different beliefs. She understood I loved my Dad but she was an atheist and clearly stated she would never forgive or forget what he had done.

I was hopeful when Gramps went to see my Dad in prison. Forgiveness had a chance. I don't know what they talked about, he didn't talk about it on his return. He just said he wasn't going there again. I imagined prison must have been an awful place. Gramps said he would provide the transport for his family and us to visit him though. At least my Dad would have us to cheer him up, I thought.

Winson Green prison was a strange eerie place, it gave me nightmares. We would go to the visitors centre first. It was an old shabby building situated across the road from the prison. For the first time in my life, I felt humiliation as I walked through the doors. I tried my best to hold my head high. The other visitors either distanced themselves or talked to each other about the crimes that had been committed, their injustices in life and their experiences with the penal system. It was an attention-grabbing world for a child exposed to such an alternative curriculum.

I listened to their, out of the ordinary, conversations, their language was terrifyingly captivating. I heard swearing in every sentence; God's name used in vain; anti-authoritarian comments; talk of drug addiction, theft and violence and I noticed they all depicted prisoners as victims of circumstance. The only real comfort was the amount of chocolate bar choices we had at the counter and the bottles of fizzy pop we could consume. Ray and I munched through several bars whilst we waited nervously to see our father.

The first time we left the visitors centre and went through the huge prison gates, a convict was hanging his arms through a first floor barred window and I wondered if it was my Dad. I stared up as I walked along but I couldn't see a face. There was a white wall in the yard that appeared to have excrement smeared over it and I naively speculated if they had enough toilets. Another emaciated prisoner with a bald head was sweeping the yard, I wondered if we could trust him. Peculiarly, on the next few visits to the prison the same man was there, sweeping the yard, I wasn't as scared and the vilification of the establishment started to fade.

We stood in queues and watched the adults being checked for drugs. I didn't know what drugs were, but I knew some of the adults didn't like being treated like criminals. They were angry towards the prison officers and let them know so. The prison officers didn't care that I was frightened. They didn't even smile when I looked at them. They seemed quite heartless people, empowered by their uniforms and the huge bunch of keys attached to their waist bands. I hated the place, but I felt I had to go there and suffer a few hours, out of duty to my poor father who had to live there every day.

We would sit in the visitor's room at a table, whilst all the other prisoners sat down with their families. Then after a while, from another door Dad would appear. I wondered why he never came in with the other prisoners. I noticed how they would pause their communication with their visitors and glare over at him with evil in their eyes. I assumed he came in separately because he wasn't really a criminal like the others were. I thought it must have been hard for him being in prison with such horrible, bad people. I was oblivious to the fact he was actually segregated because he was the serious offender. The other prisoners, like ordinary folk, didn't approve of men who murdered their wives. I just sensed they were bad people and worried about my poor Dad being with them.

I was always relieved to see him walk through the door, he was still alive. He would have a big beaming smile, pleased to see me. It seemed as though he appreciated us more as he held his arms out for a cuddle. It was obvious he must have made a mistake, he must have been sorry. He became the doting father, publicly displaying how much we were loved and I liked that feeling. He never actually spoke about what had happened. I never brought the subject up, we just talked about trivial things. He would ask how Mom's family were but I could never tell him the truth. I would always say they were OK. I sheltered him from the reality because if he had known the truth, I know he would have killed himself. I was hanging on to my only living parent.

He looked remarkably smart in his prison uniform. He was always sober and he worked out in the gym so he looked fit and well. For the first time in my life, I felt really proud he was my Dad. During the short visit I would feel like a normal child with her father. We would eat more chocolate bars, drink more fizzy pop, my aunts gave Dad cigarettes and everyone on the surface appeared to be happy. Ray and I would play in the children's corner whilst Dad spoke privately to his sisters and then he would give us a loving kiss and a hug goodbye. His sisters would hug him with tears in their eyes, knowing he was returning to his cell. I felt so guilty knowing he had lost everything and I was free to return to the warmth of my family.

On the way home, Ray and I were sitting very quietly on the rear seat of the car, with Aunt Joan. Gramps tried to encourage a conversation and asked how 'Ron' was. Aunt Hilda said he seemed OK but said it was disgusting that we only got half an hour a month with him and then she complained about the time spent travelling and waiting to see him. The car abruptly came to a halt and we all jolted forward. "How dare you complain about the time you had with him. I will never see my daughter ever again!!!" Gramps bellowed. He never took us to see my Dad again and who could blame him, how insensitive was Aunt Hilda. She had no idea how hard it was for my grandparents to deal with their loss. After that day he would drop us off at Aunt Joan's and we would take the humiliating prison bus to the prison.

I listened with the glass on the bedroom wall for regular updates. I heard that our home in Cheslyn Hay was eventually sold and Dad's bank balance was accruing interest whilst he served his time in prison. I assumed this meant those nasty prisoners were interested in spending his money. Dad offered to give Gramps some money for looking after us. I thought that was a kind gesture as they were struggling financially to buy us clothes and pay for school trips etc. Gramps refused the offer of help and said he didn't want any of his 'blood money'. My Dad was trying his best to look after us. They preferred us to do without rather than take from a murderer.

I heard Gramps talking to Nan about divorce settlements and how my mother was entitled to fifty percent but because he was charged with manslaughter, he received all the money. He raised his voice "That man has made money from her death." This information didn't make sense, the money was no use to her if she was dead but Gramps was fuming about the injustice.

Dad, on the other hand, was devastated about the selling price, he told Aunt Joan, on a visit, how he had lost thousands and believed it was worth much more, after the work he and my Gramps had done to it. I thought about the extension they had built, the modern fitted kitchen, the stone fireplace and the beautiful tarmacked new driveway. Then, I wondered if my mothers' blood was still in the garden and if that had put people off buying it. My poor Dad had been ripped off and Gramps spoke about it as some kind of windfall. I didn't understand their difference of opinion and like most ten year olds, I was oblivious to inheritance law.

During all of our trauma, education had continued. We got a new school uniform and went to Claregate Primary. Gramps told us what to say. He didn't think it was right to lie but, in his experience, children were cruel, if they knew the truth, they would turn nasty. We were told to say that our Mother had died of cancer and our Dad worked abroad. The children were friendly but naturally curious about where I had come from. They were very nosey and wanted to know all of my business. As I told my lies, I was soon introduced to John Purcell, another boy in my class who had also lost his mother to cancer, comforted by our common bond, John tried to befriend me. I hated lying to him and fooling my peers.

The lies proved to be more difficult when I went to a friend's home after school. Her father had asked me where and what my father was doing abroad. Gramps hadn't told me what to say so I nervously said he was a builder and he was building a house somewhere. He wasn't abroad, he was in prison but he was building a house, it was made of match sticks. I didn't like lying to people and felt so ashamed, especially with the high publicity, on the television and in the newspapers, those inquisitive adults probably already knew my Dad had killed my Mom. They most likely thought I was delusional and had adopted some kind of coping mechanism by fantasising about a perfect fictitious life.

I thought it was bizarre that none of the school teachers spoke to me in private about my mothers death and the situation I now found myself in. No-one asked how I was coping. I wasn't offered any support but I needed it. I was sure the teachers would have watched the news and read the newspapers and known all about it. Perhaps they didn't want to get involved with the daughter of a murderer. I thought my grandparents might have told the headmaster the truth but they were traumatised and I didn't clarify what had actually been said to him. It just seemed odd to carry on regardless.

My music teacher, Mrs. Nicholas seemed to know something. She looked at me reassuringly, her eyes showed concern but she never said anything. She told the class we were going to learn a new hymn and began to play the tune on the piano. I put my hand up with excitement and said " This was my favourite song at my old school." "Would you like to sing it with me" she said. She patted her piano stool calling me over. She smiled triumphantly as I stood at the piano. Everyone was sat waiting to hear the new girl sing but no sound came from my mouth. I stood there full of embarrassment. I couldn't 'ask the Lord his strength to lend'. I couldn't ask anyone to help me. I had lost my singing voice, along with my faith.

I asked God to prove his existence, that night, in my bedroom. I asked him to move something in the room. I looked around but nothing moved. I asked if he could see me. I was invisible and needed more than the Lord's strength to get through this nightmare. Life was going on without my mother and I was finding it harder and harder to simply pretend nothing had actually happened. Even God, didn't want to help me. He didn't love me. How could he? I didn't even like myself, my Dad was a prisoner, he had killed my Mom and I had become a liar.

It seemed absurd, after my mother's murder that I sat alongside my class mates making a Mother's Day card. Everyone wanted to make a card for their mother, except for me. I said nothing but felt confused. The teacher didn't acknowledge my dilemma. I created a beautiful flower on the front, inside I covertly addressed it to my Nan. She received it well, after all she was my mother's mother but it was still a heartbreaking moment for both of us. Mother's Day had now become something that signified loss for both of us. It warranted a two-minute silence in her memory but there was never any recognition, it was like she had never existed.

I started to learn to play the recorder. Music took my mind off what had happened. My grandparents kindly tolerated the piercing shrieks as I practiced upstairs in the early days but I soon got quite good with Mrs. Nicholas's help. Nan sat crying in the town hall when I performed a solo, playing the theme tune to Watership Down, in front of a huge audience. It was ironic that the song 'Bright Eyes' was about the suspected death of a loved one. It was a special memory my Nan treasured. She was very proud of me that day and she told me my mother would have been too. I doubted Mom was proud, I had forgiven the man that had killed her and I was lying to everyone, covering up her murder.

I wanted to know what she thought of me so I experimented with a Ouija board. There were five of us in my friends shed, sat around the table, when the glass began to move. It spelt the word Mom and then flew across the table onto the floor. Everyone thought it was John's mother who had really died of cancer that had made contact. I couldn't get out of the shed quick enough. Terrified by the experience, I never went near the shed again. I was scared of my mother's angry spirit and needed to be with someone all the time. I never told my grandparents about the experience with the Ouija board. It was something I sensed I shouldn't have dabbled with. It wasn't the normal thing to do at a friends house and I didn't want them to think I was possessed by evil.

In the summer holidays I would go with Gramps to work in his office, whilst he organised the builders on site, giving them tasks and referring to the building plans. I felt important sat in his office with a paper and pen, making notes for him. Other times I would go with my Nan to Aldersley stadium to help her out with the cleaning. I enjoyed seeing the athletes' practice. Tessa Sanderson would chat with me sometimes whilst she was training. I didn't tell her my Mom was dead or that I had won a gold medal that year. I didn't think she would want to know as it wasn't for throwing a javelin.

I admired her as I watched her practice. I watched her on TV avidly when she was competing. She encouraged me to focus on athletics but javelin wasn't for me. I tried gymnastics for a while and took part in a county competition. I noticed how stiff my previously supple body had become. Nan had been giving me comforting puddings everyday and although I didn't look overweight, I felt heavy. I became a member of Claregate Primary's netball team instead. I started to find myself and supported by Mrs. Nicholas, I even discovered my singing voice again and joined the school choir.

We spent a week in Cornwall with our grandparents, accompanied by Great Uncle George and Great Aunt Kath. The adults spent a lot of time eating and chatting and it was good to see my grandparents smiling again. Nan and Kath played bingo for hours. We sat and watched Gramps and George play lawn bowls. We visited the local tourist attractions and spent time on the beach. Gramps was worried as Nan, a non-swimmer had disappeared on her lilo inflatable. We walked along the beach together, she was nowhere in sight. We thought she was gone for ever. She had dozed off to sleep in the sunshine and was luckily noticed by a ship's crew as she drifted out to sea. They woke her up and brought her back in a rescue boat. We were all relieved to see her back on dry land.

Soon after, I was on another holiday in Aberdovey with my school friends and the wonderful headteacher, Mr. Rouse who always made me smile. The days were spent developing team building skills, walking, in our kagool's and back packs, reading maps, making fires, building camps and canoeing down river, it was so much fun. We learned a Welsh song and sang proudly in the church hall. I helped clean the dormitories and washed our pots and pans, all in the name of building resilience. I noticed how my cleaning experiences at Nan's had put me ahead of my peers. It was a relief to get away from my traumatised family and just be a normal child like everyone else. It wasn't the trip to France that Mom had paid for but I felt blessed to have a school holiday.

My bedtime talks with Aunty June continued. We would talk about my friends at school or her friends at work. There was a man that liked her, she told me all about him and asked for my advice. She deserved some happiness so I insisted she went out with him. She had found a wonderful, caring man and she became quite loved up. I was pleased to see her go out and enjoy herself with Mick. Like me, she still missed my Mom but Mick had brought her happiness. It had taken me a year to settle into my new life and I was finding it easier to hide the prison visits from my new friends. Like Aunty June, I had started to live my life but things were about to change again.

My grandparents sat us on the sofa, where they had first told us Mom had been killed. I knew something bad was about to happen. Gramps, again, had the duty of delivering the news. "We think it would be better if you move in with your Aunt Joan" he said. Despite behaving well, being helpful around the house and trying to cheer them up, they didn't want us to live with them anymore. I couldn't understand why our loving grandparents wanted us to leave them.

Gramps went on to explain "Your Dad is moving to Featherstone prison and he will be getting weekend releases." Nan interrupted him "I DO NOT want your dad, after what he has done, turning up on our doorstep!" she said. They had initially said they understood that he was our Dad and we loved him. They had said it was OK for us to see him but they didn't say there would be a future cost. It was our choice to continue contact with the man that had killed their daughter, consequently, we could no longer live with them. I longed for my life to return to normal but as the daughter of a murderer, I had no choice, I now had to deal with their rejection. I didn't know what to do or who to turn to.

Chapter 3
Ronnie's Babby

We moved to Aunt Joans that weekend. We didn't get to say goodbye to our school friends or our teachers. I had just disappeared from their lives, just like I did when my mother was killed. My brother and I were taken to the community centre in Featherstone for a medical check. We were asked to remove our clothes, down to our underpants and asked to go into the large hall. I felt very embarrassed about doing this. My breasts had begun to form and I didn't really want to show them off to anyone. I walked nervously into the hall with my arms folded to conceal my breasts.

Three very serious looking strangers were sat behind a row of tables. They looked very official, smartly dressed and equipped with clip boards, paper and pen. They asked us individually to cough, turn round and then told us to put our clothes back on. The official strangers did not explain the purpose of this humiliating experience. I assumed it might have been something to do with Dad's weekend releases or Aunt Joan becoming our foster parent or maybe they wanted to check we had no bruises from physical abuse from living with Nan and Gramps. As a vulnerable child, you just do what you are asked to do without questioning. I felt degraded and confused by the whole experience.

Aunt Joan, was also my Godmother, apart from the prison visits, she was almost a stranger to us. She was married to Uncle Geoff and they had three sons, Paul, Stephan and Martin. Ray no longer played alone with his dying soldiers. He enjoyed spending time with his cousins and playing marbles seemed to give him a new lease of life. I was relieved to see such a positive change in my brother. He shared a bedroom with the boys and I had the little box room. It was strange lying in my bed at night listening to my cousins calling out "Goodnight Mom" from their beds. I was conscious of how dissimilar our lives now were. They had both their mother and father at home. My Dad was in prison. I had no Mom to kiss goodnight and I felt very alone in that box room.

Gone were my comforting bedtime talks with my Aunty June and the warmth and security of my Grandparents home. I missed them so much my heart ached. I understood that things were difficult for my mother's family. In a way I thought my sacrifice might make them happier, after all, we were a constant reminder of what had happened. Gramps had said they thought it would be 'better' if we lived at Aunt Joans, perhaps he meant, they would heal quicker without us and their lives would go back to normal, I thought.

There were no family talks ending in tears at Aunt Joan's house and no-one appeared to be grieving for my mother. We didn't go to the crematorium to lay her flowers. Instead we were all looking forward to Dad's release date and counting down the weeks. We could have simply forgotten my mother had ever existed but I started to think more about her whilst I lay in bed at night. I thought again of how I could have helped, if only I had been there for her. If I hadn't have gone to some stupid dance competition Mom would still be alive, I thought.

I opened my jewellery box to hold her rings and feel close to her but they were gone. I searched through all my belongings but it was pointless. The rings weren't there. I had lost the most precious things in my life and I felt heartbroken. I didn't say anything to anyone. I didn't want anyone to know I had not looked after them properly. Now all I possessed was her old Tupperware box. I looked inside and noticed a spare bottle green button, for my old school cardigan and a big brown one for my Dad's cardigan. I placed the brass thimble on my finger and tapped the top of my bedside cabinet. It was something so small and irrelevant but it had belonged to my mother and it provided protection from pain.

Aunt Joan was a kind and good hearted mother. Just like my Mom she kept a perfect home. She seemed to have a hard life, washing and ironing, cooking and cleaning and caring for her frail mother as well as five children. She really was the English version of Super Woman and Super Nanny couldn't have done a better job. She amazed me how she could knit someone a jumper using a pattern, click clacking away ten to the dozen, and still hold down a conversation whilst watching TV. How she did this I wasn't sure but that was the nearest she seemed to get to relaxation.

She would give us 10p every day for a treat and we would walk down to the sweet shop together. She didn't have a lot of money but I guessed it got the children out of the house for a while and gave her a break. Featherstone village was in desperate need of regeneration. The air was polluted with smog and it smelled of burning coal. The old grey council houses were blackened with soot. The estate had been built to house the miners that worked at the local colliery but this had now closed and many people were unemployed.

We would walk past The Red, White and Blue. It was the only pub in the village. Whilst the locals expenditure on alcohol maintained the effects of poverty, The Blue, as it was known was a prosperous business with a ferocious reputation. The Featherstone folk stuck together in tough times. They were hard faced people and they all knew my Dad. "Ere's Ronnie's Babby" they would say in their Black Country common accent, the one my mother had trained us not to use. Maybe I was a snob but I didn't feel I belonged in Featherstone. This was where poor people lived but nevertheless the sweets at the shop reassuringly tasted the same.

Uncle Geoff was a very mysterious man. When he was at home, he never said a lot. He would read the newspaper or watch horse racing on the TV. He didn't do anything to help Aunt Joan but demanded she waited on him. My Dad had been the same. I assumed that was what women did but I was confused, it had never felt that way in my grandparents home or at my Aunt Linda's. Uncle Geoff scared me with his grunts of disapproval and how he shouted at his boys, so I kept out of his way.

I was spending a lot of time with Aunt Joan, she was teaching me to knit and I enjoyed developing a new skill. One day her eldest son, Paul, for some strange reason, tapped my glass whilst I was drinking and he hurt my lip. He laughed triumphantly. I waited for him to take a drink and I returned the joke to teach him a lesson. Unfortunately, his lip exploded with blood. "What have you done to him" Geoff bellowed. Despite the split lip being an accident, he thought I was like my father, trying to murder his son. He chased me around the house ranting and I thought he was going to kill me. I was terrified and remained in my room until he had calmed down.

Whilst at Aunt Joans, we had no contact with my Mom's side of the family. I missed them so much. I knew they knew where we were and hoped that sometime they would visit us or at least call for a chat on the telephone. I thought they would want to make sure we were ok. I had some stupid internal belief that they really did love us. We were in their family album. It didn't make sense. I couldn't understand how they could simply forget we existed. I knew in an instant they had stopped loving my Dad but we were their daughters children, surely they couldn't just stop loving us too. As the weeks turned into months, I was devastated, as I realised they didn't really care about me or my brother.

Mr. Jeavous, Dad's probation officer was the one and only professional person who actually spoke to me and that was only on one single occasion. He asked how I felt about my Dad moving to Featherstone prison, of course the conversation was all about my Dad, but it was nice that he was interested in how I felt. I was happy we didn't have to go to the awful Winson Green Prison any more. This prison was much nearer to Aunt Joan's house and the visits were much more child friendly, frequent and longer. I didn't tell Mr Jeavous how sad I felt about not seeing my family, he was there for my Dad, not me. My Dad seemed really happy and he loved the new gym so the move to Featherstone prison was a positive move.

I didn't enjoy moving to my new school though. St. Johns Middle School was a lot larger than Claregate Primary and somewhat terrifying. I travelled to school by coach. Again none of the teachers asked if I was OK, no one mentioned my mother and I assumed that teachers didn't really care about children's home lives. They didn't seem to notice how terrified I was about meeting new people and what I should say. They were all busy and didn't have the time to talk to me. I thought, perhaps they knew who I was and were ashamed to work with the daughter of a murderer. The school was so unprepared for my arrival that I spent the morning in Year 6. I had found the work quite difficult so I was relieved to find out I was in the wrong year.

In Year 5, Donna Nichols was assigned to look after me and show me around. Donna seemed a popular girl and she introduced me to her gang. The tall, red head was desperately thin, very loud and had an evil laugh like a Tommy gun. Her friends were all quiet and shy. Donna's Dad didn't live with her and she lived in a council house close to the prison. She had an uncle in the prison, serving time. I was pleased we had things in common. I told her my Dad was in the prison for killing my Mom. Gramps had warned me that children would be cruel if they knew the truth but my Mom had always told me to be honest. "No-one like's a liar" she had said. I wanted to be liked, I didn't want to lie anymore. It felt good to be honest, at least now I would get the peer support I was so desperate for.

It turned out, Donna was the school bully and the thoughtful teachers had put me in her care. They didn't like Donna and perhaps they thought the daughter of a murderer would be some sort of hard knock, that was tough enough to sort her out. Donna laughed at my expense, which came as a welcome relief to her gang members who were all terrified of her. I was extra vulnerable so she bullied me the most. "At the gates" she would say and I knew she would want another fight. When school ended each day, I would run as fast as I could, to the safety of my coach, my heart pounding. Donna would watch me and fire her evil laugh.

My rumbling appendix pains would start as soon as I got out of bed. My stomach seemed to know I had to spend another day with the bully, Donna Nichols. Gramps had been right, she was cruel. I should have lied but it was too late. I never reported the bullying to the teachers for fear of reprisals and another beating. I didn't want to worry Aunt Joan, she had enough to deal with. I told my Dad on the next prison visit and his advice was to simply hit her back, twice as hard. His advice wasn't helpful. I wasn't that brave.

The bullying continued and I spent most of my break times hiding in the cold toilets. I made friends with Jayne, who lived in Featherstone with her mom, sister and her nan. We caught the coach together and chatted on route to school. She was in Donna's gang too. She said she wasn't scared of Donna but she wasn't brave enough to stop her bullying me. I liked Jayne but Donna was very jealous of our friendship and tried desperately to break us up. Having Jayne to turn to made my life a little easier. She was a good friend.

Weekend releases came and I can't say they were anything special, unlike how I had imagined them. I had longed to spend quality time with my father but it wasn't to be. We would go for drinks in the Blue and then go to Nan Benton's home, a traditional rundown council house in Hilton Road. Aunt Joan did her best to keep it clean but it had a horrible musty smell, everything was old and worn and it made me feel depressed.

My Dad's older brothers were still living at home with their mother. Trevor and Bernard were bachelors and barely grunted in conversations so it didn't surprise me that neither had ever found a wife. Trevor was very thin and distant, despite being my Godfather, I was lucky to get a smile or a greeting from him. Bernard was massive, he always wore white shirts, bursting at the buttons and trousers, held up by bracers. He spent his days proudly printing newspapers for the Express and Star and his evenings sat watching TV, gorging on masses of food. They both appeared to care for their elderly and frail mother though.

Nan Benton was a very strange old lady, she had no teeth and sat in a rocking chair. She stared at the TV with her tongue hanging out. Her name was Doll and like an old neglected doll she slept with one eye open, a false eye that stared right through me. She wiped her weeping eye socket with an old handkerchief. I watched her false eye fall and roll across the floor. Dad picked it up for her, she cleaned it off and popped it back in. I didn't know why she had a false eye but it made me cringe.

She would neurotically rock in her chair, prodding a smelly neglected spaniel with her walking stick. She would talk to me as if she was in another world with people I couldn't see. I never understood who she was talking to and she startled me with her weird comments. Dad would just tell me to ignore her, saying she wasn't of a sane mind. I was frightened to speak to her and didn't want to get poked with her stick so I would sit still, in silence, next to her. I would stare at her in bewilderment, she was nothing like my other Nan.

Dad was sleeping on a sofa in her front room during his weekend releases. There were boxes of our stuff stored everywhere ready for when Dad got out of prison. I was pleased to see the boxes as there was a chance of finding my bear but Dad asked me not to open them. We ate well but the cutlery was old. I noticed a green tinge and a peculiar smell so I used my fingers to eat. We drank gallons of fizzy pop from the kitchen pantry. I never wanted to go upstairs to use the toilet as it was dark and spooky. In emergencies, I'd use the outside toilet, without touching the damp blackened walls, using torn strips of newspaper in place of toilet paper. We washed our hands with a strange smelly carbolic soap.

Ray and I would play at the bottom of the garden getting covered in coal dust and nettle stings. We would find a dock leaf to heal the pain. We went out of the gate and ran down the alleyway, quickly returning as scary strangers walked towards us. I also had a phobia for Nan's nasty black cat that had clawed me several times when I had tried to befriend it. We would endure an afternoon of watching football and wrestling on the television and then suffer the monotonous football results. The three brothers would mark off their pools coupons and whine about not winning anything.

Sometimes we visited Dad's sister's home, escaping the boredom of the grunting uncles and Gran's deranged hospitality. Aunt Hilda's welcome wasn't much better. She wasn't the prettiest woman but she couldn't be blamed for her looks. When she bent over, her 1960's crimplene dress rose along her fat thighs to reveal her backside, you never, ever wanted to see this by choice, I would always turn my head in disgust.

As common as muck with a stern look she'd say to my Dad "Ow do Nippa, yow ay got long now av ya?". Nippa was Dad's nickname as he was the baby boy of the family. I looked around her shambled home, full of dirty piles of washing, worn dirty carpets and grimy walls. I never knew where to sit, always avoided the toilet and felt the need to wash when I left her home. Although her sofa was the identical make to ours, I assumed it wasn't ours because it was dirty, ripped and burnt. If my long lost bear was in her house I wouldn't have wanted it back.

Aunt Hilda was always shouting at her kids and bossing them around. I felt so sorry for her children having to live with her in such poverty and squalor. She was quite a terrifying woman but Dad said she had a kind heart when you got to know her. She hadn't been kind hearted to Gramps so I never really wanted to know her. The showmen from the fairground on the field at the rear of her property used her electricity. They seemed to like her. They paid her lots of money and gave her free goldfishes. She was also a widow and I guess being a single mother, life was hard for her so she needed that tough persona just to get by.

I was toughening up myself. I suppose, having four boys in the house, I was a little outnumbered when it came to our pastime activities. Across the road was a wood and we spent our hours climbing the horse chestnut trees in the autumn. I remember stretching across a branch at the top of a tree to acquire a fine-looking conker and taking the quick way down, leaving pieces of my skin on every branch I hit. Battered and bruised, back on solid ground, I showed my boys the champion conker, I still had in my hand. It remained victorious for about three weeks.

We also used to have arm wrestles and play peanuts, a knuckle bending exercise where the word peanuts signified submission. Ray and Paul were both pretty strong contenders but I stood my ground and beat them both on many occasions. It was a shame I couldn't do the same with Donna Nichols at school. I would see her whispering to others and hear the Tommy gun laughing at me in my lessons. I found it difficult to focus on my work when all I was concentrating on was surviving the day.

Meanwhile, Dad completed a NEBs Diploma in business management. I praised him, I thought he was sensibly thinking about our future and I asked him what business he was going to set up when he got out of prison. He laughed in confusion and said it just looked good and passed the time. As a twelve year old, I thought he could have shown more responsibility. I knew my Dad was never going to be a respectable business man. He wasn't as clever as I had once believed. He was just a prisoner who quietly passed his time building matchstick models. He made me a jewellery box, lined with velvet, with my name painted on the front in beautiful letters. He then made me a sewing box, with draws, again lined with velvet. We liked his masterpieces and he ended up making a Windmill for Ray and gypsy caravans for his sisters. None of my friends had unique handmade gifts like these so those constructions made me feel unusually special and loved.

I threw away Moms old Tupperware sewing box and placed the contents in my new specially made box. The buttons, press studs and cotton reels, I had inherited, might be useful in the future, I thought. I had acknowledged that my father would be released from prison and we would be an ordinary happy family again. We planned to return to our village in Cheslyn Hay. I could finally rekindle my old friendships and I hoped my life would at last get back to normal. My Dad had shown the prison officers exemplary behaviour and they had all seen what a good father he was. He was getting released early as planned. Dad had served eighteen months and from my perspective that had seemed such a long time. I believed he had served his punishment to society. I counted down the days to his release when I could finally leave St. Johns and be free from my suffering, of that evil bully, Donna Nichols.

Chapter 4
Living With The Murderer

Whilst I had escaped Donna Nichols, my hopes were dashed again. We didn't buy a nice new home in Cheslyn Hay and live happily ever after. Instead, we moved into a council house in the next village. It felt like we were back in Featherstone, living in dire poverty. The dreary old house was a third refusal, which meant three families had turned it down and I could clearly see why. The grass was almost as tall as I was, concealed by an overgrown hedgerow and separated by a hidden concrete path accessed by an old rusty gate. The kitchen had an old solid fuel stove. The lounge had an old coal fire. The whole house was filthy and it needed decorating completely. I felt ashamed to move there. I thought about my old home, where I lived with my mother, the perfectly manicured gardens and inside a modern clean abode.

I began to unpack our things, searching for something of sentiment connected to my mother. There were no handbags or high heels, no hair brush or rollers, no perfume or cosmetics. They had disappeared from our lives. Even her Tupperware containers had gone. I held an ornament she had told me to be careful with. I drank from the porcelain cup she had drank from and sinfully ate from the plates she had treasured for special occasions. I had outgrown my Sindy dolls and most of the other toys she had bought me. My growling bear wasn't there to comfort me. I felt disappointed, lost in the remnants of a past life.

The house didn't feel like a home, it was just an address where we officially lived. Dad wall papered the walls, fitted a new kitchen and carpeted it throughout. He had done his best to transform it to a liveable condition but something seemed to be missing. It was still very empty. I felt cold in my bones like never before. My teeth chattered and my body shivered. I would see shadows in every room. There was a ghostly presence that I tried my best to ignore. I knew it was my Mom, I was convinced she was angry that I was living with my Dad.

At bedtime, I could see and hear her moving around and I would hide under the blankets. She terrified me. I left the light on to stop the shadows and played loud music to keep her away. I would stay awake for hours to avoid my nightmares. I could never see who was trying to kill me but I would run so fast to escape them, I would take off the ground and breast stroke through the dense air, swimming to the sky for safety. I would wake up crying. I felt like I was going crazy. I told my Dad that I thought my Mom was haunting the house. He said he had seen her in the town, she was haunting him too.

During the day, Dad had a labouring job and I instinctively took over the role of mother, washing, cleaning, lighting the fire and gardening. I soon realised it was hard work running a home. It took a lot of time and effort. Added to a lack of sleep, I felt exhausted. The coal stained my hands and the ashes from the fire got in my hair. I looked a mess. Cooking wasn't easy. I forgot to put the water in the pressure cooker so it exploded. I cut myself peeling potatoes so often we ran out of plasters. I couldn't boil an egg but I tried my best. Dad gave me a few lessons and I soon proudly mastered egg and chips, which we ate most nights with gallons of fizzy pop. I drank so much pop I needed a tooth filled, every time I visited the dentist.

We were given the keys to the house so we could get in when Dad wasn't around. Our neighbours called us the "latch key kids". We weren't normal kids, we had to grow up fast and assumed we could look after ourselves, yet most of our time was spent in our neighbour's houses, someone's mother would always feed us. The children on the estate were all rough and ready, wearing hand me downs, living on crisp sandwiches and tap water they called 'council pop'. I found them quite intimidating at first but they welcomed us. We had great fun playing 'Knock and Taz', 'Kerby' and 'Tag' and we soon adjusted to their way of life.

Ray and I were outside in the street with our new friends when Gramps pulled up in his car. It was so lovely to see him again after six long months and we both ran over and hugged him. I was devastated to discover he hadn't actually come to see us. He just wanted to talk to my Dad in private. I hoped that they would talk and settle their differences but he didn't stay long. After his private word with Dad he got back in his car, slammed the door and sped away without even looking at us or saying goodbye.

Gramps was the only visitor we had and he never came again. I realised that no-one wanted to visit us because of my Dad and what he had done. I didn't think it was fair on me or my brother. Our grandparents had always been part of our lives. We were now ostracised by them and desperately missing their love. I spent hours sat on the floor in front of the open fire, watching the flames, trying to find warmth in a cold, haunted house.

Every Friday night, Ray and myself would get on our bikes and ride round to Aunt Linda's house in Cheslyn Hay. I was lucky she lived so close and that kept us going. Our young cousins, Tracey, Melanie and Scott used to jump up and down with excitement when they saw us, we had such a close bond. We would take them over to the local park to play, it gave my busy Aunt a break. There was usually a ton of washing up to do and I would just get stuck in and help out, just like my mother would have done. We would stay there all weekend, it felt like home, it was warm, welcoming and safe.

When her children had settled to bed, we would sit and talk for hours. She told me that Mom had hidden money from my Dad to pay the bills. He had spent all his money on beer. My Dad hadn't been a good husband. It was no wonder she was so unhappy. We talked about the day it had happened how Mom had left home and gone to her house. I wanted to know all the details. Dad had telephoned her and told her to go home and talk. Mom hugged Aunt Linda and told her she loved her. She said it was like she knew she was going to die when she left that day. I noticed Aunt Linda had a bottle of prescribed Valium tablets in her bathroom, she smoked lots of cigarettes and she drank whisky to mask her pain.

She thought it was strange that Prince had been locked in the shed. "Why would your Dad have locked the dog in the shed?" she asked. I couldn't answer that one. It wasn't a place we had ever kept the dog. The more she told me the more I started to think my Dad hadn't accidentally killed my mother, it was premeditated, it was murder. I felt confused, why had the judge said it was Manslaughter? I couldn't undo my forgiveness for his accident, especially as I was now living with him but I felt relieved to finally know the truth.

I babysat with another local girl on Saturday evenings, whilst my aunt and uncle went out for a drink. Linda would give us money and we would buy sweets from the off licence of the Woodman Inn, a short walk from their house. My cousins would stay up late, watching TV and then settle to sleep. Uncle Malcom, nicknamed his eldest daughter "rent a trap" as she never stopped chatting. I would top and tail with Tracey, she made me laugh how she continued to talk in her sleep. Ray would bunk up with Scott. It was strange, I never had nightmares when I slept at Aunt Linda's house.

Uncle Malcolm had a market stall selling bread, biscuits and cakes. We would sneak into his garage secretly gorging on the broken biscuits he had in storage. It was every child's dream to fix a manifesting addiction to sugar. Aunt Linda laughed each time she caught us both with a mouthful of biscuits, she never told us off. She was kind and I knew she loved me. We would go through her wardrobe together finding nice clothes I could have. We even had matching cardigans specially knitted. I still wanted to live with her more than anything but I knew it would never be. Just being there with her at weekends was a great comfort.

Their house soon went up for sale. Aunt Linda said she was moving to be nearer my grandparents because there were too many bad memories in Cheslyn Hay. I hoped she didn't mean me. I felt she wanted to move away from my Dad and I didn't blame her for that. She had lost her big sister and the man that had killed her was living close by. It must have been hard for her and I understood. I didn't want her to move. I felt sad when I arrived to see the 'sold' sign in their garden. It took me some time to get used to her not being around.

Uncle Malcolm picked us up occasionally so we could still see them but it wasn't the same. We did get to visit my grandparents whilst we were at Linda's. Nan would cry as I walked into their house, saying how I looked like my Mom. They always seemed pleased to see us but things were so different. I felt they were torn and didn't want to have a relationship with me because I had foolishly chosen to forgive my Dad. I missed them and loved them all so much. I just wanted my normal family life to return but deep down I knew things could never be normal again.

We started Moat Hall Middle School and I was pleased to see an old friend again. I had known Adele from my first school, Glenthorne Primary. She told me how much she had worried about me for weeks and how everyone at our primary school had known my Mom had been killed. She said she would have sent me letters, had she known where I was. Adele was a kind friend who made it easy for me to settle into school and make new friends. Jayne had moved schools too and I was pleased to see she was also in my class. We had both escaped Donna Nichols. I didn't want to ever get bullied again. With no family support I felt blessed to have some good friends in my life again.

Dad reinforced the need for me to stand up for myself and hit the bullies back. The thing was I didn't like hitting people. I did whack Spencer Clayton over the head with a meter rule one day and was sent to see the Headmaster. When I explained that the jobs worth school prefect had refused to let me in when it was pouring with rain, the Head started laughing and told me not to do it again. I did apologise to Spencer but he never kept me out in the rain after that day.

On school days, Dad would get himself up for work and call us as he left the house. We would usually drift back to sleep and then wake up late for school. Luckily, a friend would knock on my door and I would quickly get dressed and rush off to school without any breakfast. Sometimes I skipped school altogether. A truancy officer visited one lunch time. He asked why I hadn't been to school that morning. I explained that I didn't have a clean blouse to wear so I had taken the morning off to do the washing, he seemed surprised but that was the truth.

I had noticed when I hung up my blouse, how dirty the collar was in comparison with the other blouses hooked on the pegs, as we changed into our PE kits. I hated the dirt marks on my collar, it symbolised not having a mother. I had the worst attendance record in the school that year. My Dad put pressure on me saying I would get him into trouble if I had any more time off school. So I made sure the washing was done in the evening and I went on to have 100% attendance. My efforts to juggle housework and school were acknowledged. I proudly received my certificate of merit.

On Mother's Day, I went with my Dad to the crematorium. It was my idea to visit and he willingly agreed to go. It was a beautiful sunny day and I proudly showed him where Mom's little slate was. Dad's mother had also died by this time, so we found her slate and we placed flowers for both of them. Dad didn't cry and neither did I. He had never been there before and I felt the need for him to see Mom's slate. Perhaps I wanted him to make peace. I didn't feel she was angry with me that day. The wind didn't howl. She even stopped haunting the house and let us move on.

My Dad started to go out with André's Mom, Lynn. André was another good friend of mine, so when Lynn moved in, I was really happy. Lynn was so like my Mom it was unreal. She was house proud and organised. Her presence made the house feel like home. She treated me like her daughter and it was a relief to feel loved again. André had two sisters and a brother and we lived together as one big happy family. André and I went on a school holiday together with our matching clothes and sleeping bags, we were like real sisters and we had a great time.

A few weeks after our school holiday, quite out of the blue, I came home and they had all gone. Lynn had left me a note on my pillow. "You'll understand when you are older" it said. Dad said Lynn had used him for his money and now it was all gone she had left him. Perhaps he had done something to her and he didn't want to admit it, I thought. I wished she had taken me with her that day but I wasn't her daughter and there was nothing I could do about her leaving me behind. It wasn't the same coming back from school to an empty house, with no laughter and no dinner.

After Lynn left, Dad started drinking heavily. He had been going to the pub straight after work and coming back drunk. I had asked him what he had done to drive Lynn away. He swore at me, said I was cheeky and threatened to belt me. Although his drunken temper frightened me, I stood my ground and threatened to report him to the NSPCC. I had contributed money from a sponsored walk for the Charity and I had learned that they looked after children who were abused or neglected. The NSPCC, didn't look after me, they didn't even know I existed but mentioning the NSPCC to Dad seemed to save my life.

I had tried to convince myself that I was still Daddy's girl even though he had stopped the hugs and kisses as soon as he had been released from prison. I just thought that was because he didn't miss me anymore. In fact he had stopped calling me 'Daddy's girl' after killing my mother but I still believed he would never physically hurt me. He wouldn't have wanted to go back to prison. He gave me an evil look and gritted his teeth in anger, I wasn't going to take the chance. I span around and fled, too frightened to look back. I ran to André's house for safety. Lynn gave me a hug. " Oh dear Diane, you can't stay here" she sympathetically said. She took me back home and had words with my father, telling him never to treat me like that again. I liked the way she stood up for me. Then she went back to her house. I felt rejected and never saw her again.

Dad got some support from an organisation called Gingerbread. He said it was for single parents. I needed support too, but there was no support for someone like me. I turned to my friends instead, they knew my life was a struggle, aware of what my Dad had done. Most of them couldn't believe that I was living with him. Some said "I would never talk to my Dad again if he killed my Mom." I didn't know what to think. I wasn't a child seen to be in need of support. I was just a child without a mother, living with the man who had killed her. It wasn't a big thing, yet all my friends thought it was. I was trying to be normal, under very abnormal circumstances. My Dad wasn't supportive, school kept me going, but still no one, apart from my school friends asked how I was coping.

I sought support from a family that lived close by, Brian and Hazel ran a jazz band and had seven children and a lodger living in their three bedroomed council house. Four of their children had been adopted as they had been neglected by their mother. I became best friends with Lisa, she told me how she had been left starving, locked in a room with her brother and sisters whilst her mom went out taking drugs. My Mom hadn't taken drugs or locked me in a room. My Mom had always looked after me. I felt sorry for Lisa. She wasn't happy living with Hazel but we both enjoyed marching in the band, playing the lead kazoo's and harmonising. Ray played the drums and we practiced twice a week. Then at weekends we travelled the country taking part in competitions. I'd found another substitute family just like the Gingham Girls, I had become a Wyrley Bird Parader. I could again put on a show in public and feel proud of myself.

Although I had plenty to occupy my mind during the daytime, I still felt very alone at night. When I was asleep I would have my recurring nightmare that someone was trying to kill me. I would hide in different places, always running away as fast as my legs could manage and taking off the ground, swimming through the air, where no-one could hurt me. I was always safe in the sky. Ray said he was having a similar dream but he pedalled his BMX so fast it took off, and he would pedal through the air to safety. Stephen Speilburg later stole his idea for the film ET.

I thought it was strange that we had such similar dreams, my friends didn't dream about escaping from a killer. I wanted to know what these dreamed meant. At the school book club, I found a book about dreams and placed an order. This book was the first of many that helped me come to terms with my life. I began to analyse my dreams and listen to my subconscious mind. I felt relieved to know that I was able to rise above my problems according to the interpretation.

Not long after moving up to Great Wyrley High School, I had a dream that my Mom was standing by Moat Hall school gates and I went over to her. She was wearing a pure white polo neck jumper and her trendy blue PVC jacket. She had a baby in a pushchair and a dog on a lead. She was stood there in broad daylight. She was waiting for Ray to come out of school. My initial surprise of delight, quickly turned to anger. "You have been here all this time, making me think you are dead. You're just carrying on with your life as if nothing has happened" I said to her.

She completely ignored me. It was as if she couldn't hear me and had suddenly become deaf. I begged her to acknowledge me "Look at me Mom" I called out her name again and woke myself up crying. It was the first time I had dreamt of my mother, since she had been killed and it was the most vivid dream I had ever experienced. Maybe, if I had been nice to her she would have talked to me. I just couldn't help being angry. My dream book said I was either missing my mother, or it was a spiritual visit either way she didn't want to know me, just like the rest of my family. Not having my beautiful mother, in my life seemed so hard.

I worried over what to wear to the school disco. I got upset because I had nothing nice to put on. My mother, Aunt Linda and Lynn would have made sure I had suitable attire for those special occasions but they were no longer in my life. Dad told me not to worry and said he would buy me a dress whilst he was in town. I knew he had absolutely no fashion sense and had no idea how to make me look good. He handed me a brown paper bag, on his return. A tacky, navy blue dress lay inside. It was made of see through nylon, V necked, with an elasticated waist and it made me look pale and fifty years older.

He insisted I wore the dress that he had bought. Even though I hated it, I wore it because I felt guilty for being ungrateful and he said it looked "fine". It was a very humiliating experience as my trendy friends all whispered and laughed. I felt so embarrassed, I disappeared into a dark corner and I didn't dance all evening. I never wore the dress again and asked my Dad to give me the money to buy my own clothes after that day. With no maternal guidance, 'Jackie' and 'Just Seventeen' magazines became my mentors.

Still feeling lonely at home, I persuaded my Dad to let us have a dog. It was a little black puppy, I called her Mitzi, she reminded me of Prince. I felt safe in the house with a dog and she snuggled up to me and kept me warm. We loved each other and enjoyed going for walks. Steve, a lad in my year, had a dog called Whiskey, who always roamed the streets. He followed Steve onto the school grounds most days and annoyingly followed me when I walked Mitzi. One day, she got out and before I knew it, she was connected rear on rear to Whiskey, outside our house.

She was stuck in that position for around twenty minutes and cried in pain each time she tried to break free. There was nothing I could do to separate them. Dad said it was my fault she had got pregnant because I had left the door open. My Dad hadn't wanted to waste money on an operation to prevent her from becoming pregnant. She had six pups and was a dedicated mother. I kept everywhere clean in their outhouse but my Dad got rid of them all. "Let that be a lesson" he said. Poor Mitzi had gone and I missed her. I had lost my mother, Prince, my family, Lynn and Mitzi was the final straw. I started to despise my heartless father, everything I loved he took from me.

I found a way of coping, I started smoking cigarettes. Dad bought boxes of cigarette tubes, two hundred in each and handed me the tobacco and the stuffing machine to make the cigarettes for him. He didn't seem to notice how many I stole from him so I didn't mind making them. I also bought cigarettes on the way to school, 5p a single. I was only thirteen but no-one really questioned you, even in a school uniform. I would drag away on my cigarettes like an adult, walking down the street openly showing the world how hard my life was but no-one seemed to notice. My peers just thought I was cool.

My affluent school friends went clothes shopping with their mothers and I envied them. I would get some money off my Dad and go to town with Lisa. We couldn't afford to buy make-up as it was really expensive so we began slipping the odd lipstick, eye-shadow or mascara into our pockets. It was really easy to do and we moved onto the shoe stall as soon as our make-up collection was complete. These shoes had all been worn by models and were exceptionally cheap. The market stall was so busy we would take off our old worn shoes, try the new ones on and then simply walk away.

With very little effort I moved on to clothes shops, I stole a complete new school uniform. It was like I was going shopping with my wealthy mother, anything I wanted I could have, money was irrelevant, if I liked it, I would try it on and then simply put it in my bag. The money I saved paid for Lisa and me to have a burger meal. I didn't have days out or treats with my mother, like my friends did. I deserved those treats and it felt so good. However, as easy as it was to steal, I felt ashamed of my actions and sensed my mother was watching me. I knew it was morally wrong. I didn't want to risk being arrested so I decided to stop shoplifting.

I reflected on my behaviour. I wrote a poem, my Gramps had always made up poems to make us laugh when we were children and he had inspired me to do the same. Poetry became another way of coping but this one reflected my guilt.

One wet and windy day I thought, can I go out, a battle brought
Rain laid down on weeping tree, and soaked my heart with misery
Sat by the fire, the warmth of love, a hand held out, I stole their glove
A moments song, soon does pass, truth lies barefoot on the grass
And in the rain, you hold my hand, guide me please to sunshine land
To ask for help, I know not how and maybe you can see that now

I sealed the poem in an envelope and placed it inside my bible, hoping for forgiveness.

For my fourteenth birthday, Dad bought me a sewing machine so I could make alterations to the clothes I bought from charity shops and jumble sales. I had all the clothes I wanted, beautifully tailored to fit my body and my peers started to notice how independently fashionable I was. Tight short skirts were a must and I soon had the keen interest of the opposite sex. I craved their love and attention but my Dad ruined every relationship I had. He would take delight in shouting at them if they dared walk me home. Knowing he had killed my mother they would run off and were too frightened to come to my house a second time. He would laugh triumphantly at my heartache and loneliness. I began searching for someone that wasn't frightened of my father, the kind hearted boys I had dated couldn't handle him. My Mr. Right was proving hard to find, they would need to be a tough character who would stand by me.

The 'lipstick effect' may have been a psychological phenomenon but it boosted my confidence and made me feel physically attractive. Wearing make-up changed my self-esteem, my attitude and my personality. In school, I was forced to remove it. I would look in the mirror, at my pale face and the noticeable dark circles under my eyes. I hated my pasty complexion as others would always ask if I was ok. The stress of life and my sleepless nights had made me look less youthful and more haggard. I felt naked and vulnerable being my natural self. Make up empowered me.

One morning, I saw someone in my year, walking down the street with her mother holding hands, they were both smiling, their bond was publicly evident. I remembered the day I walked back from the hairdressers holding my mothers hand, feeling glam and special. Nicola, kept herself to herself but that day I felt jealous of what she had. I noticed how she got away with wearing make-up and fashion accessories, despite the compulsory uniform code that I was forced to follow. I protested to the teachers about this injustice on several occasions but they did nothing about it. Nicola seemed to be a favourite, her rule breaking practices were never challenged so I took action against her, just like Donna Nichols had with me. "At the gates" I would say and I would watch her run for the bus at home time. I got a satisfying feeling seeing someone frightened of me.

Eventually she retaliated in the outdoor quad and I grabbed her. I didn't know where the anger came from but I couldn't stop hitting her, punch after punch. I made a mess of her innocent pretty face and then I dragged her by the hair across the Redgra surface, shredding her tights and grazing her legs. The teachers were watching the fight from the staff room above, I was so violent, they didn't dare intervene. I was sent to the deputy heads office. I told them she had called me a bastard because I had no mother. My disclosure, a cry for help, wasn't acknowledged, I was just seen as a problem.

Nicola's mother asked the head mistress to expel me. My father was proudly summoned to the office. Word got out about the fight and my ferocious temper and everyone said they never wanted to get on the wrong side of me. Nicola had a few weeks off school to recover, I never apologised to her but I left her alone. Nicola never really deserved to be bullied. I had detention and lines to do and admiration from my father, that I was now, at last, sticking up for myself. I was a "chip off the old block" he claimed.

I stopped going to band practice, I felt too old to be parading the streets. I spent my time with Jayne round at Griff's house instead. We used to watch videos, mainly comedies and I enjoyed them but then we started watching horror films. They used to terrify me, especially 'The Exorcist'. Oh my days, why did I watch that film? I had nightmares again.

After some pleading, my Dad gave me the money to go and buy a boxer puppy for my fifteenth birthday. It was on the condition it was not female to avoid any future unwanted pregnancies. I named my puppy Sergeant. My grandparents new Labrador was called Major so I found a name that linked the families together, despite the lack of contact. Even with the love I received from the dog, I still felt isolated. My hormones were going left, right and centre. I was becoming a young woman and I had no mother to talk to about female issues.

I started my periods and didn't tell my father. I couldn't talk to my Dad about him murdering my mother, that was a bloody conversation and so were my periods. The pain was immense and would stop me from walking. I thought this was normal. I relied on my friends to supply me with sanitary towels for the first few months. My neighbour told my father, due to her unnecessary expenses and he told me he didn't want me getting pregnant. He presumed I was having sex, even though I wasn't and he wanted me to go on the pill. He said he didn't trust me and persuaded me to go to the doctors. So to keep my father happy, I pretended to the doctor that I was having sex and began the daily ritual of taking the contraceptive pill.

It was around this time Dad told me he had met another woman. "Her name is Sandra and she is coming round tonight" he said. I was shocked he had met another woman and was introducing her so quickly. Maybe, it was hard for him being a single father having to buy sanitary towels but I couldn't face being rejected by another mother. I had no time to prepare myself for another mother figure in my life. That night I walked into the lounge to find an overweight, ugly woman sat on our sofa. She had no idea how to apply makeup, she had blushed red cheeks and bright red lipstick that looked hideous. She reminded me of Aunt Sally from Worzle Gummidge.

I looked her up and down. She had no dress sense, she looked like a man in drag, wearing a curly wig and an outdated, white cheesecloth dress. She had a deep voice and spoke in that despised Black Country accent I hated. I tried to be courteous but it was obvious we had absolutely nothing in common. Her objectives were transparent, she wanted my Dad, she had no intention of forging a relationship with me. After she had left I said "I don't like her Dad". He laughed, he didn't care about my feelings, he just wanted a woman to make his life easier.

Chapter 5
The Murderers Wife

Within six weeks, we had moved into Sandra's house and they had got married. It was against my wishes. I felt embarrassed that people might mistake her for being my mother. I don't remember any wedding dress, bridesmaids or wedding cake. I have blocked that day from my memory. Their occasion, resembled a rushed affair with a ritual pretence in a registry office. However, there were positives to consider; her house was relatively new and had a gas fire, with central heating; I wouldn't have so much housework to do; and my delighted friend's, Fiona and Jayne, lived close by so I considered the move to be socially convenient.

Sandra disclosed to me how she had never wanted to have children. Her daughter had been an accident. What an awful thing to say, I thought. And now she had unfortunately gained two more unwanted children. Her life couldn't have got any worse. Luckily for me, Sandra said she never wanted to replace my mother, she just wanted to be my friend. I didn't actually need friendship. I had plenty of friends already. She had no intention of getting to know me or fulfilling my needs. I didn't take it personally as she didn't like her own identical twin sister as she got more attention from her mother. Consequently, she didn't like her mother either because her twin was always favoured.

I thought her twin sister had a great sense of humour and was easy to get on with. She made me welcome in her home and we would sit and chat. Sandra's mom was a beautiful step-nan to me, she often bought me sweets when she visited. She would ask how I was with a genuine concern for my welfare. She lived by the school and asked me to call in, each time I visited her, she insisted she made me lunch. They both thought Sandra was an insecure woman, with issues beyond their support.

Although Sandra was a lot younger than my Dad, she seemed much older because she had Rheumatoid arthritis. Her hands were deformed and her legs and arms were swollen. She had retired from the police force in her early twenties, pensioned off due to ill health and had never worked again. Ordinarily, I would sympathise with anyone suffering pain but not with this undeserving woman. She waddled around the house like a penguin but retained her authoritarian police approach to everything. This worked in my favour on one issue as she over ruled my father and allowed me to smoke in the house on the legal grounds that I was sixteen. I didn't think to associate her kind-gesture as something perverse. I soon became a heavy smoker, coughing and spluttering and having regular tonsillitis.

I felt ashamed of the way she dressed, the way she walked and the way she talked. She caught Fiona and myself in hysterics when we checked out her coat cupboard, mocking her out dated hippy clothes. She knew I didn't respect her, she never attempted to be my friend, in fact she became my enemy, ignoring my existence in the home. She referred to me as "the spoilt bitch" and said that I thought the world revolved around me. I felt despised and irrelevant. I continued to call her Sandra to her face but outside the home, I referred to her as "the wicked step mother of the west".

Rebecca, her daughter, was a pretty but over weight, frumpily dressed child, idolised by her mother in an extremely overprotected way. I could tell she was a very anxious child, lacking some social skills but I thought she would enjoy having a big sister around. I wanted to spend time with her and get to know her. I offered to take her out shopping and buy her some nice trendy clothes. My step mother of the west discouraged such a positive sibling relationship. I felt like her mother wanted her all to herself and I soon gave up trying to be a big sister.

Rebecca had shared the double bed with her mother since her parents had separated and being very immature, she couldn't cope with the change in circumstances. We shared a room and had bunk beds. Each night she would cry, finding it hard to settle on her own. I tried to talk and reason with her but she always ignored me. It was as though she had been told to disassociate herself from me. She just wanted her Mommy, it was a classic case of separation anxiety. When I was her age I had dealt with the death of my mother, had a dad in prison and a traumatised family to support. She really needed to get a grip and grow up.

I would pretend to be asleep, despite the crying, when her mother entered our room. "Come on my darling, stop crying, goodnight my little princess, mommy loves you, I love you darling, goodnight my angel, I love you my sweetheart." She would kiss her and walk out the room. Sandra never spoke to me with any affection and that hurt. She knew I was awake and deliberately rubbed salt into my wounds.

She wasn't consistent with her parenting approach to Rebecca either. Sometimes Sandra would lose her temper, she would hit her or rant at her. She foamed at the mouth and would spit with anger. I wanted to intervene but I feared she would then start on me. Other times Rebecca's cries were completely ignored. I was taking my exams at school, I needed to sleep and my step-sister's constant crying kept me awake. She drove me crazy, I would prod her mattress from the bottom bunk and tell her to stop crying and go to sleep.

She went to see a psychiatrist with her Mom to discover what was wrong. Did she know my father had killed his first wife and was she worried my father would kill her mother? Did she think we were all murderers? Had her mother abused her all her life and made her neurotic? The woman who didn't want children wasn't a good mother. They said the psychiatrist couldn't discover what was wrong....mmmm perhaps they should have spoken to her when her abusive mother wasn't there to talk for her. Poor Rebecca just had a mother with serious control issues and I could do nothing to support her.

We were two families in one house and Dad was in the middle, allegedly, with the role of "keeping the peace". He wasn't successful and the not so happy couple spent plenty of time arguing between themselves. I was watching television and I could hear my Dad and Sandra in the kitchen having an extremely heated row. "Give it back to me now" she said. I had visions of Dad holding a knife about to kill her. Despite not liking my step mother, I instinctively raced to the kitchen to intervene and prevent another murder. They were wrestling over a scrubbing brush on the floor, arguing over who was going to do the cleaning. I was relieved there was no knife but I felt angry they didn't consider the impact their fights had on me. I told them they were pathetic parents.

I found it particularly difficult to tolerate their major arguments, I expected my Dad to kill her as she tried to control everything he did. She was very aggressive in her demeanour, treating everything as an incident for the police woman to deal with. They were oblivious to how their behaviour consequently affected me. I purposely stayed out of the house as much as possible. I apprehensively came home from school each day, expecting to find a bloodbath or a corpse. I would change out of my uniform and hurry off to work. I just didn't want to be there.

My mental health continued to deteriorate, I felt so alone in the house, living on my nerves. I spent most evenings crying myself to sleep, listening to them argue. I couldn't breath or swallow and my tonsils were always swollen. I regularly visited the doctor and was given antibiotics time and time again. To solve the issue I had my tonsils taken out. My Dad and my step mother visited me in hospital but it was my friends and school that I missed, not them. Having my tonsils removed didn't cure the problem. I had awful migraines instead. My doctor diagnosed sinusitis, the pain wasn't going away, it had simply shifted to another part of my body.

Regardless of my health, I started selling Avon cosmetics door to door and combined my time running a tote raising funds for Cancer research. I was an excellent sales woman and most weeks I was earning £50 or more. I also babysat for neighbours, looking after children came natural to me. I saved my earnings to buy Ray and my Mom's family birthday and Christmas presents. I liked to give them gifts and see their eyes light up. Aunt Linda would always get me a nice present. June and Nan would always give me chocolates. I would also buy presents for my

Dad, Sandra, and Becky, they didn't deserve presents but I thought giving was an act of kindness and it might have been returned by them. They didn't give me gifts, just money so I could go out and get wasted.

I also worked in the local chip shop from 4.45pm- 6.45pm. This money paid for my weekly expenses; cigarettes, alcohol and youth club. I would swing a sack of potatoes onto my shoulder and fill the potato peeling machine, release the chips into a bucket and carry them in ready for frying. It was back breaking work and I had to tolerate the sexual exploitation from Nick, the charming, greasy proprietor, who was old enough to be my father. His wife would be serving the customers whilst he groped me in the back room, hugging me from behind, kissing my neck and thrusting an erection up my backside, that was restrained by his work clothes.

Fortunately, she never left us alone for long. I always managed to slip away from him and get on with the tasks I was actually being paid to do. I would make enough chips for the night and then I would grab some fish and chips and a can of coke, and sit on a bench outside. It was worth suffering his advances to have a free meal each day so I didn't need to eat Sandra's awful tasteless budget meals or listen to them argue.

I was often first through the door at youth club, so I would help the staff set up, they were always pleased to see me and appreciated my support. I encouraged lots of people to attend the youth club and the place was always buzzing with happiness. Ray would arrive with his friends and they would play darts and pool. A nice lad called Dan Clarke taught me how to use a cue and I had fun playing pool with the lads and chatting to friends in the warmth. I enjoyed watching Top of the Pops, Not the Nine O'clock News and The Young Ones on television. Youth club was so important to me, it was therapy, a safe place and available five days a week.

I served in the tuck shop on the nights there was nothing worth watching on TV. We could help ourselves to food and drink as a sweetener for serving the other young people. I enjoyed the responsibility and the social aspect of chatting to my customers whilst I upped the sales. One day, I thought, I would run my own pub and earn a fortune. After the youth club closed I would hang around the chip shop for another hour and then go home to sleep.

During the school holidays and weekends, I had nowhere to go. I hated that. I would hang around the shops in all weathers until someone I knew turned up. I would stay in bed until midday and get on a bus with a day tripper ticket and travel on the buses for hours, watching the world go by. I usually persuaded someone to come along, and we would look around the town together but on many occasions, I sat on my own, it provided a good time for thinking. I just couldn't bear being at home with the murderer and the murderers wife.

Friday nights were the highlight of my week. I would dress up to the nines and meet up with my friends. We'd sit on the precinct knocking back a cheap bottle of wine and a two-litre bottle of White Lightening Cider. I always had plenty of friends who were eager to get drunk with me, before we headed off to the community centre disco, to dance the night away. I loved music, the lyrics about loss and pain gave me an outlet to express my feelings. Songs like "Mama Said" by the Shirelles, Genesis "Mama" and BoneyM's "Mother and child reunion" swept me spiritually towards my mother and uplifting songs made me feel alive and happy. I may have been a drunk dancing queen but it was a wonderful escape from my dysfunctional family.

I had to be in before 11pm so I would leave my friends and stumble home bare foot, with my high heels in my hand. I wasn't allowed a key to this house as they said I couldn't be trusted. I'd knock the door several times and wait for my Dad to wake up, standing there rocking my knees, or rushing off to have a desperate pee in the back garden before he eventually opened the door. He would moan if I was five minutes late and I would just trot off upstairs saying "Yeah, goodnight". I would lie in bed with the room spinning, I'd rush to the toilet to vomit then settle off to sleep.

One night I found a bottle of Bells whisky at a house party and I got so intoxicated I couldn't remember a thing. I had returned home with a strange man that I had called Frankie but my Dad said it wasn't Frankie, it was a stranger. My Dad undressed me and put me to bed. The next day I couldn't straighten my arm. I had a huge friction burn both sides of my elbow as though I had been dragged along the floor. I couldn't understand how I had got the injury, as my coat and top were unmarked. None of my friends knew who had taken me home. I could have been raped that night. Luckily, I cannot remember what happened but it put me off whisky for ever.

Alcohol made me forget my life and provided me with the courage to flirt with the boys. I was promiscuous and rarely without a boyfriend. My relationships never lasted long, due to my father. Other girls would say I was a slut and a slag, because I went out with lots of boys, despite still being a virgin. I was very popular but I couldn't face the pain of losing my virginity no matter how much alcohol I had consumed. I had seen how Mitzi had suffered. The boys spoke about 'breaking her in' which to me seemed frightfully painful. They appeared to like to be teased and I loved to turn them on but I would never go all the way. I was very choosy, I never dated a Tom, Dick or a Harry but in hind sight, I was totally incapable of finding my Mr. Right.

I was desperate for love but I had no idea what love was, my Dad hadn't been a good role model. I started going out with Dan Clarke from the youth club. He was different, in a nice way, he had a trendy haircut like Fergal Sharkey, had good morals and was courageous. He had a great personality and he made me laugh. I admired his work ethic, racing round on a chopper bike, to complete his paper round and earn his money. He had interesting hobbies. He liked going fishing and making go carts. He came from a large family and they were all notably very close.

We spent evenings at his brothers house and we babysat his nephews, he was sensitive and caring towards them. There was a warm welcoming sense of family love surrounding him. It reminded me of how I felt at Aunt Linda's house. I didn't tell him about my family, he knew my brother Ray and that was it. I couldn't take him home to meet the murderer and the wicked step mother of the west, to witness their arguments. I couldn't let him know how depressed I was living there, I didn't want him to feel sorry for me or judge me. When we were together we were like soul mates. I felt happy and safe as we walked the streets hand in hand. He was the perfect boyfriend, in a stable loving family but I was embarrassed to admit to him that I came from a very different environment. I was lured away from him when I was told someone else fancied me.

Chapter 6

The Rebellion

I compared my options at the youth club as they both stood together. Dan's 'hand me down' trousers did him no justice, he had no visible bottom. Steve Morley on the other hand, had a great physique, with a really sexy bottom, the type I wanted to pinch. I finished with Dan and made a move on Steve. He had just come home from borstal, I knew he was a bad boy, the most deviant teenager in the village. I watched him impressively defeat the police in a chase, by jumping off the railway bridge and running up the railway track. He taunted them because they could never catch him. I loved his mischievous ways.

I never told my Dad who my boyfriend was. Steve thought it was best not to mention his name. So he was a secret boyfriend, which made the relationship even more exciting. One night, I heard my step mothers cries from their bedroom and attempting to save her, I entered their room. My Dad wasn't trying to kill her, he going down on her. It wasn't a pleasant sight. I quickly left the room, shocked and disgusted. I couldn't believe they were having sex at their age. I took advantage of their need for privacy and told my father I was staying at a friend's house for the night. My Dad never checked up on my whereabouts, he didn't really care, if I was out of the house, they could have sex and play happy families. I'd stay out all night with Steve and a few others. He looked after me and I provided cash and cigarettes for him.

Steve was streetwise and he knew how to survive. He used to wear his mother's tights under his trousers and when I was shivering, he advised me to wear layers to keep warm. He would go on a survival hunt, returning with food if we were hungry, robbed from someone's house or clothes if we were cold, stolen from someone's washing line. We drank cider and lit fires and snuggled up together to keep warm. We made camps along the railway banks and found dry places to sleep in wet weather. The police would often try to catch us but we always got away. We would lie on the ground and stare at the night sky. I was fascinated with brightest star and wondered what it was called. Steve told me it was the North Star but it was actually Sirius. Whilst my peers were safely cooped up in their beds, I had freedom in a vast universe. I felt relaxed and alive.

I gave up my Avon and tote jobs and lost my babysitting job because of Steve. People in the village didn't like him. He got my brother and a few others to help him raid the cake shop one night. Dan Clarke and his brother, Phil had seen them and had sensibly walked away, not wanting to be involved with their criminal activities. The next day Dan moved to Torquay with his family to run a bed and breakfast business. The culprits involved in the raid were all caught. Steve told the police it was Dan and Phil . I couldn't believe that he had put the blame on two innocent people, he had no morals at all. My ex-boyfriend and his brother had to come back for the court case but were found not guilty and after a few days they returned to Torquay. My heart ached for a second chance with Dan, how different my life could have been if I had stayed with him. I would have loved to have moved to Torquay with him. I had lost a loyal boyfriend, over a sexy bottom and chosen a different path in life. Steve was sent back to Borstal, Ray received a caution and my rebellious life continued.

In my final year at school I instigated a school strike and managed to get four hundred or so students from my school to join me on a protest. "We are going on strike, just like the miners" I told them as they turned up for school. I led the march to Cannock Park, meeting up with crowds of other students. The media were there and I felt part of something very special. I noticed the organisers all wore a matching badge. They said they were 'militants'. I listened intently to their speech. Margaret Thatcher, had tried to make the Youth Training Schemes compulsory. The militants wanted positive change for young people being financially exploited.

Contradictory to what they said, I actually admired Mrs.Thatcher. She was our first female prime minister. I liked her philosophy of people getting on their bikes and finding work. I was very proud of The Iron Lady and wasn't quite sure what they were ranting on about but I had done my bit to help them. The next day, I tried to explain to the head teacher that this was a democratic society, we had a right to be heard and had to fight for justice. I was excluded from school for the rest of the week for organising the strike which had disrupted the school day. On my return, some of the teachers told me they had enjoyed that day, not just because it was quiet but they thought the publicity was warranted.

I might have caused some disruption here and there but school was my place of safety, where I felt able to challenge adults without the fear of death. I did smoke behind the bike sheds but I was out of sight and I never got caught. I felt the need to speak up for others who lacked in confidence. I'd get isolation for being 'loud' and they would force me to write lines, I wasted so much ink and paper it was ridiculous and pointless. It was also so damn hard for me to concentrate in class, if I lost the thread of the conversation, my mind would wander and I switched off.

I knew I had some sort of disability but no-one had ever acknowledged it. My Mom had taken me for a deafness test when I was eight. I thought I was just a bit deaf due to the number of backhanders I had received for talking like my father. I had a lot going on in my head and I was also very addicted to nicotine. I needed a regular fix to relax and learn. One day, a cover teacher asked me to concentrate, everyone was talking about their family in a French lesson. I thought, do you know my Dad has killed my mother and my family is fucked. I looked her in the eyes and translated my thoughts "Mon père a assassiné ma mère, ma famille est foutue. I had, luckily, taken the time to learn the swear words from the French exchange students. She burst into tears and left the room, she couldn't handle a perfectly capable and honest student like me.

I disclosed nothing to the other teachers but I had a reputation. I was blamed for excrement on the toilet floor, which I had no doubt had been deposited by 'Whiskey', Steve's roaming dog, who had been seen in the toilets that day after I did some investigations. I received no apology, they thought a dog would be unlikely to do such a thing. I was fuming. "So you're saying I would, you're disgusting for thinking that of me" I said. Yes, I had a fight and I stood up for young people who had no voice but I had always shit in a toilet and wiped my bum, like everyone else. What sort of animal did they think I was? Their prejudice towards me was ridiculously evident.

On another day, I was told to stand outside the deputy heads door and start praying. Despite having lost my faith after my mother was killed, I recited the Lord's Prayer out loud until Mrs.Charles returned. She said I was insolent, accused me of putting a used sanitary towel on her office chair and threatened me with exclusion. When the actual culprit heard I had been accused, he apologised to me and confessed he had done the deed. It was the same lad that had blasted all our clay models off the shelf with a fire extinguisher, he liked to have a mischievous laugh with the teachers. I received no apology from the deputy head mistress so I gave her dead eyes every single time I saw her after that day. I intimidated her and made her feel uncomfortable. She deserved it. I mean come on, her accusations evidenced how much respect she had for me.

Parents evenings had fallen by the wayside, I would analyse my own reports, from my mothers perspective. Most comments were favourable from the teachers I liked. My maths teacher, Mr Hopkins, loved what I brought to his lessons. I brightened his day and made him laugh. He was a strict, old fashioned fiery redhead, who most students were terrified of and he only taught the top group. John McFarland and myself sat next to his desk, but we couldn't keep up the pace. I may have done better if I had still sat next to Sarah Wood, but our lives were becoming so different I couldn't sit with her or the other girls. They had things easy, they had supportive parents and their career plans forged. Despite liking them all, they made me realise my life without my mother was so different to theirs.

After my shocking mock results and a lot of pleading, Mr Hopkins agreed to let me drop down a group, he was sad, his maths lessons would never be the same, but I was relieved and it was the best move I had made. Group two, was a slower paced lesson, I was top of the group and sat with my dear friend Adele. I spent many a lesson helping her and spent hours into the night doing homework. I loved maths, you know where you are in life, 2+2 is always 4, algebra is just shorthand and fractions are a piece of cake, it all makes total sense to me.

I did well in Child Development and Art, subjects that interested me as they provided me with awareness and therapeutic tools. Mr. Hinton was my social studies teacher and had previously taught me history. He liked me too and I excelled in his class, my interest in society grew. I complained to my new history teacher, Mr. Oldfield about the inequalities and unfair treatment in his class on many occasion. He spent more time with the O Level students studying English history. I had opted to study world history by choice. I knew my memory wasn't as good as my peers so avoiding exams where possible worked in my favour. The CSE group was second rated. Mr. Oldfield, was married to a German lady and yet he had no time to spare to talk about Germany. He said he had cried in his sleep over me, as he struggled to deliver two different qualifications in his class. I had empathy for the man, I did give him a hard time but I was hungry to learn and he wasn't feeding me the information I required.

I refused to waste any more of my time in his lessons. I spent the last six weeks studying Hitler, compiling a non biased project, in the library. Hitler was a fascinating man, to go from being homeless, living in hostels, selling stamps to running a country seemed quite an achievement. He changed the education system which captivated my attention. I included a poster from a schoolbook which in English translated to "Who wants to live has to fight, and whoever refuses to fight in this world of eternal challenge has no right to live." For different reasons these words made me think about my life, my fight with eternal challenges and the need for a perfect world, a world of happiness and safety.

Hitlers ideology was, of course, crazy, the power and control went to his head. He caused trauma and destruction in people's lives, just like my father. I knew he had killed so many people from my chats with my Gramps. I was more fascinated with his relationship with Eva. She had met Hitler when she was just 17 and she had stood by him for years. A family member said she was the unhappiest woman she had ever met but she had never left him. She liked dancing and buying clothes, just like me and my mother. Eva eventually married Hitler but it was a hushed affair and then apparently, she poisoned herself. She was alleged to have died from suicide, shortly before her husband, it stank of a domestic homicide to me. She was oppressed and manipulated by an evil monster who killed her and then himself.

Mr. Hinton would casually pass by, checking I was working and he would glance over my project and wink and smile in admiration. We would have a brief conversation about my findings and off he would go. Other teachers weren't so supportive. There were the ones that gave me the disapproval look, the ones that didn't want to know me, their comments on my reports were very different. To them, I was immature, challenging, rude and insolent, and of course, my grades reflected this.

I wasn't in the house to revise like my school friends were, and my mock parents weren't at all supportive. I had nowhere specific to study and received no encouragement from them to do well. As long as I vacuumed and polished upstairs, cleaned the bathroom and changed the bed sheets every Sunday they stayed off my back. They just didn't care about my academic achievements. Despite the lack of revision, I still managed to pass all my exams.

My friends were all amazed at my grades since they had been forced to stay in for weeks to revise. I would have got straight A's if I had made the effort. It was thanks to Mr Hooper and my treasured calculator that I achieved my best grades in Maths. On the last day we wrote on our school shirts, had egg fights and got drunk to celebrate the end of an era. In the midst of all the fun, I sat alone, I wasn't sure where I was going in life and how I would cope without school.

I wanted a place just for me and my dog. My step mother said she didn't like dogs. She didn't like Sergeant because he was mine. She would cruelly strike him with her walking stick just for sniffing her smelly worn carpets. I would tell her she was evil, I knew she was deliberately upsetting him. Suffering her abuse, he began to gnaw things whilst I was out. She said it was my fault because I wasn't walking him enough. Like me, she didn't make him feel welcome, show him any love or want him in the house. The unemployed housewife might have found the loving dog good company if she had bonded with him but she preferred to go out every day instead, spending time with the mother or the sister she didn't like.

I started to walk him more but it didn't cure the problem. I tried shutting him in the kitchen and he emptied the rubbish bin, causing her an exaggerated two hours of cleaning when she returned. It was always my fault. Out of desperation, I placed his food and water on the floor in the downstairs toilet and I locked Sergeant in, assuming he could do no damage in a toilet just to keep the wicked step mother of the west happy.

I hadn't known the consequence of confining a dog to such a small room. When she returned that day, she said the "little shit" had scratched the door to the toilet trying to get out so without any prior warning Dad parcelled him off. I came home to be told the sad news and how I was to blame. I took his redundant bowls and his leash up to my bed room and cried my heart out. It was quite a conscious decision to get rid of the problem regardless of the hurt. They claimed I would get over it, they were both very heartless people.

I went over to Wolverhampton visiting family, armed with Christmas presents for each and every one of them. It was a lost cause, hoping to regenerate the love on my mother's side. Aunt Linda and Uncle Malcolm introduced me to their new baby daughter Carrie-Ann, who they described as my mother reborn. Aunt June and Uncle Mick introduced me to Suzanne, their baby daughter. My Nan welcomed me with tears of joy and told me again how I looked just like my mother. My grandad said I was always welcome but clarified he would never visit me because of my Dad and what he had done.

They wouldn't let me forget that my father had killed their daughter and that's why we were suffering. It had been my choice to forgive him. I had made my bed. I had to lie on it. There was no going back. I gave Major a love and lay on the floor with him. He had no idea how lucky he was to be loved and cared for. I said my goodbye's and walked back to the bus stop in tears. I missed them all so much. It was time I made a life for myself, away from the man who had ruined all our lives with his selfish actions.

Opportunities adrift, I gave up my job at the chip shop and signed up for a youth training scheme. It was a community care scheme and I had several placements. I helped prepare and serve dinner to elderly people at a luncheon club, having little contact with my grandparents I enjoyed the contact with older, wiser people and they enjoyed my company too. Some of them told me they knew who I was and they would hold my hand to comfort me. They made me feel like I was part of their family. I also worked at the church preschool with children. I'd studied child development and had plenty of experience with my younger cousins and all the babysitting I had done, so the staff thought I was great and the children were always happy to see me.

I worked in a special school with some aspirational children with disabilities. I took them swimming every week. It didn't matter to them whether they had arms or legs, somehow they could still swim length after length of the pool. I loved being with them. My perspective on life started changing. My placements gave my life a purpose. I helped disadvantaged people to enjoy their lives. It raised my self-esteem but the money wasn't good at just £25 per week. I now understood what the strike had been about, cheap labour with no security of a job at the end of it. Despite thoroughly appreciating my YTS experience, I wondered what I was going to do at the end of it. I paid £15 each week for board and I wasn't able to save any money to move out.

I started a new relationship and this time it was steady. I went out with Quilly for a year, and I lost my virginity. It turned out to be quite a painless experience and one I actually enjoyed. I spent most of my time at his house, as part of the family and regardless of being quite fond of him, my friends felt we had become too serious and they missed my friendship. I ended the relationship based on their advice. He moved on but when I saw him with the lovely Deana, I charged over and punched her in the face, causing a nose bleed. He couldn't understand why I had responded that way and I couldn't explain my reaction.

My Dad had killed through jealousy and I didn't want to be like him, I didn't want to be a violent person with a crazy temper. I had dumped Quilly so I couldn't have really loved him. I followed the trail of blood and apologised to Deana. Donna Nichols sent me a message through the grapevine stating she was going to kill me for hurting her friend. I wasn't frightened of her anymore and I sent a message back inviting her to come and see me. She didn't show up.

My next boyfriend, was known locally as Nigger Taylor. Being the only black lad in our village Mick encountered a lot of racial hatred but he stood his ground and won many fights. I suffered the discrimination too. My friends started to call me the 'nigger lover' and I felt ostracised once more. He had white parents but we never talked about how they had ended up with Mick. I thought perhaps his mom had an affair. I got on well with them and I would call in on my way home from work each day. Everything was going ok until we went to the post office to get our passports for our holiday to Corfu. I had my birth certificate and I was engrossed in my mother's name, featuring once again, in my life. Mick asked to see his and his Mom reluctantly handed him the paperwork that disclosed he was adopted. He was shocked and really angry with his parents. He was in so much pain he refused to talk to me about it.

My Dad said I could only go on holiday if I shared a twin room with his mother, so our sex life was off the agenda. I didn't care, this was my first holiday abroad and I couldn't wait to get there. The first night I was awake, fighting off the mosquitoes that had taken a liking to my blood, when I heard Mick sneak out of the apartment. I was curious as to where he was going. The next day he denied he had left the apartment and said I was hearing things. That night he did the same but this time I followed him and found him chatting up a girl at the bar. He saw me and came over to ask why I was spying on him. I was heartbroken, how could my boyfriend betray me whilst we were on holiday together? We went quietly back to our rooms and I lay in my bed crying silently, his mother broke from her snoring and turned over. The next day it was my 17th birthday and we went out for a special meal. Mick bought me a bracelet, the first real gift any boyfriend had given me and all was forgiven but my trust in him had gone.

Not long after the holiday he beat me up for allegedly giving him a sexually transmitted infection. I knew he had caught it elsewhere. I wasn't sleeping around to catch anything. I walked home with a black eye and a split lip and told my Dad I had got into a fight with another girl. Dad proudly laughed it off, "Chip off the old block" he said again. Luckily it was summer time so hiding behind sunglasses whilst I was out wasn't suspicious. I loved Mick and because I was innocent, I tried to fix the relationship. He refused to have sex with me after that day and became more abusive. He had also started to hit his mother and we were both walking on egg shells totally confused by his aggressive outbursts. He eventually told me he had another girlfriend in Birmingham, she was black and she was pregnant. I wondered if he was hitting her too. In a way I felt relieved. I had escaped a violent relationship. I never saw him again.

At the end of my YTS I started to work in a clothing factory, purely for the money but I hated every second I was there. During my six-week trial, I was moved from one department to another. I found the work tedious and the days extremely long. It was a modern-day equivalent to the work house. My mind would drift as I watched the women working their fingers to the bone on piece work. I thought about my mother working in the factory and how she hadn't wanted me to follow in her footsteps and I could understand why.

After the trial, the boss, the dynamic, formidable Debbie Frankham-Wood summoned me to her office. She sat at her desk, like a movie star, made up to the nines, smelling of expensive perfume, wearing her high heels and glad rags. She said she didn't feel I was interested in the work and she was terminating my employment. I wasn't sure what this meant at the time and I blushed with embarrassment. She said "In other words you have been given the sack" and I recall feeling a wonderful sense of freedom. I left the factory with a smile that day and vowed never to return to factory work.

I was on a low ebb but Steve's Mom welcomed me into her home and it was good to have a friendly adult to talk to. I told her how I had hated working in the factory and how my mother had wanted me to get a career. She asked if I missed my mother and she thought it was awful the life I now had at home with the wicked stepmother of the west and my neglectful father. She knew I was lonely and told me Steve was due to come out of Borstal. She hoped I could keep him on the straight and narrow.

He didn't seem that interested in me when he got out. He said I had lost my appeal. He had heard I had lost my virginity after going out with Quilly and Mick. I felt I had hurt his feelings forgetting about him whilst he was in Borstal. I hadn't visited him or sent him a letter. Out of guilt, I wanted to make things up to him.

I would wait at his house chatting to his mother, neither of us knowing what he was up to. Steve would never state where he had been. "Who are you, a copper?" he would say. He was a mystery and if ever I was to help him stay on the straight and narrow, he needed to trust me again. I gave him cigarettes and money, like I had before. He didn't show any appreciation but he let me into his dangerous and strange world.

Steve was still a petty criminal but he now had a new pass time, abusing solvents. I sat with him in his den whilst he sniffed his glue "Why do you do this?" I asked. He told me if I had never tried it, I wouldn't understand. I watched whilst he glue sniffed in front of me, he was drawling and staring into space. When he was high he started to speak to me, telling me I was a good girl, he stroked my hair and smiled. I was fascinated with the way he lovingly talked to me even though he was off his face.

I decided to take a carrier bag and try glue sniffing for myself. At least then I could say I had done it and stop him from continuing the habit. I waited for him to go into a trance and then I scooped some of his glue into my bag and began inhaling the fumes having learned by observation. I could hear thudding echo's almost like I was inside my body and then I saw my mother standing in front of me. She was looking at me and smiling. She was wearing her white polar neck jumper and her blue three quarter length PVC jacket, the same clothes she wore in the dream I'd had. It was a wonderful experience to see her again and I wanted to stay there with her forever but it was quickly shattered in an instant.

Steve was glaring in my face "What are you playing at, you thieving bitch". He pushed me onto my back, snatched the bag off me, picked up his pot of Evo and continued to walk up the railway track sniffing his bag. Glue was something he obviously didn't share. I was shocked by his selfish and brutal nature. Glue sniffing provided me with a rapid and cheap way of escaping my lonely worthless life. Evo was readily available in B&Q and was totally legal to buy. I knew it was dangerous but my life was so shit I didn't really care if I died. I had great dreams but sometimes they turned into horrific nightmares. I wasn't addicted but I desperately wanted to see my Mom again. Perhaps she didn't want to encourage me because she didn't appear again.

I told my curious friends what glue sniffing was like, they were fascinated but I told them not to do it. I hung around with Steve's mates and we glue sniffed together. I had woken up from one session being sexually abused by one of them. I felt so ashamed, he was such an ugly boy who grinned with pride. I decided to sniff on my own after that. I had no recollection of how I had walked a mile up the railway and realising the risks I asked a friend if she would stay with me to make sure I was safe whilst I sniffed. When I couldn't get glue I would sniff butane gas. My image began to change. I started wearing Doctor Martin Boots and I turned into a punk. I was so proud of my image and my Mohican hair style, although it cost an awful lot of money to maintain in hairspray.

My rebellious ways attracted a lot of attention from the wrong type of friends. I sniffed a glue bag on a train with one brainless girl. It had been her stupid idea but once I saw her getting high I had to get there too. The passengers complained as they sat inhaling the fumes in the confines of the carriage. We were removed from the train by the police and taken to Walsall police station. We weren't arrested as we hadn't broken the law. We were just a couple of anti-social kids.

The young officers found the whole incident quite amusing. I apologised for what I had done and told them in future I would only glue sniff on the railway, not on the train. It had, after all, been a very stupid thing to do. They didn't inform my parents because I was seventeen. My friend's parents were notified and luckily for me, she was banned from ever associating with me again.

On my eighteenth birthday, there were no celebrations. I sat on the wall by the shops and Steve came over to scrounge a cigarette. I reluctantly gave him one. He looked into my carrier bag to see what he could steal from me. He grabbed a can of hairspray and as I tried to get it back he sprayed it towards me and lit the gas with a lighter. The flames hit my face and I naturally bowed my head. He singed all my hair and just laughed and ran off. He was the devil in disguise.

I felt like getting off my face after that incident so I bought a pot of glue and sat on the floor in an abandoned garage behind the shopping precinct. Dan Clarke was visiting from Torquay and he walked past and saw me in all my glory. "What are you doing, you idiot" he said in disgust. I needed him to rescue me from my destructive life but he just looked horrified. I was beyond help. I blew the bag up, inhaled a few more times and returned back to dream world.

My next-door neighbour knew all about my Dad killing my mother and my unhappiness at home, she didn't know how I coped. She said she had often heard the rows and didn't blame me for always being out. The shouting worried her sometimes. She had no idea that I wasn't coping and my only escape was a pot of glue. I would use the mirror in my local pub toilets to peel the glue from my face before returning home with a mouthful of mints so no-one suspected a thing.

My neighbour was in a toilet cubicle one night, she smelt the glue as I walked in and recognised my voice. She sat in the cubicle listening to me moaning to my friend about the spots all round my lips. She stared at me as she walked out. I could see she was shocked and concerned about my welfare. When I got home, she was sat on our sofa with my Dad and the wicked step-mother from the west. I openly admitted to them that I was a glue sniffer. My genuinely kind hearted neighbour apologised to me for getting me into trouble and said she had only told them for my own sake. My step mother said "You should be ashamed of yourself, you reprobate" and added "You are a stupid crazy girl who needs to see a psychiatrist." My step mother had such an excellent way of expressing herself. I didn't need a psychiatrist, I just missed my Mom and nothing in my life made sense.

My Dad gave me the worst punishment he could, he grounded me for a week. I lay on my bed crying for nights, listening to their constant arguments, wishing my life was over. The only aerosol gas I was able to inhale was the left over's in my hairspray cans and despite the high, the odd taste of hairspray was bloody revolting. Ray tried to cheer me up. He said Mr. Oldfield had shown the class the best example of a history project he had ever seen. Ray was proud to see it had my name on it. "That's my sister" he said. I realised how much I missed school. There was no further mention of a psychiatrist or any kind of support. I decided not to abuse solvents again. Getting off this planet wasn't changing my life; it was just adding to my problems and above all it was ruining my complexion.

I was glad of some respite from the glue when we went on a fake family holiday to Pontins. It was an opportunity to pretend to be normal. There were plenty of activities for Ray and Rebecca but being that bit older, I found the week quite tedious. I really wasn't interested in the Barney Bear facade that put a smile on every youngster's face. I didn't find playing bingo with Dad and my step mother exciting and I tried to avoid the embarrassment of the Red Coats dragging me onto the dance floor. I did however want to see the adults only show. I loved to watch the Comedians on TV and Mick Miller was one of my favourites and he was the highlight of the week. Neither my Dad nor his wife could be persuaded to join me. "Go on your own" they said, so I did.

I sat there with no-one to talk to, like 'Billy No Mates', observing all the happy families that surrounded me. I half expected Sandra or my Dad to come in and sit with me but I knew deep down they wouldn't bother. I got quite tearful whilst I waited for the show to begin but fortunately Mick Miller instantly cheered me up. He bounced onto the stage with his funny walk and I began to smile. He seemed to notice me immediately and he remarked on my Mohican hairstyle being the opposite of his. He would wink at me whilst he reeled off his jokes. He went on, joke after joke, the audience roared. I laughed so much my cheeks and my stomach ached. It turned out to be one of the happiest nights of my life.

My Dad reminded me when we got home, that I had board to pay and being unemployed, I needed to go and sign on and look in the job centre for work. I walked a couple of miles to Cannock and entered the smoke-filled room of the DHSS. I looked at all the people struck by poverty and ignorance queuing to claim benefits and I turned around and headed for the Job Centre instead.

It was 1987 and the Iron Lady seemed unstoppable. Despite the closure of our local mines and the working-class whinges of a labour community, I was going to be one who got off their backside and got a job. No one was going to look after me or find me a job. I had to do it myself. There was nothing I could apply for with my limited work experience so I contacted a company who wanted a car cleaner and I arranged an interview for that afternoon.

I walked back towards my village penniless and the heavens opened. My Mohican hair style flopped to one side, whilst my mascara ran down my cheeks. I decided to go to the church toilets to make myself decent for the interview. I didn't think God would notice or mind me using his facilities. I washed my face and scooped my hair back with my fingers, detangling the dissolved hairspray from every strand on my head. I looked dreadful. As I left the church, I looked at Jesus on the cross "I know it's a hard life but please help, wish me luck" I said. It was still raining and by the time I arrived at 'The Motor House' my shoes squeaked with water. I advised the impeccably suited sales man who I was. He introduced me to Phil. "Can you start tomorrow" he said. JC, thank you, we got ourselves a job!

I began a new phase, I was at the bottom of the ladder, cleaning the toilets, making the tea and cleaning all the cars but I was needed and appreciated. I also got a fantastic tan in the summer months and wearing my hot pants, I drew the punters in like a prostitute which resulted in more sales. I did have to suffer the sexual harassment from a fat middle aged salesman who each day conveniently appeared in the kitchen when I was making a brew, he would groan with delight as he held my hips and squeezed past me. Nick at the chip shop had been bad but this man made me feel sick. I said nothing and put up with his predatory perverted behaviour because with the money I was earning I could afford to have driving lessons and save a little towards getting my own place.

Chapter 7
Vulnerability

I started going to Cannock at the weekend and enjoyed meeting new people. It was good to be out of the village. I tamed my image and I felt quite grown up. One evening the old school bully, Donna Nichols showed up. I followed her into the toilets and candidly offered her out. She knew I was no longer frightened of her. How the tables had turned, she was now petrified of me. She denied saying she had made threats to kill me. I reminded her of what a bully she had been at school and told her that I had now realised how easy it would be for me to beat her up. She was like a stick insect and I could have snapped her in two. "What goes around comes around" I said. It was satisfying to know I had stood up to the bully that had made my life such a misery.

I walked out of the toilet with my head held high and went back to dance with Shaun Green. Shaun was much older than me but we had often danced together at the community centre discos. We both had a passion for music and dance. He was also popular with all the girls as he worked on the fair ground as a Waltzer boy and he would spin us round to make sure we all had a good time. I loved the fun of the fair. It was another escape from my life. Shaun knew my Dad had killed my Mom and that didn't bother him because he had been in prison too. He said I needed a real man, someone who would look after me.

He told me he had beaten Steve up and told him to stay away from me. He thought Steve had been a bad influence and I was better off without him. I hadn't asked him to do this and I didn't want Steve hurt even if he had singed all my hair. It was just Shaun's way of showing me he cared. He kept chatting me up and asking me out on dates. He was a new romantic, had a job modelling clothes, drove a white Ford Capri and really was the Mr. Charming. He didn't drink, smoke or take drugs so I thought I was the luckiest girl in the world that he was interested in me. I was whisked off my feet.

We were so in love. He would do all he could to make sure I was happy. It was his idea to subscribe to the monthly "Joy of Sex" publication, so we could joyfully experiment based on our new found knowledge. We got engaged and had a huge party. My Dad and and his wife came along for the free buffet food and sat on a table away from us all. I didn't care I had a real loving relationship. After Shaun's modelling work stopped, I got him a job at the Motor House and he picked me up for work each day in his Ford Capri. We spent all of our time together. The sales men persuaded him to buy a bright red Sierra on hire purchase. I don't know if it was posing around in the new car that made him feel like getting a new woman but he soon started having affairs.

Even though I was 19 years of age, I still had to be in at 11pm. Shaun would visit nightclubs after he had dropped me off at home. When I asked him about the other women, he became violent. It was a gradual process, typical of domestic abuse. He wore away my confidence, accused me of having affairs, told me what to wear, spent my money, isolated me from my friends and totally controlled me. I tried finishing with him but he would put the charm on and I would go back to him. I was vulnerable and he was the only person in my life who actually said they loved me, I needed him.

I challenged him one time after he had given me verbal abuse as we were going for a night out. "Don't pretend to everyone that everything is ok in front of our friends" I said. I remembered how my Mom and Dad always put on a front in public. He decided to show me up instead and called me a miserable cow. I turned round and landed a punch on his chin. I hit him so hard he landed on the floor. Everyone laughed out loud but when they saw the rage in his face, they all went silent. They were all frightened of him and I feared I would later be punished for showing him up. I got off lightly that night, he beat someone else up instead, someone who arrived after the incident and said he deserved a smack in the face for the way he beat his ex girlfriend up. Shaun had a history of violence against women and I had naively thought it wouldn't happen to me.

After the next beating, I went to see a solicitor to get an injunction. The solicitor said he would write to him and warn him that if he did this again, we would seek an injunction. I left the solicitor to do the letter and was given no further advice or support. Several days later I was at work cleaning the cars on the forecourt. The sales men had just finished their tea break. I watched them rush out competitively together to prey on a willing punter, both with hopes of earning their commission. But this was not a punter looking to buy a car, it was Shaun looking for me.

Waving the solicitors letter, he stormed over towards me and grabbed me by the hair, rebounding my head off the car roof I had been cleaning. I glanced over to see the salesmen looking at me and scurrying back towards the office. "What the hell is this you bitch?" he yelled. He pulled my face towards the letter. He ripped it up and sprinkled it on the floor like confetti, kicked my soap bucket all over me and threatened to kill me if I ever dared take him to court for an injunction.

He got back into his car and wheel spun away. I sat on the floor in tears, totally traumatised, soaked and publicly humiliated by him. I had just wanted him to leave me alone but the solicitor's letter had made things worse. The salesmen came back out and rushed over to see if I was alright. They claimed they hadn't seen the incident happen. I knew they had turned their backs on me. How can men ignore a young woman being attacked and pretend they know nothing about it?

I learned, as a victim of domestic violence, you couldn't rely on others to help you, most men were cowards and wouldn't get involved. My boss thankfully, decided to terminate Shaun's employment as his attendance had dropped off at work due to all the late nights he was having chasing after girls. At least not having to see him at work helped. I went back to the solicitor, by the time it went to court, Shaun had persuaded me to tell the court I didn't want to press charges. I got confused as I stood in the dock, they used language I wasn't familiar with. I thought an adjournment meant an end to the case. Shaun turned on me when we got outside. He said "You stupid bitch, you have just said you need more time to decide whether you want to get me sent down". I didn't go back to the solicitor. I just tried to avoid contact with Shaun.

My Dad and the wicked stepmother of the west laughed at my suffering and said I would get over him. I was so upset by their neglect in my time of need but I noted my step mother actually sat beside me and gave me a sympathetic hug. I was shocked, it was the first hug she had ever given me. "There's nothing worse than heartbreak" she said. It wasn't the breakdown of the relationship that caused my distress but the knowledge that Shaun was going to give me a beating the next time he saw me. She had no idea how many times he had already beaten me. I couldn't turn to her for help.

I walked down the street with a hammer up my sleeve for several days. I didn't feel any safer, knowing he would probably take the hammer from my hand and hit me with it. I hid behind a garden wall when he pulled up to ask my friends where I was. "Tell her she's in trouble" he said. My heart was pounding whilst he drove around like a maniac trying to find me. I crawled up to someone's front door and asked the residents to call the police. The lady wasn't sympathetic and told me to get off her property or she would call the police to arrest me for trespass. I cut across a field onto the railway track and headed towards home.

My Dad had seen Shaun at the petrol station and had called him over to talk. He said Shaun was a coward and he had scurried away. I was surprised that my Dad cared but that did not take away my fear. My Dad, like the solicitor had just made things worse. Everywhere I went I was looking over my shoulder. I would panic if I heard a car horn or a wheel spin. He had made me a nervous wreck. Dad advised me to stay clear of him and not to come back to the house saying we were back together.

The next time I saw Shaun he smiled and apologised and said he was really missing me. He gave me a loving hug and told me how much he loved me. The only way I felt safe was to know we were back together. Perhaps this time he had learned his lesson, I thought. I couldn't tell my Dad we were back together he wouldn't have understood. I didn't really want to live there anyhow. Shaun said it was time we moved away and got a home together. "We need to get married, I can't live without you" he said.

We went to my home to get all my belongings, our engagement presents and my sewing machine. We drove all the way to Dover and went to the social services looking for somewhere to live. We were advised to go back home. We slept in the car for a week. The nights were cold and I couldn't get comfortable lying on the passenger seat. My back ached. I longed to sleep in a bed but I wasn't going to return to my Dad's house. Shaun asked his mother if I could stay at their house and she sympathetically refused. She knew my Dad had killed my Mom and didn't want any trouble. I spent another week sleeping in the car on their driveway.

His mother brought a Sunday dinner out to me. I sat in the passenger seat of the car trying to eat it whilst crying. It was the first homemade meal I had eaten in a long time. Shaun's Dad, the king of their council house, clarified the terms of a temporary arrangement and agreed to let me stay in the single bed in Shaun's box room. We finally unpacked the car. My Dad came to Shaun's front door to tell me work had called and he was concerned about my job. He never asked me to go home. I never went back to the Motor House, I felt too embarrassed to admit to them that I was back with my violent boyfriend. Instead I went to the DHSS to sign on, so I could pay board to Shaun's dad and I cancelled my driving lessons.

Occasionally, I would sit on the sofa and watch TV, trying to forge a relationship with the insensitive Mr. Green. I observed how controlling he was with his nervous wife. She was tied to the kitchen sink, at his beck and call, constantly walking on eggshells avoiding confrontations. His six children were all fearfully respectful towards him. The atmosphere in the Green's house wasn't pleasant but I was used to it. I spent most of the daytime visiting the job centre, reading the situations vacant in newspapers, walking around industrial sites, cold calling on businesses but every employer wanted experience or qualifications, it was demoralising.

Shaun wasn't worried, he started to do burglaries and joined forces with Steve. Influenced by a martial arts TV programme, they both wore intimidating black Ninja outfits, so they couldn't be identified. They aggressively branded swords and nunchakus. It was as though they were possessed by the devil. My friends thought they were hilarious posing around in their new attire. I was terrified they would kill me. I knew they thought they were invincible.

They booked flights to Tenerife with the funds they had made from their crimes. Shaun said he was going to get work and find somewhere for us to live. He asked me to sell all our engagement presents whilst he was gone, to raise the funds for my flight and our new life in Tenerife. I was relieved and excited. I boasted to all my old friends, as I sold our gifts, that I was leaving England for better weather. I thought I could start a new life abroad, Shaun's life of crime would be over and we would live happily ever after.

However, a week later, I was woken in the middle of the night by stones hitting the bedroom window. "Open the door you silly cow" Shaun whispered. He told me that all his money had been stolen from the safe in his room, so they had to come back home. Steve pulled me aside, the next day and told me how they had actually enjoyed a crazy week of sex, drugs and rock and roll and I believed Steve.

All my dreams of a new future were lost. The man who I had left home for wasn't faithful and he didn't want to look after me. Sleeping together in an extra small single bed had taken its toll on our relationship. Neither of us could get comfortable or sleep. Shaun became more abusive. He left me in the box room, took the money I had saved and didn't return. I assumed he had gone out to a nightclub to dance and meet another woman. I knew he would be out enjoying himself. I had hit an all time low. I couldn't take anymore. I took an overdose of Paracetamol tablets and lay on the bed, expecting to drop off to sleep and die.

I had cramps in my stomach, they got worse but I didn't die. Shaun came back to find me crying in agony. He just said I was stupid and stormed back out. I was stupid, I had taken the full bottle but I couldn't even kill myself. I felt so alone. I needed love and support. The only person I knew I could turn to was my Aunt Linda. The next day I got Shaun to take me to visit her and I told her we were looking for work and somewhere to live.

Chapter 8
Reconnected

My aunt and uncle were so pleased to see me after such a long time. They were a little shocked by my appearance, even though I had actually tamed it down. Aunt Linda seemed happy to hear I had stopped talking to my Dad. She had predicted the day would come when I realised the reality of what he had done. How different a life I might have had if it hadn't been for my Dad's selfish nature. Why didn't he just get divorced? I told her how much I missed my Mom. I didn't tell her about my drinking habits, the glue sniffing, the overdose or the violent relationship I was in, I felt too ashamed. All I wanted was her love and support.

They offered me a job at their bakery and helped us find a furnished bedsit in Wolverhampton. I said goodbye to Mr. and Mrs. Green and thanked them for letting me stay. They seemed relieved to know we had found somewhere else to live. I spent most days in the bakery happily chatting with Aunt Linda about the past. We would visit my grandparents on the way home from work. It was a huge comfort to be back with my family. We both worked hard in the bakery. She appreciated my help. I would serve the customers and run errands for her and it took the pressure off her.

My uncle showed me how to make all the cakes and I had a great time. I would jam the doughnuts and eat one, chocolate the éclairs and eat one, ice the buns and eat one and cream the other cakes. Then I would burn off the calories cleaning and mopping so I maintained my slim figure, whilst keeping the working environment immaculately clean. I telephoned Ray to tell him where I was living and how happy I was. He said Rebecca now had a dog called Barney, ironically, Sandra actually loved this dog. Ray described 'their family' as being complete. Ray had left school, had no direction, no support and was alone. He claimed Steve was 'looking after him'. I felt guilty, in my own effort to find happiness, I had abandoned my brother.

In bedsit land many of the occupants were either students or down and out loners. We rented a large room in a Victorian house. It was on the ground floor and had French Doors that opened out onto the drive. I borrowed some extra tall step ladders from Gramps and began painting the ceiling. I became quite disorientated whilst on them happily layering brilliant white paint on a ceiling which probably hadn't seen any paint since the day it was built. As I stepped down the ladders, I realised the steps were on the other side and holding the pot of paint and a roller I fell back onto the French doors. I could have easily gone through either pane of glass but somehow, I managed to land between them on the door frame. I sat for a moment, with paint dripping down my face, assessing the situation. Despite having wobbly legs I got back up and completed the task.

As soon as the paint was dry, Shaun hung his Samurai swords and nunchakus up above the fireplace, against my wishes. He disregarded my phobia of knives that symbolised death. He humiliated me and asserted his control. The Samurai swords were used now and then to frighten me and to keep me in line. I hid the abuse from my family and was grateful to be in their company. Shaun got himself a job working in a warehouse and sold his Sierra to a gypsy. He bought a flashy racing car with the cash. Two men turned up one day, as my aunt dropped me off at home. "Who are they?" she said. The men were trying to look like normal people hanging around but I knew they were plain clothed police. They told me Shaun had stopped his payments on the car and a warrant was out for his arrest for fraud.

Whilst Shaun faced a court case my uncle Malcolm was in a lot of pain with an abscess. He explained about the hardships of running your own business and how he had to continue baking or he would lose contracts. I said I would cover for him and we eventually persuaded him to go into hospital. I worked continuously for three days and nights to keep the bakery going. On the fourth day, when Uncle Malcolm was due back at work, I sat down on a stool and fell asleep. His father woke me again and asked which house was mine as he dropped me off. I was so exhausted I didn't know I had got in his van. I went to bed and slept straight through for twenty-four hours.

During this time, Shaun had begun an affair with the office receptionist at his depot. I found a letter in his jacket pocket. The girl said she had felt guilty having sex in our bed and that she had been looking at my photographs and wanted to call things off. I rang her office and told her she was welcome to him. My Aunt Linda had seen the evil side of Shaun that day and said I could live at their house. My Uncle Malcolm called the police and asked them to meet us at the bedsit so I could collect my belongings without being attacked by Shaun and his Samurai swords.

We pulled up outside the bedsit and waited for the police. The light was on and I assumed Shaun was sat inside. I did not want to get my things without police protection. I was terrified I would end up like my mother. Had I have known he wasn't there, I would have had plenty of time to get everything out. About an hour passed and Shaun arrived. My uncle advised me to lock the car and he would keep him talking until the police turned up. He walked towards him armed with a baseball bat, hidden in his jacket. They seemed quite relaxed towards each other, laughing and joking about what women were like. I couldn't believe my uncle was being so disloyal, knowing what had happened to my mother on the day she left my father. I thought he didn't care if history repeated itself but he was just biding his time, waiting for the police to come.

The police arrived a few minutes later and spoke to Shaun. They came over to the car and asked me to get out and talk to him. I refused. They said I was being 'silly' and he wasn't going to hurt me, not while they were there. You find with the police that they seem to think they know the perpetrator better than you do and I foolishly believed them. I unwillingly unlocked the car thinking I was safe. Shaun opened the door and asked why I was leaving him, almost like he had done nothing wrong. I told him my reasons and he called me a bitch. He leaned into the car and began to strangle me. I wasn't too sure how long I would last with his hands around my throat, choking me.

It seemed a long time before the police got him off me. I sat there gasping for breath whilst the two officers with their truncheons and my uncle with his baseball bat, beat him until he was crying like a baby, curled up in a ball. It was somewhat satisfying to see him being beaten for a change. I felt a sense of relief which quickly passed to a feeling of dread. I watched them handcuff him and get him into the police car. He didn't need to say a word, he just glared. He will definitely kill me now, I thought.

Despite the safety and warmth of my Aunt's home, and the bruises to my neck fading, I lay in bed quietly crying each night, worrying over the court case and what he would do to me. Uncle Malcolm took me to court and I sat in a corridor fretting that I would see him. I was a nervous wreck. Strangulation was the single biggest predicting factor of future homicidal behaviour of men towards women. It was attempted murder, and should have been treated as such. However, my solicitor had said Shaun was pleading not guilty to a charge of common assault. This made me feel more nervous and somewhat despondent, even the British justice system seemed to be on his side. My stomach churned in preparation for his evil glare as I walked towards the court room to give evidence. "It's OK, you don't need to go in" the solicitor smiled. Shaun had changed his plea.

Not knowing the system, I asked if he had been sent to prison, but another date had been set for sentencing. He was however held in remand so I felt a temporary sense of security. A month later he was sentenced to nine months for the fraud charge and was to serve two months to run concurrent for strangling me. Ironically, the car was worth more than me, and to add insult to injury with good behaviour and his remand time considered Shaun only actually served six months. During this time, I wrote him a letter. I had probably written around twelve versions to ensure what I was saying could not be misinterpreted. I hoped that he would read this in his cell and leave me in peace when he was released.

I began having driving lessons again. As soon as I had passed my test, I bought an old Morris Marina van and began my own bread round. The van had allegedly got twelve months MOT and was a real bargain. I learned how to knock my starter motor on with a hammer when the van stalled at a junction and how to get the handbrake cable tight so I didn't have to park it in gear. I haggled at the scrap yard for cheaper bits and even treated her to four new tyres after the police had pulled me over pointing out to me that my worn tyres resembled Brillo pads.

The money I earned wasn't good and I struggled but it was my business and I was proud to be self-sufficient at last. With my aunts and uncles support my self-esteem was rising every day. I was grateful for they had given me somewhere safe to sleep but as I was approaching twenty-one, I felt I needed my independence. My uncle asked if I would be interested in running a second shop for him. He said it had a flat that was vacant above the shop. I jumped at the chance to expand the family business and naively thought my uncle was trying to help me gain my independence.

My three bed roomed flat was inhabitable. Despite its condition I made it home. I removed the fungi off the walls and negotiated a reduced rent with the landlord when I tried to open a window and the window frame fell out. I bought a second hand mattress, sofa and a wardrobe from a junk shop. I had also found some material enough to make some curtains. I went back to my father's house when I realised I hadn't got the foot for my sewing machine.

The wicked step mother of the west answered the door. I politely asked her for the foot for my sewing machine. This was absolutely no use to her and it was pure spite that she refused to let me have it. She told me that as far as my Dad was concerned I was dead and she told me never to turn up on their doorstep again. I returned to my flat and hung the material over the curtain rail and pulled it off in the day time. I got some free paint from the recycling site and began restoring the property so it was habitable.

During the day I worked in the cake shop but trade was slow and I spent most of my days sat in the back room privately writing letters to Steve. He was back in prison and he was lonely too. I wrote to him every day this time. He wrote back now and then. I was so pleased to receive a letter from him it made me feel loved, in a crude sort of way but I was still lonely. My uncle ceased the opportunity to take advantage of a vulnerable young woman, living on her own. He confided in me about problems in his marriage and then spoke about my energy and motivation. He put his hand on my leg and said "if only I was 15 years younger, eh?"

I couldn't believe that my own uncle was coming onto me. He made me feel physically sick. He was willing to betray his wife, a woman I loved more than anyone in the world and there was no way I would have entertained the idea of having an affair with her husband. I made my feelings clear there and then. I contemplated telling her about his advances but I didn't have the heart. She had been through so much already. I kept silent and I tried to forget the incident had ever happened. He said she was suspicious that we were already having an affair.

She sensed something had happened and I felt awkward not telling her the truth, she didn't seem to trust me but he was just the man that paid my wages and the slime ball I had turned down.

Chapter 9
MeasureMENt

Living on my own, in a multicultural area was exciting, there were interesting people from different backgrounds all around me and I was keen to make new friends. I spent most evenings chatting to the staff in the chip shop next door. Mardi, the owner, was a Iranian Muslim who drove a flashy new Mercedes. He was completing his degree in architecture and impressed me with how intelligent he was to be studying in a foreign language. He had a warm and humorous personality which made me laugh. He employed two members of staff, Bali and Omar.

Bali was a lovely Indian guy who lived round the corner with his wife and children. We were invited to his house on special occasions. I always sat in the lounge chatting and drinking alcohol with the men, whilst the wives prepared feasts for us in the kitchen. The ladies were gracious and hospitable and refused to let me help them because I was their guest. The men were all noticeably over fed but I observed how respectful and appreciative they were towards their wives. Bali's wife had a laborious lifestyle yet she seemed content washing her clothes in the bath tub "We wash clothes in the river in India, the water is very very bad there" she told me. She came to my flat to teach me how to make a traditional Indian curry from scratch.

Omar was an asylum seeker from troubled Iraq. I was fascinated by his culture and realised how much he missed his family. He was a constant flirt but I warmed to his charms and romantic gestures. He took me out to classy wine bars and made me feel like his princess. One evening we ended up back at his house, a property he was renovating. There were planks of wood everywhere and I was interested in his development plans. We sat on the sofa chatting like we had known each other all our lives. He took my hand and guided me to his bedroom. He was gentle, kind and loving and I felt my loneliness and despair melt away as we made love.

The next morning he popped out to the local shop to get some milk, whilst I took a shower. I heard the door knock and thought Omar had forgotten his key. Dripping wet and wearing only a towel, I opened the door. On the door step stood a young woman with a baby in her arms. She asked for Omar. I explained he had gone to the shop and quickly closed the door. I got dressed and I peeped through the net curtains as they talked on his drive. I noticed a water rates bill on the window sill, it was addressed to Morfuk Sadir.

It turned out, she was his girlfriend and the baby was his daughter. I ended the relationship with Morfuk. The man who lived up to his real name. Mardi had warned me Omar was full of bullshit and then he asked if he could take me out, just as friends, we had no future, he said it was forbidden for him to marry a Christian but we did love each others company. Again, I was fascinated with his cultural background and surprised when he showed me a family video, he had come from a palatial home, fit for a king and now just like me, he lived in a grotty flat in Wolverhampton.

His oblivious wealthy father had given him far too much money for his living expenses. He wasn't legally supposed to have a business but he invested the excess funds in the chip shop and it was very profitable. With his surplus cash, he would dress to impress and take me to the casino to lose some dosh and we would often laugh on the way home at how much we had won.

Mardi was a charming carefree gentleman, who opened doors for me and insisted on paying for everything, buying me alcoholic drinks and toasted sandwiches. I knew he took other women out and that didn't worry me, he liked having fun and flaunting his cash. I called it a day when he shared his crabs with me. Much to my embarrassment, a shameful trip to the VD clinic was called upon. I had every test going just to be on the safe side. I remained friends with Mardi but I wasn't going to risk catching anything else.

I took in a flatmate. Marie was a good friend at first and eased my lonely life by hosting parties. A friend of Shaun's came to one party and told me he had visited him in prison. Shaun had asked him to pass on the message that he was going to kill me when he got out and that he blamed me for having to do time. On the day of Shaun's release, I drove to his house with Marie. He was stood outside with his father and was initially surprised to see me driving a van. I told him I had come so he could kill me and advised him that whilst he served his time for murder, I would sit in his cell and haunt him. He started to laugh. "Let's let sleeping dogs lie" he said. I drove away knowing at last I was safe.

On my twenty first birthday Marie bought me a case of Diamond White Cider. By this time, my flat was a mess and she wasn't contributing any money towards the bills as we had arranged. She owed me a lot of money and was clearly taking advantage but I wasn't going to argue on my birthday. My brother Ray and all my friends from Cheslyn Hay came to the party. I went to bed when my flat began to spin with the hastily consumed cider, leaving Marie to supervise things.

The next day I woke to find the usual aftermath of the night before and began to clean up. Marie returned some hours later. She told me she had left the party early to sleep at her boyfriend's house and was claiming her room had been raided. There had been no-one at the party that would have stole anything but it gave her an excuse to move out. I never got the money she owed me and we never spoke again.

Shaun decided to pay me a visit, with tears in his eyes, he said he couldn't live without me. Before I could blink, he was there in my life again. I couldn't bring myself to tell Aunt Linda that we were back together. I knew it was a stupid thing to do, but I was lonely and he said all the right things at the time. I fell for it time after time and nothing ever changed. One night after we had been to a firework display, he left me babysitting his sister's children and disappeared. I thought he was seeing another woman again and when his sister returned, I decided to catch him in the act.

It was 2am in the morning and I was walking the streets looking for his van. An old school friend was in a car on his drive. I walked over to him and persuaded him to take me home. It was a foggy evening and it was very difficult driving conditions. I was shocked to see Shaun's van parked outside my flat when we eventually arrived there. How dare he bring a woman back here, I thought, but when I got up to the lounge, I was even more shocked to find the flat full of electrical equipment. Shaun and Steve had decided to raid an electrical shop as the weather reduced visibility. They had completely emptied the shop and drove off into the white fog never to be followed by anyone.

The next day their loot was bundled back into the van. I had given them a choice "Either get rid of it or I am calling the police." I couldn't believe he could involve me and think it was acceptable to use my flat for storage. I felt like a criminal because I hadn't told the police. The electrical shop reopened with security cages up the window. As I walked past, the owner was standing on a window sill holding the cage and rattling it. It was like he was an animal in the zoo trying to escape. He had been driven crazy by having his business broken into time after time. I wanted to go in and tell him who had stolen all of his goods but I couldn't. I was too scared of Shaun.

I felt used by Shaun and I refused to have sex with him that night. He accused me of having an affair. Ray and Steve were in my kitchen chatting and I decided to get out of bed and give Shaun the cold shoulder. I thought he would drop off to sleep. Ray and Steve had been boiling magic mushrooms and Steve had scalded himself with the boiling water. He removed his wet T-shirt and showed me his red stomach. I gave him a cold compress to apply. The mushrooms didn't turn out to have any magic qualities but a nightmare unfolded. We sat down to watch TV and then Shaun charged in with his Samurai sword. He slashed the TV we were watching, then the fire and then he attacked the arms of the sofa. We all froze in terror, hoping to survive the psychopath as he demonstrated his directed anger. I could never refuse sex with him after that night.

The flat above the bakery was up to let and I thought if I was to move there, I would be safer. I needed £400 deposit and my previous landlord eagerly gave me the money to get me out so he could make more money renting each room as a bedsit. I did feel a lot safer above the bakery. My uncle and the other baker were there every night baking so Shaun couldn't use the flat to store stolen goods without being seen, I thought this might deter him from involving me in his criminal activity. Malcolm was keeping his eye on me and it wasn't long before he knew we were back together. Aunt Linda thought I was crazy and deserved better. I agreed with her but I was too frightened to finish with him.

Then one night, in the early hours of the morning Shaun come home drunk with lipstick on his collar. It was a classic sign of adultery. He had obviously been with another woman and I questioned him. He stumbled to bed, laughing at me. I took the kitchen knife from the drawer and went to the bedroom. He lay fully clothed in bed, sleeping with a smile on his face. I stood at the foot of the bed with the knife in my hand. I wanted to cut off his testicles and wipe the smile from his face. I hated the way he treated me. As I leant back on the wall, I slid down and collapsed on the floor. As much as he deserved to have his testicles removed, I knew I would go to prison just like my father. He wasn't worth it.

The next day, whilst Shaun was at work, I packed all his belongings and took them to his mothers and said I never wanted him in my life again. I handed the Samaria swords to the police and told his mother I had done this to avoid being killed. She collected them from the police station and told me that she had buried them in the garden. It's strange but it was his infidelity that made me finish with him. I had learned my lesson. I would never have another relationship with a violent and unfaithful man again. I was worth more.

I would visit Great Wyrley at the weekends, drinking in the local pubs, wondering where I would sleep. There was always a sex starved someone who couldn't resist me, who was keen to take me back to theirs for a night of passionate sex. They were satisfying and respectful mutual affairs. I enjoyed sex and being close to someone in an intimate way made me feel loved and wanted. I felt in control of my life, I had turned the tables on men, I used them and that freedom felt good for a while.

I couldn't continue that kind of lifestyle for ever so I cut myself off from my past, from Great Wyrley and all my old friends. I went to a club in Wolverhampton and I asked Ray's friend to fix me up with a man. He told a guy I liked him and he came over to talk to me. I took Ian home that night and he told me how he had just separated from his wife because she had been having an affair. He already had two children and was heartbroken that he had tried to be a good husband and father to them. We talked for hours about his life and his hardships, and then we made love.

A few weeks later, I didn't have a period and told Ian I thought I might be pregnant. He was furious with me and insisted I have a termination. I spoke to Uncle Malcolm and Aunt Linda about the situation. Aunt Linda was glad to see I had got psychopathic Shaun out of my system and this was a new chapter in my life. Uncle Malcolm felt I was best to have a termination as I couldn't do my bread round and look after a baby. I don't know if it was my hormones or my emotional state but being pregnant made me feel different, I felt stronger. Ian finished with me and I went ahead with the pregnancy regardless.

I visited May Morley for a catch up when I was about seven months pregnant and I bumped into my Dad walking up the road. He pointed at my stomach and said "What's this then?" I sarcastically explained it was a baby and we started to talk. It was his grandchild I was carrying and I thought at first he was genuinely interested in my welfare. He asked why I hadn't been in touch and I reminded him of what my step mother had said. He denied saying I was dead and stated all he had said was that I had made my bed and had to lie on it. My father had never been one for comforting words. I had lost count of the number of beds I had laid on since I had left his house. I politely said goodbye and went on my way.

Eight months into the pregnancy, I was physically struggling to get through the doorways with my bread trays and a bump so I gave up my bread round. Uncle Malcolm gave me a few quid for working on the markets selling cakes and bread. I was looking forward to being a mom but I worried about finishing work and how I would survive financially. I knew I would have to give up my flat, I wouldn't be able to pay the rent. The flat wasn't practical for a baby, having to carry pushchairs up stairs would have been a further strain. I applied to the council for housing.

Ian had almost forgotten I existed but his family stayed in touch and reassured me he would come round once the baby was born. I hoped he would, I didn't really want to raise a child on my own. Ian earned good money. He spent plenty of it on beer drinking sessions but the skinflint saved the rest like a miser, he wasn't going to look after me.

I settled for a comforting Christmas with Nan and Gramps. Nan's delicious dinners, home made trifle and warm mince pies went down a treat and my bump was at bursting point. New Cross Hospital offered a cheque for £1000 for the first baby born in 1990 so desperate for money, I tried all the old wife's tales to trigger the onset of labour. I had hot baths. Nan cooked me a spicy curry, with extra pineapple and insisted I bounced around the house, we laughed at my efforts but the baby wasn't budging.

Chapter 10
The Single Mother

On January the 7th, I was enormous and the horrendous contractions finally started. Nan had told me I wasn't in labour and reassured me I was ok. She rubbed my back and seemed determined for me to have a home birth, confident in her midwifery skills. The ambulance drivers were on strike at the time and the army were covering for them. When the contractions became more regular, I decided to ring Aunt Linda, she had given birth to four children and I felt more secure with her taking me to hospital than a young naive soldier.

We arrived in the hospital when I was ten centimetres dilated just how the midwives liked it. They kept telling me to push. "I am bloody pushing!" I replied. Aunt Linda held my hand as my son eventually tore his way out of my body. The midwives were shocked at his size, handed me my baby and set about stitching me back together. I had hoped, throughout the entire pregnancy, to have a sweet little baby girl. I tried not to show my disappointment as I lay there, relieved the labour was finally over.

The next day after some rest, I held Nathan in my arms, I should have been a happy new mother but I was overcome with a torrent of uncontrollable emotions. I shed tears of sadness not joy. I was now a mother with no mother, submerged in grief. I looked at his face, my father's angry features glared back at me. He kicked and waved his arms as he shrieked in discontent as I perversely tried to breastfeed someone who looked just like my Dad.

The milk didn't flow as I expected it would. My breasts were hard, full of solidified milk, my nipples were burning red with soreness as my baby tried in vain to feed. He was the biggest baby on the ward, with the loudest cry. I couldn't cope that he didn't like me or my milk. I asked the midwife, who intervened, if I could go for a cigarette. I stood outside, tears rolling down my face, dragging away on a cigarette, regaining the courage to return. I was surprised and relieved to see he had settled back to sleep.

Over the next few hours I observed the midwives whispering and looking towards me. They openly displayed preferential treatment towards the happily married mothers. The woman opposite me was smiling with pride as she handed her baby to her husband. He proudly kissed his wife on her cheek. I felt alone, disrespected and undignified. I glanced at my baby sleeping, with my fathers face. I went outside for another cigarette. The daughter of a murderer was now a predictable single mother surviving on benefits. I returned to find a midwife bottle feeding my baby. My wishes to breast feed were irrelevant. She gave me a harsh lecture that Nathan had jaundice, justifying her need to bottle feed him. It wasn't the first bottle they had secretly given him without my consent. I gave up trying to breastfeed.

I wasn't allowed home for three days as I had a water infection and a high temperature. During my time on the maternity ward, I was upset but not surprised that Ian didn't turn up to see me or his son. I received a beautiful bouquet of flowers which I naturally assumed he had sent. I read the card "Congratulations Diane, on the birth of your son, love from Dad and Sandra." I had never been given flowers before and I felt oddly special. Then on the evening, my mothers family visited bringing flowers and gifts and Nathan was passed around, to each one of them, all desperate to hold the families first great grandson. It felt good to have them around me.

People often talk about single mothers deliberately getting pregnant to get a council house. I hadn't thought about getting pregnant at the time I had sex, let alone to get a house. Getting a house wasn't really a privilege. I was offered the worst place to call home, for me and my son, yet another third refusal, which due to being broke, I gratefully accepted. It wasn't a beautiful house in the country, nor was it a nice place by the sea, it was on an intimidating, rundown council estate in Bilston.

I didn't have enough housing points to have a house near to my family. I wasn't offered a choice. After two years, they said, I could exchange so I moved in. The council gave me the keys, enough money to decorate some parts of the house and a grant which paid for a few rooms to have carpet. I again hoped that Ian, as a painter and decorator, would come to my rescue, but I was clearly on my own as a single parent.

Once home, I plummeted into a deep dark depression. I thought it was just my hormones at first or the baby blues but it went on and on. I mourned the loss of my mother each time I said "mommy's here" to my son. "I wish you were here Mom" I said. For twelve years I had tried to cope without her but now I needed her to show me what to do. I yearned for her to help me as I cried during the long lonely sleep deprived nights, trying to settle a new born baby. This was the first time I had really grieved, as adults do, for the loss of a loved one.

It was Aunt Linda who came to my rescue and really supported me. She bought all the expensive items for Nathan and made sure he never went without. She loved him like her own grandchild and she showed me how to be a mother. Without her love and support I don't know if I would have got through the early weeks of my sons life. He was an innocent baby born into a tragedy but genetically I could not sever the ties with my father, when he looked so much like him. I tried my hardest to do what should have come naturally, I loved Nathan and he was never neglected but I was an emotional wreck.

When Nathan was six weeks old and I had done most of the decorating, Ian came to visit. He held Nathan in his arms and I felt the warmth of love he had for his son. He had bought a racing car for him. It was marked up with a Woolworths reduced sticker and he placed a fifty pence piece in his hand for luck. I sticky taped the coin to the car and kept it as a memento, along with his baby book and lock of hair. Ian did move in with me for a while but it was only for his convenience, he didn't love me. I tried to talk to him about my life but he wasn't interested. He thought I was crazy when I cowered when he raised his voice. I would wash and iron his clothes and cook his evening meal. I tried to play the happy family but Ian always went out without me and it wasn't long before I felt the need to end the relationship.

When I could afford it, I would catch two buses and visit my grandparents and my aunts. I would take walks around the park when the weather was nice but we were socially isolated, I didn't have any friends in Bilston. I didn't take Nathan to a mothers and toddlers group because I felt ashamed of being a poor, unemployed, single mother. I met up with Donna Nichols once again in the local health centre. Mrs Patel, as she was now known, had two children, a husband, a mortgage and seemed very settled. She boasted about her children being spoilt by their grandma. I could have arranged to meet up with her but I wasn't that desperate for human company. I just needed some direction in my life.

A Government scheme allowed Nathan a free nursery place, so he could socialise with other children whilst I was able to continue my education and that opportunity was a blessing. After completing a home study course for a GCSE in Welfare and Society, I started an Access to Social Work Course. I enjoyed the learning experiences and doing something for myself. It was a welcome break from being the penniless single mother. I studied social work and social welfare.

Homelessness, the poverty trap, discrimination and mental health issues were all things I had personally experienced so I enjoyed learning more about these subjects. I was shocked when a tutor gave me feedback on an equal opportunities assignment. She had ripped the work apart, underlining words insinuating I was racist. She was the first black tutor in my education to date and the first person to challenge my ignorance. I learned from her about indirect discrimination, micro aggressions and attitudes that reflected white supremacy, she changed my perspective completely. I confronted my prejudices and changed my thought processes, resubmitted my work and passed. I thanked her, for what she had done was more important to me than any assignment. She had opened my eyes to prejudice.

My doctor diagnosed I was suffering from depression, not the baby blues, he didn't know my life history, nor was he aware of the trauma I had suffered over the years. He knew a cheque for £1000 might have helped but all he could give me was antidepressants. My grandparents had never benefitted from pill popping after my mother's death and they'd continued to take them ever since. I didn't bother taking mine. Anti-depressants can't work if people need them forever. I set myself some longterm goals; to complete my degree, get a good paid job supporting others and buy a house by the sea. As much as I struggled with poverty and the hardship of being a single mother, in a time where huge stigma existed, I wanted my son to have a better life and to be proud of me.

I went in to town to cash my family allowance and benefit money. I topped up my gas and electricity meter cards for the week, made my council tax and water payments, bought some saving stamps towards my next TV licence and counted what little remained for my weekly shop. My cousin had come with me and she was pushing Nathan in his pushchair. I was totting up the total in my mind, trying to be miraculously thrifty. I was rummaging in a freezer when my cousin asked if I knew the two women that were giving me funny looks from over by the check out. I glanced over but didn't recognise them. I continued to do my shopping. When we came to the check out, I realised my purse had been stolen from my bag. The two women must have thought my cousin had seen them take my purse but she hadn't. The cashier told me not to worry and she would put all my items back.

That was all the money I possessed, I was penniless. The token cards for my gas and electric meters had enough credit on them to get me through the week and pay off the emergency supply I had already used. I had lost enough TV license stamps to get my next license. We had no food, Nathan had no nappies and my front door key was in my purse. I was devastated. I called the council and waited for them to send someone out to change my locks and stayed at Aunt Linda's for a week until I could cash my benefits again. I needed an income if I was to improve our lives so I thought about ways for surviving poverty. The gas board owed me £360 as they had overcharged me on my meter but I was prosecuted for not having a TV licence. The court appearance was a humiliating experience. The well spoken witness said I had opened the door and said "I ay got a TV licence" in the broad Black Country accent I never used. The fine was coincidentally £360.

I walked to Bilston to enquire about some part time work, my college tutors had told me about a post supervising offenders in a probation hostel. Naomi Swannel, introduced herself. She was a probation officer and the manager of the hostel. She asked me to tell her a bit about myself. I told her I was a single mom, living on a council estate, taking a college course, hoping for a career in social work and determined to escape poverty. She showed me around the hostel and introduced me to some of the residents and asked me for my thoughts. As I responded she handed me an application form "It's great to have you on board" she said. I felt somewhat reassured that my luck was changing.

I returned home to find I had been burgled. I assumed it was some of the local lads who had been watching my movements that day. I had noticed the sun shining on the lenses from their binoculars, from their window. They had only stolen my microwave. I had nothing else worth stealing. I marched round to the squat where the lads sat sniffing glue, they seemed surprised I wasn't intimidated by their behaviour. I asked who had stolen my microwave. They all denied it and offered me a choice of two others from their kitchen, which were rusty and covered in mouldy splattered food, I declined their offer.

I notified the police who gave me a card to contact Victim Support and a crime reference number so I could claim on my insurance, not that I could afford home insurance. I was shaken by the burglary. I felt violated and found it difficult to sleep for several nights knowing someone had been in my house. I paced around the lounge expecting them to return. I called Victim Support and a man who lived in my street visited me. As a victim of crime it was helpful to talk to someone. Although it seemed unjustified attention, when a ten year old child got no support in the aftermath of a murder. We had a chat about how vulnerable I was. He knew the lads that broke into my home and he knew they had no morals.

I reluctantly, sold my old Morris Marina van to the scrap man to raise some cash to replace my microwave. I knew the van was falling apart, the tax had ran out and it would never have legally passed another MOT but not having transport made me feel more isolated in Bilston. I began working in the hostel supervising young men who had been sentenced to live in the probation hostel by the courts. As I talked to them I noticed how many had suffered trauma, had chaotic home lives and a poor education. It seemed predictable that they would be there.

I enjoyed the opportunity to steer these young men into education or work, for their next stop was prison, if they didn't do something positive with their lives. They reminded me of my brother. I wondered how he was coping as they told me about their role models in life. The pay at the hostel was extremely good and with Nathan having free nursery places, child care wasn't an issue. I had started to get my home in order with the extra money but it would have needed £1000's to make it look attractive.

I was studying hard at college and working so I decided to treat myself, once a week, to a night out whilst my cousin babysat. I met plenty of worthless characters. I started seeing the caretaker from the college who turned out to have a heavily pregnant wife. I met a boxer who moved in with me for a week to make his wife jealous, he returned to her. Then there was a guy who got back with his girlfriend and another whose girlfriend knocked on my door to tell me she was pregnant. I just couldn't find a decent man. I wanted someone who would love and treasure me and my son.

A wild romance started with *Dick**, (I would name and shame him, but he is still a serving officer and he could lose his job) He was the brother of a college friend and was a police officer. We went out together on several occasions. The criminals on the estate would warn us off, if we drank anywhere local. "Can you smell pork?" they would grunt. *Dick** stood his ground, he wasn't intimidated by the low life. One night, as we left a nightclub, I sat down next to a man, I was concerned about him because he was crying. I asked him what was up. He told me his wife had left him and he couldn't cope. *Dick** told him to move on. The guy turned nasty and said "Who the fuck, do you think you are". *Dick** flashed his badge to show him who he was. The man moved on. I tried to explain to *Dick** that the guy was upset, his wife had just left him. "And why do you think she did that Diane? he said.

*Dick** knew good from bad and I really did feel safe in his company. I had finally managed to find someone with good morals and a respectable profession. He seemed to enjoy spending time with me and my son. I admired him and felt proud of our relationship. I visited my grandparents and told them the good news. My Gramps, who had also been a police officer, before he worked in the building trade, tried to let me down gently, he warned me it wouldn't last. He said he would look into my background and being the daughter of a murderer this would taint his conduct. I didn't believe the police force would discriminate like that.

*Dick** wasn't bothered about conduct. I had a police car parked outside my house most days, whilst PC *Hadaway** paid me a quick visit. I couldn't resist the man in uniform. The sex was great, we got on great and I really liked him. Then out of the blue, he said he was seeing another police officer, she didn't have children and our relationship had to end. I felt disappointed but wise Gramps had been right, yet again.

On a night out with college friends I was asked if we wanted some VIP passes to a private function at a local nightclub to join the Wolves footballers. I was hungry and asked if there was a buffet, there was, so I accepted the invitation. Of course there was only one reason why a bunch of ladies were given VIP tickets. I got stuck into the buffet whilst one of my friends had sex with the main *Wolfe*, another had sex with a young Wolfe* in the ladies toilet.*

The *Blue Eyed Wolfe** started to chat me up. He persistently offered me a drink and tried to engage in a conversation. I told him I could buy my own drinks and he was wasting his time on me. I hated football it reminded me of my Dad. In the end I said "You footballers, think you are all God's gift to women, all you do is kick a ball around a field." He was offended and sloped off through the back exit, probably to return to his wife. My baby sitter thought I was crazy to have snubbed such a wealthy and successful footballer. *Young Wolfe** and his wife were on the front of the Express and Star a few weeks later, celebrating the birth of their son. I began to think that all men just totally exploited women.

I started seeing Quilly again as a safe option. He was good with Nathan and it was good to have contact with his parents again. They treated Nathan like their own grandchild and were very loving towards him. I had foolishly allowed Quilly to have sex with me when I had run out of contraceptive pills. He said he would be careful but he forgot to be, in the heat of the moment. We had a major row and I told him I wanted him out of my life because he was not responsible enough. There was no surprise to see the pregnancy test show positive but this time I asked the doctor for an abortion. I was already struggling, I couldn't afford another baby and I was about to start university. I told Aunt Linda and she tried to talk me out of a termination but I felt I had no choice. Quilly had no idea and I left it that way.

No one on my college course got onto the social work degree course, we had all put the wrong code on our application form. My second choice was Psychology. By the time I had started university, I had pretty much given up on men. I felt very proud to be the first in our family to further their education. Gramps said he didn't understand why I wanted to study psychology and that those in the white coats were meddlesome people that caused more harm than good.

This perspective came from a man who was a prisoner of war, who exchanged his wedding ring for a piece of bread because he was starving, who dressed as a German officer and marched his fellow soldiers through two villages to freedom. I was tremendously proud of him. He was so traumatised by his experience he bluntly refused praise and would refute the idea that he was any kind of a hero, when so many men had lost their lives. He received no psychological support on his return. Then he suffered the trauma of losing his own daughter. I knew his heart ached but he wasn't proud of me wanting to study psychology to help people who were traumatised.

With the student grant and a loan I was able to afford a cheap little Mini to get Nathan to the nursery and myself to the campus each day. With lectures here and there, I couldn't continue my work at the hostel so I paid my rent upfront and had a little left for food. I knew money was going to be tight but I was investing in my future. Despite missing out on some lectures that were outside the nursery opening times, I learned a lot during the first year. It was hard completing assignments with a toddler in my life and my grades reflected this. I would often study into the early hours of the morning whilst Nathan slept.

Psychology helped me become a better person. I learned more about myself and others. I studied emotions, thought processes and human behaviour. I learned so much about ethics and different theorists such as Freud, Piaget and Jung. I knew how to gather, organise, analyse, and interpret data. I became a better communicator, learned how to resolve conflict and how to build healthy relationships. My new found knowledge was proving helpful in my own life and one day it would help me to help others.

The wicked step mother of the west had thrown Ray out for something quite petty and he had spent the night on the streets. I took him back to their house. I stood up for my brother as he had none of his belongings and it was winter. I told her she was a cruel woman. She became very abusive and attacked me. My conflict resolution skills were put to the test. I received four claw marks across my face and we were all locked out of the house. Dad knocked the door begging her to open, just as a police car was reversing up our street. I asked the officer to help. She soon opened the door for the police. I seized my opportunity to get the foot for my sewing machine back. Ray got all his belongings and moved in with me. They sold their house and down sized to a two bed bungalow to avoid either of us ever thinking we could live with them again.

Having Ray living at home with me made me feel less vulnerable. He got himself a well paid job, steel erecting and I managed to get an evening job working in a petrol station. One busy Friday someone left the forecourt without paying for their fuel. The manager docked my wages because we were supposed to take the number plates of all the cars but at busy periods we didn't have the time to do this and serve customers simultaneously. There was no CCTV. The manager's philosophy was if you haven't got a number plate then it looks like you have stolen the money. I couldn't afford to work for nothing and drive offs were getting quite common, so I resigned.

Every Sunday I would work with my Uncle Malcolm on a market stall to raise the funds for the family to go on a fantastic and well deserved holiday to Florida. Nathan was too young to appreciate Disney World and was traumatised by a ride where a massive King Kong grabbed our vehicle and shook it. He would scream when ever he saw a little King Kong teddy after that. When we returned home, two weeks later, I found out Ray had been hanging around with the local lads, the ones who had stolen my microwave and Ray being the only one with a job was persuaded to help them raid his depot. He consequently lost his job and then sold his TV and Video player to buy food and drugs. He ended up living in the probation hostel I had worked at.

My uncle Malcolm sold his bakery and started a new business with bouncing castles. Most weekends I would be standing on a field, at a car boot sale, earning money for him. Nathan was happy bouncing away all day. I had a very pleasant child friendly job. Malcolm would buy us food and drinks and he gave me a small wage which helped me make ends meet. I knew he was making a lot of money out of me but it didn't matter. I liked helping them, I felt part of the family business.

Gramps on the other hand seemed depressed when I visited him. He spent most of his days lying on the sofa, with emphysema, he couldn't enjoy his retirement. I asked him if he would build me a brick fireplace in my lounge. I thought it would be nice to have something that he had made for me and it would get him out of the house and make him feel wanted. Gramps agreed and I gave him a key to let himself in whilst I was at university. I bought the materials and he began to build the fire place.

The following day I returned home to find the fire place completed and a note from Nan saying "GONE TO HOSPITAL" on the mantel piece. Gramps had suffered a heart attack. I felt so guilty, it was April 15th and I had got an ill old man working on the anniversary of the day his daughter was killed. We sat in the hospital talking. I was shocked to discover this was his second heart attack, the first had occurred on April 15th 1979 when we had just moved into Aunty Joan's house and Gramps was heart broken. This explained their lack of contact with us at the time. Having a near death experience himself, he went on to tell me why I couldn't go to my Moms funeral. My Dad had asked to go, tempers were running high and if he had turned up it would have been awful for us. I understood he had just been trying to protect us. I held his hand and whispered "You're my Gramps, the best man I have ever known. I have always loved you and always will." He smiled and asked me to pour him a glass of orange juice.

Chapter 11
The Con Man

I was on my way home from university when my car broke down. I looked underneath the engine and could see the fuel pipe dangling. I had no idea where it was supposed to go. I called my brother from a telephone box as Nathan and I walked towards home. Ray said he knew a mechanic who could help, he lived in the hostel. We were almost home when I gave Ray my car keys, relieved that this man could fix my car without me having to suffer the cost of a breakdown recovery truck. I hadn't realised I had given Ray my house key too. It was dark, so we walked to the fish and chip shop and when they returned with my Mini, I was sat on my doorstep with Nathan, eating a bag chips.

Pete looked much older than he was and reminded me of the man I had often seen at Winson Green prison sweeping the yard, he was gaunt and bald. I invited Pete and Ray in for a cup of tea and we got talking. Pete refused to accept any money for repairing the car as it hadn't cost anything but time to fix. He advised me that the car was in a dangerous state and he couldn't believe it had passed a MOT. Despite not being attracted to the man there was something intriguing about him. He seemed very intelligent despite being down and out. He visited me for several weeks and we would talk for hours. He was different to all the other men I had met. I wasn't sure about him and turned to my Aunt Linda for advice. She said it was up to me. He seemed to care about me so we began a relationship.

Pete told me someone had smashed his car window and stole his tools and a bag of precious photographs, he appeared distraught. His ex wife had taken the car. I saw her in a beautiful Mercedes, with their son Ronnie, they were talking to Pete. Here we go again, I thought. Pete reassured me that their relationship was over and that the car she took had belonged to her. She appeared to be quite wealthy. Pete, on the other hand, had nothing. I borrowed some money from the Provident as an investment so he could buy himself some tools and go to work, he was shocked by my kindness.

He moved in and I depended on him as the mechanic to get me something more roadworthy. He said he had sold my Mini for scrap and I believed him. He bought me something else with the money, something he said was safer. But the brakes didn't appear to work. And so began many years of trust in a man who claimed to be a mechanic. I never had a decent car in all the years I was with him. I was forever breaking down and he would come to my rescue. I was never quite sure if he was deliberately tampering with the cars. He would always buy and sell motors but he never appeared to make a profit from them.

I wanted to know all about his past and he told me how he had been adopted. He had always felt like a failure to his very successful brother, who was ten years his senior. He had served twelve years in prison and gave me a justifiable story which explained why he had ended up in prison. He said he had been set up by the Free Masons, robbed of a briefcase full of Rolex watches and almost killed. He had the scars across his head to prove it. He told me he spent six weeks in hospital recovering and planned a revenge attack on the man who had apparently organised the robbery. He didn't get away with what he did and received a ten years sentence for robbery. He went to Gartree Prison as a category A prisoner and because he would not be a model prisoner, his sentence was extended.

Pete was a perfect gentleman, he would open doors for me and treat me like a princess. "Manners maketh man" he would nobly say. He gave me gifts, a gold necklace, a ring and a bracelet, the other men in my life had always taken from me, I was glad to have finally found someone who would look after me. My Grandparents seemed to like Pete too. He turned up at their house with a snow shovel and cleared their path of snow without even asking them. When Gramps was in hospital he insisted on taking my Nan to visit him and paid for her tea in the canteen. She too thought he was a right gentleman.

Pete convinced me to rekindle the relationship with my father. He said my mothers family were biased in their perspective and I shouldn't give my Dad a hard time. So I let my Dad back into my world. He made me a study desk in my bedroom and noticing the worn mattress I had, he offered to buy me a new bed. He said Becky was always having his money and I had never asked him for anything. I felt like a charity case but I accepted his offer and as Nathan had outgrown his cot he bought Nathan's first bed too. Pete said my Dad just wanted to make things right between us but it seemed such a fake relationship.

Pete had read a lot of books whilst he had been in prison and was very educated. He said psychology was all about statistics and that we were all individuals. When I became pregnant, he seemed delighted and he persuaded me to give up on my degree. His famous words were "It's monkey fuck monkey in this world Diane and it's a jungle out there." He persuaded me to stand up to my Uncle Malcolm for the way he was exploiting me financially and I quit working for him. Malcolm was shocked but I felt liberated saying I didn't need to work for him anymore. Pete even persuaded me to grow my hair. He felt women should have long hair.

My brother and Pete both smoked cannabis and I was anti-drugs. Pete lectured me on the harm alcohol actually did. I had stopped going out and I wasn't drinking alcohol but Pete continually offered the joint to me when we were deep in conversation "Do you want some of this?" he would repeatedly say. I was soon a regular cannabis smoker just like he was.

Ray and Pete went to collect some cannabis from a drug dealer's house one day and one of them stole some jewellery. I didn't know who to believe. Ray had stated categorically he hadn't taken it and I wanted to believe him. Pete claimed the same. Ray said Pete was a shady character, he tried to warn me he was nothing but a conman and that I shouldn't trust him. Ray and I fell out. Everything very quickly was changing in my life. I was oblivious and couldn't see what was happening.

With a baby on the way, and no income, Pete continued to reassure me things would be alright. I had always struggled financially but now our bills weren't getting paid and Pete said for me not to worry. He would go out and return home the next day with antique furniture which he would sell onto traders. He was very knowledgeable and spent many an hour studying from his Millers Antique guide price book. I found it quite interesting too. I noticed how much my long lost teddybear was worth. The only thing I had that was worth money was stolen from me as a child following the death of my mother.

One night Pete rang me and said he was soaking wet and freezing to death because he had waded through a river on the run from the police. I got Nathan out of his bed and drove to Wales to pick him up. He justified his actions on the way home as I 'nagged' him to be law abiding. He told me how he only targeted holiday homes and abandoned houses as some people had more money than sense, he believed they all had insurance cover and he was simply redistributing the wealth.

I was heavily pregnant when a police car pulled up outside my house. PC *Dick Hadaway** knocked my door. "Hello Diane" he said. He seemed proud to inform me that Pete had been arrested for a burglary and he asked if he could search the property. I invited him and his colleague in. I thought he was somehow, in a nice kind of way, trying to keep me safe, as the man I now lived with was nothing but a thief and a con artist.

Pete got released the next day and Tracey, my cousin came round asking for her dads trolley jack back. Pete said he could have it back when he paid him the £25 for the work he had done on his van. My Uncle Malcolm called and said he needed his trolley jack back as his van had a puncture. Pete told me my uncle was trying to rip him off. Aunt Linda called me and asked what Pete's game was. She said Malcolm had already paid for the work. I sided with Pete as I genuinely believed he could have forgotten to pay him. It wasn't a lot of money but it caused another rift in the family.

Aunt Linda and Aunt June thought I was better off without Pete. I had Nathan and a child on the way. They both needed a mother and a father in their lives. I just wanted a normal life. "Once a thief, always a thief" they both wisely said. My Grandparents repeated the phrase. I thought back to my school days when I was shop lifting, people can change. He said he would and of course I believed him. I felt on edge all the time, nervous about being left alone. Pete decided to get a dog so I felt safer. He got a Rottweiler bitch. She was a kind loving dog and was very protective. Pete was sent to prison for getting into hot water, stealing oil filled radiators, leaving me in the cold, with Nathan and a new dog to walk. I was so stressed I went into labour.

Tracey, accompanied me to the labour ward. I grabbed the gas and prepared myself for the next contraction. The midwife this time, was an old friend from school, Amanda Pugh. I was pleased to see her and chatted to her about school, which took my mind off the contractions. She left the room and didn't return. I assumed she had finished her shift. I took full benefit of the gas and air and got as high as I could. I heard my Mother's voice "It's a circle Diane. We're all connected." she said as I delivered my baby. I tried to explain my experience to my cousin, she thought I was just having a funny moment and I left it that way.

This time my mother had been with me and I felt so reassured by her words but confused by what she meant, perhaps my mother was now reincarnated, reborn or maybe she was trying to help me this time because she hadn't been around when Nathan was born. Knowing my mother was with me, I held my precious baby girl in my arms and instantly fell in love with her.

The prison officers told Pete the next day and he called the hospital. I had time for a brief tearful conversation before his allowed talk time was up. I was upset that yet again the father of my child wasn't present at the birth, but I didn't feel alone when I looked at my beautiful daughter. I knew we would always have a special bond, so strong that nothing else mattered.

I travelled with Nathan and Holly on the train to Liverpool to visit Pete in prison. I'd managed to mistakenly board a train to Edinburgh as my train had been late and I couldn't hear the announcement over the tannoy. It took me a while to realise I was on the wrong train. The conductor gave me some instructions and I got the children and the pushchair and exchanged trains, in the confusion I left Nathan's new coat on the overhead shelf. I couldn't handle the stress but I had to be strong for my children.

We got to Liverpool early as I had planned and we walked around the docks, sightseeing like tourists before heading for the prison. Pete was pleased to see us and reassured me that things were going to be different when he was back home. He didn't change when he came out of prison. He would claim he just needed to do one more job. I hated his dishonesty and the life we were leading, with two small children I felt trapped but he told me not to worry.

My Dad and Sandra would visit and they seemed to get on really well with Pete. They would talk about normal things and it felt good listening to them, it was like my life was becoming more settled. I was always anxious that my family were going to bump into my Dad and my Aunt Linda did on several occasions, she handled it well. Having contact with him was betraying my mothers memory and my family. Pete told me to focus on my children's lives. I knew how important my grandparents were in my life. I wanted my children to have grandparents, they were calling them Nan and Grandad but they didn't seem to have a close loving relationship with them.

My Aunt June, rarely visited me, knowing I still had contact with my father. On one of her visits, he unexpectedly pulled up outside my house with Sandra. She panicked and went into flight mode. I remained calm and tried to safely escort June away from my property. Sandra, became abusive, shouting at Aunt June for giving her a filthy look. She sat in my Dad's car crying. I tried to get Sandra to empathise, explaining this was the first time she had met with my Dad since he had killed her sister. She told me she didn't care, it wasn't anything to do with her, she felt hard done by. I tried to comfort her and asked her in for a cup of tea. She refused to get out of the car and said she wasn't going to come to my house ever again. My Aunty June, never visited me again either, despite numerous invites, if I wanted to see her, I had to visit her.

I cried after they had all left, my family was such a disaster. I was always the one in the middle, that lost out. Pete felt Aunt June had over reacted. "Anyone can make mistakes" he told me. He felt my father was a good man just not very clever. Funny really, my clever father had a better life than I had. He was settled, had holidays abroad, money invested in bonds and owned a house. When he was short, Pete would persuade me to ask my father to lend us money. "It's what families do" he said. I didn't want to borrow money from my father, especially when I knew the money was going on cannabis resin, tobacco and other drug paraphernalia. Pete saw my fathers money as an interest free loan but I made sure he always paid him back. I felt humiliated to be so desperate.

Gramps wasn't well and the hospital had said they weren't sure whether to operate on him. He had an embolism and if it were to burst it would kill him. But after two heart attacks and suffering with emphysema, his quality of life was poor. We all urged him to have the operation and were relieved to hear he was out of intensive care and on a normal ward. When I visited that day I was concerned about him. I joked with him saying he looked like a millionaire in his paisley silk dressing gown and his tanned skin. Gramps declared he was ready for the knackers yard. I spoke to the doctor about the colour of his skin and the yellowing of his eyes and questioned whether he was going to recover.

The next day he was back in intensive care as his condition had deteriorated. He asked me to pass him a drink of water. On his bedstead it said 'NIL BY MOUTH' so I checked with the nurse to see if he could have a sip of water. She bluntly refused and Gramps told me off for asking. "I'm just doing what's best for you Gramps" I said. He smiled to me and waved as I walked out the door that day. A sip of water might have been all he needed to survive, I felt so guilty, believing the nurse knew best. I was angry with myself not to have granted him his last request, a sip of water. The only consolation was that he was now reunited with my mother.

Pete rolled me a joint and told me to smoke it on the way round to my Nan's house. I had said I wanted to sleep there, I didn't want her to be alone. Aunt Linda and Aunt June were both there. "I've had a joint" I confessed. This was the first time they had ever seen me stoned. They had got the stiff drinks going, we all comforted each other and chatted for hours. When I went to bed, as my head hit his pillow, I heard my Gramps' voice roaring "NO!" I felt like he had entered my body. Perhaps he was angry I hadn't given him that sip of water or he didn't like me sleeping in his bed. It spooked me and I never slept there again. Nan said he often woke her up in the mornings but her life stood still after he died.

I refused to go to my Gramps funeral much to the disgust of my family. I told them I had promised my Mom I would never go to anyone's funeral. I had secretly gone to the crematorium earlier that day, said a few words to my mother and left some flowers. I then went round to my Nan's house to offer my support to my family. I cried when the hearse arrived, waved them off and went to the kitchen to make sandwiches for their return. His ashes were laid to rest under my mother's slate.

Losing my Gramps was hard and made me realise how short life was. I wanted to be close to my family all the time. I had suffered my two years in Bilston so we exchanged our house with another tenant to be nearer to my Nan, Aunt Linda and Aunt June. I would walk up to Nan's and sit and chat with her. "Remember that day Nan when Mom had her appendix out and I had come home the same day?" She looked shocked. She assured me that my mother had never had such an operation and said she could not recall that day. I tried to remind her about the bits on the carpet. She said my mother was very house proud but she had never been in hospital for any operation. Perhaps she was going a bit senile, I thought.

Pete hated the way my Aunt Linda would call round uninvited. He said she was prying when he saw her looking at some unpaid bills left on the mantelpiece. I didn't care, I loved it when she visited even if she knew I was struggling. Pete's son, Ronnie came to see his new baby sister and before long he had moved in with us. His mother was said to be an alcoholic with mental health issues although each time I had met her, she had seemed a really nice woman. Ronnie said she was crazy, she had embarrassed him when she had danced naked on a car in their street. He was fed up with pouring her alcohol down the sink. Pete assured me that she was very manipulative and not to have anything to do with her.

Ronnie was a typical fifteen year old and I got on with him really well. I wasn't going to be a wicked step mother and make him feel unwelcome or unloved. I helped him with his homework and talked about his future. We were quickly out growing the small two bed roomed house. Holly and Nathan shared a tiny room. Ronnie had the large bedroom with all the wardrobes and a desk so he could study. Pete and I slept in the lounge. I asked the council for a bigger house. We were told we didn't have enough points to be rehoused.

I appealed to the council and went to a hearing. The officers asked what my life was like in that house and I started to tell them and ended up crying. Holly found it difficult to get around in her walker. The pushchair was always in a door way, it was difficult to find somewhere to do the ironing, the dog had nowhere to lie down, I had nowhere to sit and apply makeup, my list went on and the council agreed to find us something more suitable. We moved to a large four bedroomed council house which we couldn't afford to carpet. We got a second Rottweiler dog called Rocky so we could breed pups and make some money. Pete got work as a recovery driver and I thought our lives were going to improve.

Nathan was calling Pete 'Dad' which pleased me as he had no contact with Ian, his real father who had forgotten he existed. Pete was very strict with Nathan and made him very nervous. He called Nathan a wimp and that upset me. Nathan started wetting the bed and Pete told him he was a dirty disgusting boy. My Dad told me it was in the genes as Ray had done the same and said for me not to worry and he would grow out of it. Nathan had dry nights before Pete moved in and I suggested that the name calling was probably causing him anxiety. Pete said I was making Nathan worse, he needed toughening up.

Chapter 12
A Weak Wife

When Nathan started school, his elderly middle class teacher warmed to Pete's intelligent conversation. She referred to him as 'Mr. Benton'. I felt embarrassed to say "we're not married". She raised her eyebrows disapprovingly. I wanted to be treated as a respectable woman so it was my idea to get married. He didn't propose. I hated my surname, it reminded me of my Dad and I needed to disassociate myself with the past. I wanted Nathan's surname to be changed by deed pole so we all had the same family name. Pete's parents had given us £1000 and with Pete having a legitimate job as a breakdown mechanic, assuring me his life of crime was done, I wanted to be that respectable married woman.

Pete insisted my father and my step mother come to our wedding as this was tradition. "You can't get married without your Dad being there" he told me. "It's up to them if they don't want to come" he assured me. He didn't like my mother's side of the family and said they were stuck up, interfering, busy bodies. They weren't though, they were honest hard working people, who did things the right way. Aunt Linda gave us a beautiful mirror as a wedding present. She bought it round the day before the wedding. I told her I wished they could all come to the wedding, I always knew the day would come and recalled the conversation I had with Gramps when I was ten years old. After she left I put the mirror up in the hall way. I looked at my reflection, who was I trying to kid? I wasn't happy, I was making do. I felt heartbroken.

On my wedding day, the day all girls dream of, my mother wasn't there fussing over me. I didn't have a wedding dress, I had a two piece suit. I looked in the mirror at my overgrown drab hair. Where had I gone? I used to look amazing and now I looked different, frumpy and old fashioned. I had bought Holly a beautiful dress with a matching hat, I must have put it on her head a thousand times, she really didn't want to wear it. Nathan was uncomfortable in his wedding attire and would have preferred to go in his tracksuit and trainers. Pete made an effort but he looked like an old man, he was fourteen years older than me. I didn't find him physically attractive, I didn't even like his face.

I wasn't getting married for the right reasons and all the wrong people were coming. My father, step mother and step sister were all downstairs drinking tea. I gave the video camera to Ronnie to record the event. My brother Ray and his girlfriend arrived and we set off to the registry office on a cold and frosty morning. Pete's family were there waiting. His brother, a high ranking civil servant, his sister in law, a head teacher and his parents both retired from the forces, all normal lovely people were introduced to my family. My Dad didn't offer to give me away. Pete had no best man. We just had the ceremony and signed the papers. We took a few photographs outside in the wind, I held on to Rebecca as I had slipped several times on the ice, what a farce I thought and we quickly headed off to the pub to defrost and have a family meal.

Pete's father decided to give a speech and toasted our future after my father had failed to get up. My Dad was oblivious to his role at the wedding. We returned home for a buffet that I had earlier prepared and we sliced the wedding cake. My father, step mother and sister left early, informing me that they had another party to go to. At 4pm. Pete was asleep on the lounge floor. He had worked the night shift before and couldn't keep his eyes open. Ray had asked if he could have some more wedding cake and I said "Of course, help yourself." He took the remainder of wedding cake with him, so I had none to give my mothers side of the family.

There was no honeymoon but we were due to go out for the evening. Just as Pete was fastening his shoes Ray called and said he couldn't babysit so we stayed in. We watched the wedding video, there was no decent wedding shots, plenty of clips of my brother and his girlfriend showing off, doing round house kicks and a shot of Holly sticking her finger in the wedding cake, pulling a funny face. It wasn't the happiest day of my life but I was now "Mrs. Diane Yates" respectfully married at last.

I reflected on my 'traditional wedding' and my fathers involvement. Knowing my Dad drove a new car and had afforded a month long holiday to Australia. I foolishly expected a surprise present, perhaps a honeymoon but that wasn't to be. He had asked us what we wanted for our wedding present and I asked for some kitchen scales, the old traditional ones which didn't cost a lot of money and that's exactly what I got. I had only invited him to the wedding due to tradition. He never gave me away. He never gave a speech. He wore an old ill fitting suit, enjoyed his free meal and was spared the traditional expense of his only daughter's wedding day. What was I doing having contact with this man? He was selfish and always made me feel so worthless.

With the profits I made from car boot sales and two Rottweiler puppies, I went into town to do some Christmas shopping. Pete had reminded me to be careful with my bag. I had the strap crossed over my body so no-one could snatch it. I was enjoying the day and was about to go to the taxi rank and head off back home. I rearranged my carrier bags, putting the smaller ones inside each other so I had fewer bags to carry. I took off my hand bag and placed it under the pushchair and then decided to just have a look in Mothercare before getting the taxi.

I picked up a pretty outfit for Holly to wear on Christmas Day and headed to the check out. My bag had gone without a trace despite the police checking the CCTV. Everything was in my bag and Pete went crazy. His life of crime started up again as a result of my carelessness. It wasn't long before he was back in prison and the debts began to grow.

I was feeling depressed and struggling to be a prisoner's wife. I would burst into tears when I heard myself as a mother saying the things my mother used to say. I would cry on their birthdays as I attempted to sing happy birthday to them, thinking about my mothers voice. I would cry on mother's day when my children gave me their cards. It was so hard being a mother without a mother. Despite how low I got I could never end my life or walk out of their lives because I knew how it felt to be abandoned and I wasn't going to put my children through that. I went to the doctor and told him how I was struggling with my mental health. He offered me antidepressants and I told him they weren't the answer. It had been twenty years since my mother had been killed and I asked if I could see a counsellor.

The NHS had never been quick for things you need done now and it was nine months later before I got to see a counsellor. I tried desperately to put my prejudices aside but she had dwarfism and I instinctively wanted to support her. It wasn't easy for me to pour my heart out to a stranger, half my size. She was professional and explained the Gestalts approach she practiced. I was asked to imagine my life as a pool of water that we were to stir, she prepared me for the water to become cloudy. I poured out my heart to her and she listened and I left. I returned the following week and we did the same. The idea was the pool would settle and the water would become clear. I needed her to tell me what to do but counsellors don't do that. I felt I was stuck in the mud, I was being sucked down, sinking in quicksand and she wouldn't throw me a rope so I could get out. I gave it four more sessions and told her I was feeling much better, of course I wasn't but counselling was doing me more harm than good.

Why do people go for counselling for years if it doesn't work, what's the point in re-traumatising yourself? It's never made sense to me. All I needed was someone to guide me. I didn't want someone to listen to me until I fixed things for myself. I had already tried to do that. I thought about how I, as a mother, guided my children in times of crisis. When Nathan cried about the boys at school calling him "Nathan, bacon sandwich" he came to me for help. Of course, I naturally laughed but it was a big deal to him. He hated his name because of the bullies. We spoke about children and why they come up with silly names and I advised him to laugh it off. "If they know it doesn't bother you Nathan, they won't say it" I got him to see the funny side and after a few days of laughing it off, they stopped calling him names. I could have just listened and left him in the muddy water but no, I guided him back on to dry land. There was no guide for me.

My Uncle Malcolm had been working at Wolverhampton Council as a county councillor. It had its perks. He could exploit his position, influence people and get a free parking space in town. His daughter, as a result of his influence, insignificantly moved into my old house. I wondered why she hadn't been forced to live in a deprived area like I had in Bilston. I envied the support she had from her parents. This was the first time she had lived on a council estate. She had been sheltered all her life and had no idea how to survive. I advised her to get a dog or she would certainly get burgled whilst she was out at work.

She ignored my advice and inevitably her home was raided. Malcolm and Linda accused my step son, Ronnie of having something to do with it. Ronnie was already struggling having his dad in prison and was really upset because they were now tarring him with the same brush. Pete was right they looked down on me as though I was scum. I turned to alcohol. I got drunk and shouted at Linda. We had a huge fall out because she didn't believe me. She said she didn't want to waste her time on me. Why would she? I was such a weak wife, standing by a con man. I realised I had no one in my life that really cared.

We moved house again when Pete came out of prison, this time to a private bungalow. I was no longer in a council house and that felt good. Nostalgically, I felt like I was back home, living in a bungalow with my mother. An old man had lived there before us and I was shocked to see pornographic magazines being posted through our letterbox addressed to him. "He must have been some sort of pervert" I said to Pete. We later broke the padlock off his shed. It was full of magazines and videos. Pete tried to get me watch them with him. I wasn't interested in seeing women being sexually exploited.

Pete got a job as a recovery driver but the bills were continuing to mount up. He encouraged me to take a job selling cockles and mussels around the local pubs. Pete felt with the stolen diesel he was putting in my car I couldn't lose financially. I endured drunken men feeling me up so I could get some commission on my sales. I felt like a prostitute but I did earn more than the other guys did and it got me out on a Friday and Saturday evenings. I managed to get work in the local Goodyear's factory as a kitchen assistant for Saturday and Sunday mornings too. It felt good to be earning money again.

Linda's house was burgled and I thought Pete would get the blame. There were no accusations this time which surprised me, because I didn't know where he had been that day. I even thought he might have been the culprit. I went round their house to offer my support. Tracey told me how upset her Mom was because my mother's jewellery had been stolen in the burglary. I told her she was mistaken as my mother didn't have any jewellery. "Well you know her wedding ring and engagement ring. It was all my mom had." she sympathetically stated. My cousin didn't realise how betrayed I felt inside.

I now knew Linda had taken my mother's rings from my jewellery box before I had moved in with my Aunty Joan. I'd felt empty and guilty for losing them for twenty years. I was so shocked I was speechless. I couldn't confront her about it, I loved her too much. I doubted if those rings had brought her any comfort, she must have felt guilty for taking them. It breaks my heart to know some thief, possibly my own husband, eventually stole them. Pete told me I couldn't trust my aunt because she had stolen from me.She claimed on her house insurance and bought a cuckoo clock, like my mother used to have. I stared at the clock, thinking of my mother, it's time to heal, I thought.

Pete started driving HGV's around for an agency that didn't realise he had no HGV licence. He was really good at conning people, everyone believed what he said. He had withheld the rent to our landlord because the house had been floor boarded with MDF and rats had chewed their way into my daughter's bedroom. Then I was knocked off my feet with a mysterious illness where my body continually shook. I felt like I was having some sort of drug induced seizures or I had been poisoned. I believed I was going to die. Pete was so worried he called the emergency doctor out. The doctor said he wasn't sure what it was but suspected I had the flu. I hadn't even had a cold but I was sick with worry about the life we had, dodging bills left right and centre with a dodgy husband. He sold both the dogs and most of our furniture and suggested we start a fresh life away from Wolverhampton, he had found a beautiful house to live in Dorset by the sea. He wanted me to see a different way of living.

This was just what I needed. My Dad was miles away and the panoramic view from my bedroom was therapy in its self. The Golden Cap and Hardown Hill framed the sea and the peaceful walk across National Trust land to the pebbled beach provided serenity from the cacophony of Wolverhampton. I began working in the local playgroup which Holly attended, and against Pete's wishes, I completed an early years diploma. I had regretted not completing my degree and needed a qualification. The proprietor, Mrs. Lawrence, was a fascinating, eighty five year old, intellectual woman. She refused to retire after years of teaching and inspecting schools for Ofsted. She had published a series of books for children learning to read and was the author of several books for professionals learning to teach. I felt privileged to be mentored by such a devoted soul.

Mrs. Lawrence also had a spiritual understanding of children. Holly now had an imaginary friend. She would sit in the back of the car, telling me about her 'Grandad' he was always in the car with her. "My Grandad built that house and that one" she would often say. I thought it was because she didn't really have a relationship with her grandparents, that she had invented one. Mrs. Lawrence assured me that children were closer to God and to the spirits around them. "We lose that gift as we age" she told me.

I thought back to my childhood and how my Gramps had told me if I saw his initial 'H' on a yellow sign, that meant he had built those houses. I would see his initial everywhere, he had built so many houses, I felt proud. For years I had believed his joke, the yellow signs actually meant hydrogen. Perhaps my Gramps was in the back of the car with my daughter, having another joke about all the houses he had built.

I learned so much from Mrs. Lawrence about how children learn to socialise, understand maths and learn to read. I realised my mother hadn't been thick, she had dyslexia. It hadn't been recognised back then and I felt guilty that as her daughter, I had felt ashamed of her learning difficulty. Like most proud and eager parents, I realised I had really messed up Nathans early learning experiences, teaching him to say the alphabet before he knew phonics caused him confusion. Writing his name, before he had developed his fine motor skills caused him frustration. Forcing him to be clever without developing the skills backfired, he would switch off, play up or cry. I admired and appreciated Mrs. Lawrence, for taking the time to teach me how to teach. I could now practice teaching Holly and other children the right way, producing happy, confident and motivated learners.

During the summer break, I woke up to see the tragic news that Princess Diana had died in a car crash, my heart broke. Like most people, I had watched a shy innocent woman have her fairytale wedding and marry her prince. Like a third of all marriages it had ended in misery and divorce. The queen of hearts, didn't give up, she found a purpose in life and found happiness. Then in an instant she was gone. Just like my own mother's death it was splattered across the news papers, and everyone was talking about the wonderful Diana. I empathised with William and Harry. I knew their lives would never be the same. As they followed their mother's coffin, I wanted to hold both their hands. They were given the opportunity to say their goodbyes, I felt like I was attending my own mother's funeral, saying my goodbyes too.

We took long country walks with our new dog and spent many days on the beach. Life was a constant holiday for the children and me. They soon picked up the Dorset tones and lost their awful Black Country accents. Nathan's best friend lived on a farm and I became good friends with his mother, Sarah. She had been privately educated, and was another very intelligent woman who became central in my Dorset life. I had always envied those who were privileged. I would have loved to go to boarding school. She told me how she had always envied children being at home with their parents, she'd felt neglected. I enjoyed her company and was happy to have her son for sleep over's.

The children were out playing one day and returned home to tell me about the new people who had moved into St. Gabriel's house, close by. I had noticed a rich man in a new Mercedes when I had walked the dog. Holly said they were really nice and I had been invited round to meet them. I took some home made bread as a gift and walked up the long drive to their home, with my children. It was a beautiful property set in its own grounds. How the other half live, I thought.

And so began a new friendship with Ann Marie. She worked as an occupational health nurse and earned a high salary. It turned out she didn't actually own the house, she rented it. The man in the Mercedes wasn't rich, he sold cars and was her friend. She had four children, with four different fathers and never had a penny in maintenance from them. She was a survivor and I admired her independence. She helped guide me a lot.

I used to look after her animals whilst she was out at work; the grunting pot bellied pig, a wild and boisterous nanny goat, ducks, chickens, rabbits and guinea pigs. She even had bottled fed lambs for a while. Anne Marie adored children and loved them to show kindness to animals. She would host parties and there was always plenty of food and wine. The children would happily play on the grounds all day long. It was wonderful spending time with her chatting but Pete didn't approve.

One day, Anne Marie had dished up a spaghetti Bolognese with garlic bread and I was stuffed. She was the type of woman, that would always put more food on your plate and your glass would never empty. We had all enjoyed a lovely day, the children preferred to be there than at home as it was so much fun. They were having another sleep over and were all upstairs ready for bed. I had thanked her for her hospitality. I had drank way too much wine and I knew it was time I headed back home. She told me how she adored my company and our conversations. She topped up my wine as I answered a call from Pete.

"Get yourself ready, we've been invited to play backgammon, with some people I've met" he said. I tried to get out of the invitation. I had drank too much wine and needed to sleep. He insisted I got in the car a few minutes later. I complained on route, I really wasn't in the mood to meet new people. "You'll like them" he said. I wondered how he came to that conclusion when he never liked any of my friends.

He pulled up outside a run down terraced property. I didn't like the look of the place. We were invited in by a happy hippy. Their house was very creative but dark and dirty. I tried not to be rude but I felt very uncomfortable. It was a drug den. We sat around a table in their back room. I didn't want anything to eat or drink but they insisted. They passed around a pipe, I didn't know what it was so I declined. I sat playing backgammon trying to focus. The room was full of smoke and they passed me a joint, I had an insignificant drag and handed it on. The room began to spin. I was handed a glass, the smell of dark rum made me heave. I pretended to sip it.

Then a dish full of chilly was placed in front of me. I quickly headed for the front door and threw up on their door step. We didn't go there again, I had utterly embarrassed him!

Pete found another friend, an interesting old fellow, that he wanted me to meet. He took me round to his house. It was beautiful, the walls were all panelled with a light wood, it had a unique Swedish influence. I complimented him on the design. He told me how he had just moved back to the UK from Sweden and this was his way of retaining the beauty of such a wonderful country. He took me into his workshop, from floor to ceiling there were television screens all along the length of the wall. "Gosh, this is like a shop" I said in amazement. "I used to have a shop, before I moved to Sweden, but I had been broken into so many times, they drove me crazy" he said. I looked at his face, the last time I had seen this man, he had been rattling the bars on his shop window, like an animal in a cage. "Well, crazy or not, you've ended up with a stunning home in beautiful Dorset now" I said. "Yes, they actually did me a favour" he smiled.

Although I have some fond memories of my time in Dorset with the people I liked, my relationship with Pete deteriorated. He seemed very jealous of the time I spent with the children round at Anne Marie's. She had told me that she had two national insurance numbers and she had been claiming unemployment benefit as well as working. She justified her actions as her children's absent fathers had never helped her out financially. I knew it was wrong what she was doing but she was always giving to her children, compensating them. Then one day, I was shocked when she accused me of informing on her and we parted friends. Someone, possibly my husband, had told the authorities and as a result, I lost her friendship.

One evening, I found Pete masturbating and looking at pornography. I was shocked. He also had a brief case hidden in the shed, that I suspected contained films and magazines. I cracked the code on the brief case and that confirmed my suspicions. I thought about the magazines and videos at the bungalow and how he had let me believe the old man had been a pervert. Our sex life had dwindled over the years. I still participated in my duty, a few times a week, like I thought most married women did. I had amazed myself that I still enjoyed having sex with him because there was no physical attraction. I guessed I deserved the odd orgasm, when the mood suited, for putting up with his negative attributes. I had no idea why he felt the need for self indulgence. I was ashamed to speak to anyone about it. He disgusted me and I completely went off sex.

Added to the marital disturbance of living with a pervert, my husband began to treat Nathan unfavourably and my mind began replaying memories of my childhood. My children were the age I was when my mother had died and little things began to haunt me. I felt like I was going crazy, having some sort of mental breakdown. At times I felt like I was floating. Experiencing vivid flashbacks made me question my parenting capacity. I sensed my mothers spirit was guiding me through a very difficult time in my life.

I was mowing the lawn one summer's day and Holly asked me for a sandwich..... I can see her mowing the lawn, it's a heavy roller mower and it's harder work than my Flymo but she is smiling, I'm tired but she isn't, she keeps going, I keep going, I want to finish the lawn, like she did, I never asked for food whilst she was mowing the lawn, I was never hungry.... I need to feed them before I start gardening.

It was Holly's birthday and we had invited her friends to a party and I was organising a game of pass the parcel....She stands by the stereo, turns off the music, so we can unwrap a layer, she turns her back so she cannot see which child will eventually unwrap the prize. "Well done" she says, "let's play musical statues now" She knew how to have fun....I need to have fun.

My house was always full of children during the school holidays. I had a large collection of games and activities which entertained them all. We would make our own play dough and bake together. We would paint and make sculptures from papier-mâché. I was just enjoying myself having fun and children love adults who have fun. Psychologically, it was hard having fun all the time but it also compensated Nathan for the troublesome relationship he had with Pete.

He had got Nathan to carry the bins full of fire wood up to the house every day, whilst he continued to chop the scavenged MDF boards up ready for his return. He claimed it was building his strength up but poor Nathan looked exhausted and would look at me and cry as he reached the house. I would try to make it up to him but it was hard seeing him struggle.

Sunday evenings the children would have their baths and watch TV before bedtime.....She's in the kitchen "Would you like some toast for supper, you two?" We sit together on the sofa to watch Charlie's Angels. Ray's licking the jam off his toast and we're laughing....my children need supper.

Pete shaved Nathan's hair to save on the expense of a barber. He said it made him look like a man instead of a wimp. Nathan didn't like it and neither did I, he looked like child in a concentration camp facing the gas chamber. I knew it would soon grow back but the hair was gone and my poor boy wasn't happy. I put a cap on Nathan's head and took the children for a walk to the beach. I tried to compensate Nathan with happier times. He loved the beach and smiled when I handed him an ice-cream. "This is a nice treat" he said. He never complained about the way Pete treated him. He was just happier if he wasn't around.

Holly wanted to get her hair cut short like mine and I took her to the hair dressers..... "Can I have it just like yours Mom but with the flick the other way so it's not exactly the same" I did love her, I was proud she was my mother and I wanted my hair just like hers and now Holly wants to be like me because she loves me... I didn't want her to have her hair the same as mine. I wanted her to be different. I didn't want her to have my life. I said she could have it in a bob. She hated her hair in a bob.

Pete had got a job as a recovery driver for Frodsham Motors. To hide the gap in his work history he lied and told Jim Frodsham that he had served time in the army and had his HGV licence but Jim, an old soldier himself, didn't believe his lies. It wasn't long before he was given the push and he came home with another dramatised sob story. I was now aware that this man could never keep a job. We were always going to be struggling to pay bills but he would always find money for cannabis.

He worked from home for a while fixing up and selling old cars. He sold a Volvo estate with a lifetime guarantee to our neighbours, then he emptied their car of petrol after doing some mechanical work. My neighbour, Pete called "Tim but dim" wasn't a fool. He and his wife, who I become close friends with stopped speaking to me and stopped her daughter playing with my children because she felt Pete was a con artist. She said I was a good person and I could do better for myself. They didn't like the way he treated Nathan either. I totally agreed with them. I was also embarrassed to be associated with his dodgy dealings and fed up with him ruining my relationships with nice people. If I'd had sufficient funds I would have left him. I didn't have the strength to stand up to him. I just felt I was an exhausted weak wife that missed having a mother to turn to for advice.

I found a support group that was based in Weymouth, an hours drive away along the coast road, which I thought might help me come to terms with my life. I cried all the way there on my first visit, admitting to myself that I needed help. The charity, Support After Murder or Manslaughter or SAMM as it is known, was set up especially for people bereaved by homicides. I had finally found people in my life, that knew how I felt. It was good to have coffee and biscuits and chat about our "death stories" with others. They offered retreats and regular meetings for those traumatised by loss. My grandparents and aunts would have found this support group beneficial, but there was an issue with me, I didn't have their full victim status. Unlike them, I was the daughter of a murderer and I sensed I was in the wrong place.

Chapter 13
Truth And Injustice

My thirty-third birthday was a significant milestone. I had outlived my mother's age, history was not repeating itself, I was going to survive. I couldn't rely on flashbacks now to help me rear my children, I was on my own. This was new territory but I still wanted to know what exactly had happened to her. I nervously picked up the telephone and dialled the number. "In 1978 my mother was killed and I was wondering if you could send me any information...It was April the 15th.....thank you" The police said they would look in their archives and send copies of anything relevant. The Express and Star newspaper said the same. I braced myself for the new knowledge I was to acquire.

I had read in a magazine how a woman had sued a drunk driver after he had killed her mother in a road traffic accident. It triggered my thoughts. I wanted to sue my father for killing my mother and benefitting financially by taking her half of the money from the sale of our home, justice money, money that should have been passed to my brother and myself in the first place. Being the daughter of a murderer, I wasn't brave enough to take action. I feared repercussions from him, his family or his friends. I also felt sickly ashamed if I dared to benefit financially from my own mothers murder.

I continued reading the magazine. The Criminal Injuries Compensation Association (CICA) had also awarded this woman over £20K for the loss of a mother. It was a tragic story but I was amazed that society compensated people for their loss. I decided to go to see a solicitor and see if I was entitled to compensation. On balance, I had surely suffered more than this woman had and although no amount of money could replace my mother or undo the loss I was still experiencing, if nothing else it could free me from the life I led. It could provide me the funds I needed to get away from my husband and give my children a more secure future.

I found a female solicitor who specialised in family law. She was well educated and she initially asked me why I didn't want to sue my own father. I expressed my concerns and she looked bewildered. It's funny, the look people give, they have no idea how the fear of death, known as thanatophobia, takes over your life. It's something I wouldn't want people to ever understand, to be fair. I had received no support from society, no advocacy and no welfare checks were ever made on me as a child. "Its society who I feel let down by" I told her. She asked me to complete some forms. I had to write down how my father killing my mother had affected me and I completed the difficult task in floods of tears compiling several sides of A4 paper.

I wrote about how difficult I felt it was being a housewife and a mother; the flashbacks I had and how they upset me; my lack of confidence and my indecisiveness; how I would panic if my husband raised his voice fearing he would end my life; my feelings of helplessness and insecurity in my own home; how I worried about my children and how they would cope if anything happened to me; how I lay in bed at night thinking about painful memories and how my family had been traumatised; how I felt no-one understood me or cared about what had happened; my guilt for thinking about myself; my restless sleep and waking up with a sense of dread for the day ahead; how I smoked 2 or 3 cigarettes before I did anything and how I was tired, miserable and irritable most of the time and only happy when I was out of the home.

I explained how I couldn't discuss what had happened to my Mom with anyone because it was too painful, so I never got any support from other people; I found it hard to trust nice people but put trust in bad people; I spoke about my hyper-vigilance; I had a terrible memory; when I heard sirens or saw blue flashing lights I had palpitations and I felt numb and cold at the thought that something awful had happened to someone; I ached all over and had little motivation or energy; I worried about everything; I had regular stomach cramps and diarrhoea; I feared confrontations and often did things I didn't want to in order to avoid confrontations; I had a phobia about knives and other weapons which to me symbolised death and pain; I found talking to my family upsetting and depressing so I avoided contact with them, but felt overpowered with guilt for not being there to support them. I believed it was my duty to cheer them up.

It was a mishmash as I read through my essay, that was me, pretty fucked! Would the reader believe me? They didn't know me, surely they would think I had exaggerated my symptoms just to get my hands on some compensation. I smoked a joint and sealed the envelope. CICA wrote back to say they were sorry but due to the fact that my personal injury occurred before 1 October 1979 and I was living with my father, as members of the same family, I was not entitled to anything at all. There was a second apology and a recognition that this would come as a great disappointment to me. The person who had written the letter felt the injustice of the 'under the same roof rule'. Eighteen months my father had served, he doubled his money, society rewarded him for his actions and allowed him to benefit financially. As the daughter of a murderer, society wasn't going to compensate me because I was his daughter. People think crime doesn't pay and justice will be served. It didn't feel that way to me.

I received the statements taken by the police, an autopsy report and every newspaper report. The truth began to unfold and things started to look very different. Dad was arrested for murder and pleaded not guilty. I read his statement first and tried to sum it up in my head.....So is this true Mom? After all I don't have your side of the story, still....You have a row and tell him you are seeing Benny, he throws all your clothes out of the bedroom window and then throws you out. He doesn't hit you. Ray has seen everything and he is in the street with his friend when Aunt Linda arrives to take you to her house. After a couple of hours he calls you and asks you to come back home to talk. Uncle Malcolm comes in with you and leaves you to chat. Ray comes back in and you ask him if he's told everyone. You send Ray to the bathroom to get cleaned up for bed, it's about 8.15pm. You both sit on the sofa in silence for about ten minutes. He offers to make you a cup of tea. He suggests that he should move back to his mothers and you should remain at home because he can't look after us and go to work. You complain that the tea is weak. The next he thing he knows is he was holding a knife that had blood on it. Ray all of a sudden is fast asleep in bed. He calls Gramps at around 8.30pm....

She had got up early that day and made me a packed lunch. Her face wasn't bruised when I kissed her goodbye. She wouldn't leave Ray in the street and go to Aunt Linda's without him not unless she was forced to. Ray would never go to bed before me, not unless he was frightened. I read the autopsy report, it's not nice but it was the only way she could tell me what had really happened. She is lying on her back on the lawn, spread eagled. Close to her hand is a coffee cup. She has bruising to her nose, lip, arms and legs. The knife has been pushed through her chest into her heart, pulled back twisted and pushed in further. Her death would have been instant.

I read some more, she is wearing a white polar necked jumper and turquoise leather jacket and ...The same clothes she wore in my dream, she wore them when I was glue sniffing, she wore them in the photograph at Nan's house, these were the clothes she died in......She has a slipper near her foot, the other is in the lounge.....So what happened in the lounge Mom?..... There is a surgical scar below her umbilical.....That's too high to have been a scar from an appendix operation. My Nan had blocked this incident from her mind. My Dad must have stabbed her before or she must have self harmed. I tried to remember what had happened that day but all I could remember was having stomach cramps at school.

I had always believed we had a psychic connection but maybe I had cramps because I was worried about her. I remembered my Nan telling the head teacher she had been rushed to hospital to have her appendix out. I pictured her walking in from the hospital guarding her wound with her hand. My Dad wasn't there. Just my Nan. I saw the stitches, days later, when she got changed. They were in the centre of her stomach below her umbilical. My Nan and my Mom had lied about an operation. I called Aunt Linda, she hadn't been told about an injury. The real reason she had a wound had been hidden from me and brushed under the carpet.

The other statements had a common thread, evidencing what a nice man Ron Benton was. Their statements were given in a shocked state, it's natural to be in disbelief mode. No wonder he got away with her murder. None of them knew his nasty side or did they? My Gramps mentioned my mother had turned up on his doorstep, a few months earlier, with my brother Ray. I wondered why I had been left behind and couldn't recall a time that Ray had visited Nan and Gramps without me. Had Ray been told to keep the visit a secret? He told her to return to her husband, fatal words, I thought.

I remember Gramps spending hours with me, lying on my mothers bed because I had a 'rumbling appendicitis' on many occasions. I thought he cared about me. He was cheering me up, telling me funny stories or was he really keeping his eye on my Dad?

My Nan's statement was pretty short, she didn't say a lot. None of them lived in my house to see the abuse. Justice Blake said at the trial that he was 'a man of good character that had been provoked, it was a crime of passion', effectively saying she deserved to die. Can we rewind the tape because I am getting really wound up here. "Fucking PROVOKED!" I'm pacing the room, breathing heavy, gritting my teeth, this isn't anger, I'm fucking raging! I'm not crazy but I know a world that is.

I wondered if Justice Blake was still alive, or had my mother already slapped him in the face with the truth about this 'crime of passion'. We don't refer to a pedophile or a child killer as committing a crime of passion, they're monsters or psychopaths and we never say pedophiles accidentally sexually abuse a child. My dad, was a drunken bully, who forced himself on her, I have no doubts that he may have even raped her. He always put her down, knocked her self worth and made her life an absolute misery. He was the king of his castle and she was his slave. He wrestled with her until she cried, to keep her under his control, week after week. These weren't isolated incidents, she was a victim of domestic violence. Where is the justice?

He manipulated me to take his side and made me think his behaviour was normal 'playfighting'. He dragged me into the abuse, he made me part of it, with his twisted evil mind. He was happy to see me taunt my mother, it made him more powerful. It was no wonder she slapped me. I added salt to her wounds because he manipulated me. He should have wanted me to love my mother not join in the abuse. He was a bad father and a bad husband. We had lived with his abuse for years and my Mom had finally found happiness, with a man who truly loved her. My Dad put an end to her happiness and left a cross on her heart with the biggest blade he could find in the house, in my book that's murder, not passion. Tell me I am wrong.

Twenty three years had passed but knowing all this it seemed even harder to carry on, life would never be the same. Pete suggested I needed to invite my Dad and the wicked step mother of the west down to stay. He thought I should reconcile my relationship with my father and forgive him for a second time. He said I was going mad and needed to sort things out. I wrote him a long letter, telling him how I felt and what my life had been like, I still said I loved him, I didn't want him to kill me. Of course it was a free holiday so they turned up quite rapidly. Pete took Sandra and the children out to leave Dad and myself to talk. Dad said he always knew the day would come, that was another guilty slip of the tongue.

The problem, masked by our fake relationship, was I was still too frightened to end my relationship with him. I couldn't handle the situation on my own. He was still manipulating me, still claiming he had never hit Mom that day. I told him about the day I was sent home with rumbling appendicitis. He said my Mom had never had an operation or gone into hospital, as far as he knew. The victim played out saying things were going on behind his back, portioning the blame onto my mother and her family. He breathed heavily and nervously smiled. His lack of knowledge confirmed my mother hadn't self harmed or had an accident. He took the statements back with him, he wanted to read them. They would convince him he was still that 'Mr Nice Guy' I never handed over the autopsy report and he had no idea I had it.

....you think I don't know what happened, you fooled everyone didn't you, the family, the judge, even yourself, you believed your sober story was the truth and you expect me to go with it...not on your Nelly father, I know you couldn't believe your wife would dare to leave you, so you punished her and ended her life.

With the truth came strength, it may have been internal anger but it was a positive time for change. I told Pete I was going to get a full time job so we had more money coming in. My children felt second best to my career but that's the consequence of being a working mother. I applied for a job as a full time Nanny and started working for the Farragher family, who owned a chip shop and a restaurant in Yeovil an hour's drive from home. I cared for their four children Monday to Thursday. I had a good bond with all of them, especially their eldest son who had cerebral palsy. When the family moved back to the Midlands, I started working for Sedgemoor College and took my NVQ for working with young people in care with severe behavioural and emotional difficulties.

As my dependence on Pete whittled away, his abuse towards Nathan intensified and became violent. He slapped him so hard he left a handprint bruise on his face. I worked in child protection, I was now trained in recognising child abuse bruises. The psychological abuse was enough but now he had gone too far. I wanted to leave that day but I lacked the funds to live independently, I felt trapped. Pete apologised and we went to the doctor for advice, he said the bruising would fade and didn't take it any further. I was devastated I hadn't protected my own child.

It wasn't just Nathan he was cruel to. He had Tyson shot by a farmer, without my knowledge because he didn't trust the vets to put him to sleep humanely. He was shot three times before he died. Our next dog, he brought back home dead after he had shouted at him to hurry up because it was raining and the dog raced into the road and got run over. He claimed to love the dogs but they were purely a status symbol, he used them to intimidate people. He may never have killed anyone but he was selfish and manipulative, just like my father.

My Aunt Linda called me to let me know my Nan had cancer and once again I felt guilty that, for a couple of years, I had hardly seen her. I needed to commute to Wolverhampton as often as I could to spend time with her and also give my two aunts a break from caring for her. I got into some debt, paying for the petrol expenses but I didn't care, I just wanted to spend as much time with her as I could. On one hospital visit, we went as a family to cheer her up. I heard her tell Linda how she couldn't stand 'that fucking man', she was referring to Pete. I was shocked how, nearing death, she had changed so much. My Nan, high on morphine, had become a swearing, born again Christian, she made me smile. I still adored her.

She spent the last part of her life at home on a hospital bed in the lounge. She was frail and didn't enjoy being moved around by the Macmillan Nurses that were so gentle with her. On the last day I saw her, Linda had said she hadn't eaten or spoken for two days but when I walked in she said "Oh hello Diane, I've been waiting for you to come" Linda looked at me in disbelief. I felt so lovingly connected to my Nan that she had purposely waited to see me before she died. She continued "I did have three daughters but because of what your dad has done, all my money will now go to Linda and June." I already knew, the money would go to Linda and June. I hadn't come to talk about money. I just wanted to be with her and hold her hand one last time. What my Dad had done, she took to her grave and she made sure she reminded me of that fact. I had no idea of inheritance law at the time or our legal entitlement to my mothers share.

Life would never be the same without her around. She had spent many hours telling me about her extraordinary life; how she had been born outside a pub on April fools day. Her mom had gone into labour trying to get her dad out of the pub, close to midnight.They said she was born after midnight so she wouldn't always be a fool. She would often joke how she was "born in the gutter." Her mom had died of cancer when she was ten, she knew what it was like to grow up without a mother. She had danced with Lord Derby and he had asked her to marry him. She was engaged to be married to my grandfather at the time. Her naivety shone through on her wedding night when they couldn't have sex. When the doctor examined her he found she had no vagina. They operated on her but said she would never have children. She told me how she had spent weeks fingering herself to keep the hole open ready for when my Gramps returned on leave. She became pregnant with my Mom straight away. She was so full of crazy stories but everyone loved her.

My Nan had always loved me and despite my promise to my mother, I decided we would go to her funeral as a family. We had decided on Nan's favourite hymn, " All Things Bright and Beautiful" but for the second time in my life, my singing voice had gone. Holly sang out loud and held my hand. Tears rolled down my face throughout the service. We spent hours together, as a family, during her wake. I felt close and connected to the remaining members of my family. I enjoyed the togetherness and felt valued and loved, the Barlow bond would never break us. The truth was, I needed them as much as they needed me.

My Dorset country walks with the children were a blissful escape from reality. I lived in my Barbour wax jacket and wellington boots and became accustomed to the sweet smell of hydrogen sulphide. Inhaling cow manure was pretty addictive. I spent many hours trolling the Jurassic beach with my pink ear muffs blocking out the wind, head down scouring for ammonites, belemnites and the devil's toe nails or a special bit of driftwood. I never went home with empty pockets.

Dorset was a treasure trove and being in my tranquil world, close to nature, I felt very close to my mother. However, our days in Dorset were soon outnumbered. I was in serious debt and Pete refused to pay the rent, whilst he was out of work. He convinced me that another move was our only option. We both had career opportunities in Cheshire. We didn't say goodbye to our remaining friends. We packed up our belongings and simply disappeared.

Chapter 14
Financial Freedom

Linda thoughtfully asked if I wanted anything from Nan's house before she had a house clearance. I walked around the deserted home for the last time, reminiscing about the warmth of their love. The pots of tea that had welcomed me for so many years were gone. I stood in my grandads shed, the dust had settled on all his displayed tools. I picked up his spade and fork that he had used to bury his emotions, seized a hammer and some nails to fix my life and placed the old oak bureau, where I had once stored my calculator, into the back of my car. I requested a copy of my grandad's beautiful poems and left.

My aunts sold the house and gave Ray and myself £1000 each. They commented on how that was 'fair' as my cousins had been given the same amount. There was nothing 'fair' about my life. I envied my cousins in a way because they had so much more, they had their mothers. Mothers who were now financially fortunate because my mother and their mother were dead. It was nice to see the happiness their inheritance brought them after all they had been through. Seeing them happy put a smile on my face. I knew they loved my Nan and were just as heartbroken as I was. I didn't get a copy of my grandads poems but I paid off my credit card debt which was a great relief. I was still Momless, broke and stuck with Pete.

I employed an au pair to care for my children and knowing they were in safe hands, I concentrated on developing a career. My patience and conflict resolution skills came in handy as I worked with some of the most challenging young people in the country. It was a stressful role but we offered these young people a wonderful opportunity to enjoy their lives. I was always out at the cinema, ten pin bowling or go-carting with them. We drove brand new cars to escort them around and the houses were stunningly beautiful, countryside retreats. It was surreal, I felt like I was a wealthy happy mother and actually preferred to be at work. I was promoted to a senior residential social worker and against Pete's advice I was able to buy my first house.

The property was across the road from a petrol station. I had noticed a hand made sign in it's garden that simply said it was for sale and a mobile number. The vender just wanted a quick sale and I quickly became the owner. It was an ex council house and I did my usual thing, I made it look nice. There was an elderly couple living next door and I had noticed them walk down the road hand in hand. How sweet, I thought. Mr. Tomlinson had seen me cutting my hedges with shears and he came over to introduce himself. He told me his wife had dementia and how much he loved her. He reminded me of my Gramps as he offered to give me some spare hedge-trimmers, he had in his shed that just needed a plug.

As I walked into his house his wife greeted me, her eyes lit up, she had a beaming smile and held her arms open wide for a hug. "Oh, this is Pauline's daughter" she said to her husband as I gave her a comforting hug. Mr. Tomlinson looked at me and shook his head. "I'm sorry" he said in embarrassment. She knew who I was and was delighted to know I had moved into the house next door. He thought I was being nice, going along with what she had said and he thanked me as I left their house. Dementia had always fascinated me. My fathers mother had spoken to the spirits around me whilst I had sat next to her. I hadn't understood the relevance at the time. The old people I had worked with on my YTS placement claimed they knew who I was and Mrs. Tomlinson even knew my mother's name.

I managed a children's home in Holmes Chapel and trained all the new staff. I didn't trust anyone on their own with my boys until I was sure they were safe to be left. Most employees didn't last long, some only managed a trial shift. It took a certain type of character to care for these children. My time with Mrs. Lawrence gave me the skills to teach them how to manage their behaviour. It's the inner child that has temper tantrums. I rarely had to restrain a child and even then it was only for their own or others safety. I held house meetings and staff meetings but the high turnover of staff was soul destroying. The boys, were frustrated with the system, they were traumatised and often lost their placements for damaging property, assaulting staff or other boys.

I managed their behaviours in an extraordinary humorous way and made them feel loved. We had to adhere to professional boundaries and most professionals didn't understand how harmful that was. You had to understand them and use sensitivity. So when a child asked me where I lived, that was their way of saying I like you and next time I'm not happy, I will runaway to your house. I would say "If I tell you that, I'd have to kill you because you will want to move in, but I will tell you it's a very posh castle". They hated social workers so I told them I wasn't just a social worker, I was a bit like Jesus. I was there to take them out to have fun, to guide them and make sure they were safe. They would laugh at my comments, it took the hurt away from professional boundaries but still maintained the principles of good care.

One morning I arrived at work and found a lad on the roof throwing slates to the ground, the staff were hiding in the house, waiting for my back up. They had used their professional boundaries to control a child they believed was bad, and lacking in skills for humanity, they had lost control. I looked up at the lad. He hadn't swam to the sky for safety but he had got as high as he physically could. "You would be excellent in a career for demolition. Did you know, brave men like you, get paid a high wage for risking their lives? I am doing a fry up if you want to come down" and down he came. The other staff couldn't believe how I got them to do what I wanted, without a fuss.

We chatted as he relaxed over breakfast. I listened to him recounting all his failed foster placements and what he had done in the past. Like all of the children I worked with, he hated being in care but he did think Sedgemoor was different and I was 'ok really'. He soon settled but staff change overs were hard to handle, some just wanted an easy life, others played power games, and a few were restraint happy, everyone had their own interpretation of discipline and consequences and that inconsistency was hard for any human to handle. I tried to train them but some just thought they knew best.

I often used an analogy in staff meetings to help staff understand the needs of the children we worked with. Imagine the child you love has broken their leg. You can see they are in pain and you know that they need to go to hospital. They cry in pain and there is nothing you can do except maybe hold their hand. The child's leg is put into a caste and gradually the body heals it self. In fact the body does such a good job that the bone is actually stronger than it was. These children haven't been taken to hospital to get the help they needed because their parents caused their injury. They may not have a broken leg but they have been neglected and have something very painful inside. Our job is to help them feel safe so they can relax and their body can heal.

The first encounter with a child in care was always the most important to me. I knew the disapproving look people gave me as the daughter of a murderer. These children knew I was different, I was pleased to meet them for a start and I would always shake their hand. That action alone, engaged the adult, the part of the child that had to grow up and look after themselves. When their inner child played out, I offered them reassurance. I knew what abandonment felt like and that silent hope someone would look after me. I never shared my story. I was paid to support them and that's what I did but just like them, I had once worn the T-shirt from some tragic childhood. Jesus didn't need training in professional boundaries, he just cared, with his heart and did the right thing and so did I.

I met one new lad, requiring an emergency placement at our assessment house, he was sweating, wearing a polo neck jumper. I said "It's hot outside, go get your shorts and T-shirt on". I was told, on the staff handover, he was a difficult child, a neglect case, with 90% burns on his body, who had been saved by a firefighter. He was actually hiding his scars. He had a beaming smile on his face when I went down to him, dressed in cooler clothing. "That's better, ain't it mate" I said. I could see his scars, but it didn't matter, I too had scars for something that wasn't my fault. It didn't make him a bad person. I taught him how to play backgammon, a game that's all about equality. You can play it safe or take risks but with a throw of the dice the game can change, like life it depends on the moves you make and the opportunities you are given.

He ate dinner, watched TV and went up to settle in his new bedroom. He had a shower and shouted goodnight. He filled the toilet with bath foam, causing a huge dome shaped bubble structure in the garden by the cesspit the next morning. "The aliens have landed outside, come and look" I said and fearing he was in trouble, he ran away. I found him lying in a field close by. I lay next to him, staring at the clouds and he told me his life story. I just listened to him fantasising about his heroic Dad. "You must feel proud of that firefighter for saving your life, not all Dads are that special, some of us get shit ones, I wished my real Dad had been a teacher" I said. He knew he didn't need to lie to me. He lit up a cigarette and told me he was only making the toilet smell nice after he had used it. We weren't allowed to leave toilet cleaner in their en-suite as it was seen as a safeguarding issue.

These young people were so troubled and I walked a dangerous path trying my best to help them. I had good communication skills, the knives were all locked away and most days I felt safe. One lad said he could rape me and no one would know. I told him not to go there and that I had enough hassle with my husband, he looked shocked but it seemed to warn him off. I refused to work with him again. A member of staff had already been raped and I didn't fancy being another victim. One lad smashed his way into my office trying to attack a member of staff who had annoyed him. The door hit my head and I needed stitches. Some days I questioned if my dedication to my role was worth it.

During my time at Sedgemoor, I had worked with around thirty emotionally disturbed children, each with a price tag on their head. Social services were paying around £3K per week to care for these vulnerable human beings. On the home visits, parents would say, they were better off in care as they couldn't afford to give them clothing and spending allowances or take them on activities. There was something so counterproductive with a child in need, depriving parents of their children because of poverty. The beautiful properties we worked in were owned by clever investors, reaping quick returns, whilst the staff ratio dwindled. The average burn out rate for residential social workers was two years and I had already done three.

When Pete 'accidentally' dropped an axle on his leg, recovering a lorry, I had more stress to deal with. He was an absolute nightmare to care for and put us all through hell with his mood swings, whilst his leg was pinned and plastered for ten weeks. I had to give up my job to look after him. I sold our home and moved all our stuff into temporary accommodation. I had sacrificed everything. Kathy Bates didn't have my issues in the film 'Misery'. I wasn't a besotted fan of resentful Pete.

Whilst I got ready for my next interview Pete went out to check my car. He cleaned the windscreen for me, checked my oil and water levels and I thought naively, he was being kind. I set off for the interview early and had just hit the countryside when my car electrics stopped working. I called Pete on my mobile, I had broken down on a bend and I was worried someone would drive into me. The hero came to my rescue, towed the car to a safe place, checked it over and said it couldn't be fixed there and then. I called a taxi and told the receptionist at Castlehomes I would be late. I arrived half an hour late and felt very stressed but the interview went well and after a second interview I was given the position of a peripatetic senior residential social worker.

Castle Homes was a breath of fresh air. They genuinely cared about their staff, so staff turnover wasn't such an issue and the children they looked after were much happier. I worked in a no frills mainstream home, with girls and boys. I soon became aware of the sexual exploitation the girls were experiencing in the community so this was high on my agenda with regards to safeguarding them. Doing 48 hour shifts in residential work, and not having reliable childcare myself, meant I was dependent on my unreliable husband. I took on another position as a project worker for young people leaving care which was more suitable. Care leavers were lucky in a way as they were given a leavers grant to set up home and a key worker who regularly checked up on them, giving them support. I reflected on my move into independence as they complained that they had it hard. Having a normal 9-5 job meant I got to spend more time at home with my children and I noticed Pete's relationship with Nathan seem worse than ever. I hated to see my son so sad and terrified of the man I was married to.

I decided to take the children and their friends to Waterworld as a special treat. I couldn't really afford to go but we hadn't had a holiday that year and I wanted to cheer them up. Pete wasn't happy about me paying for someone else's children. He went out to 'check the car over' whilst we got our swimming kits ready. We broke down on the way to Waterworld. I called Pete and he came out to look at the car. He tried to convince me that he hadn't tampered with the electrics and it was the way I had been driving that had caused the problem. We had a row in front of the children and their friends who were now deflated from their excitement. We headed back home via a tow rope, rescued by an irate untrustworthy 'mechanic'.

We moved again to a rent free two up, two down terraced property in Stoke on Trent, owned by Pete's employer. It was supposed to have been another temporary home, whilst we saved to buy our next property. I hated living there, my life seemed to be one sacrifice after another. He was earning a fantastic wage as he was on permanent call out and recovered HGV's. We were also breeding Dalmatians as they were more profitable and popular. He still had control of our finances, so I couldn't 'waste' or 'lose' money but we still didn't seem to be any better off. I just remained focused on my career.

As a professional my home life and my mothers death were never disclosed at work. When I left the house, in work mode, I became a different person. Furthermore, I would support my colleagues with their trivial issues that seemed to impact on their work. I noticed how settled their lives were, compared to mine. I booked a family holiday to France trying to do what my colleagues did to relax, trying to feel in control of my life, trying to feel normal. I was lost, nothing in my life made sense. Whether it was JC, fate, my strong character or my CV that boasted a vast amount of skills and training, I was suddenly headhunted for a new role.

Moorlands Housing asked me to take over the position of domestic violence support officer, when my predecessor was herself experiencing domestic violence and couldn't manage her role. During the three years I worked there, I supported many women and a few men who were victims of domestic violence. I had job satisfaction and overwhelming gratitude from my clients, as I helped them rebuild their lives. One male victim who I supported claimed that I was a special being on this earth. He said my body was surrounded by a yellow aura which meant he could trust me as I was a friend. I had taken him to the Priory for several counselling sessions so I didn't take much notice of his comments and laughed them off as a women who ate her Ready Brek.

As the service developed we took on another member of staff. Karen had a counselling background and we had an excellent working relationship. She also believed I had an aura surrounding me. " Don't you start" I said as I explained what one of my clients had said. Whether I had an aura or not, I remained focused on my work. I learned all there was to know about this field of work and became a specialist consultant and trainer. I was perfect for the job, I had empathy, experience and knowledge and the job was perfect for me, it changed my life completely.

Pete had apparently blown the money we had made from the last property on Land Rovers and Jeeps. I paid all the bills and bought the food and as he pleaded poverty, I suspected he was taking harder drugs, gambling or seeing prostitutes. I knew for sure he was conning me. The money had to be going somewhere. He swapped mobiles with me for some strange reason, perhaps he wanted to check who I was in contact with. I had nothing to hide so it didn't worry me but his ex wife called. "Hi Peter, sweetheart" she said. We sat chatting, she thought we had split up years ago and Pete had been living on a canal boat, perhaps he had! He was often 'away' doing break-downs, working 70-90 hours a week, but he never seemed to have anything left to show for his efforts.

My brain was trying to figure out what was going on in my personal life. I stopped smoking completely. My cabbaged mind was cleared of cannabis and nicotine. My vision and sense of smell returned. I saw an old smelly tramp, a gas lighting con artist, a liar, a bad father and a bad husband. He knew I was slipping away from him so he did what all abusive husbands do to keep their wives, he put the kettle on. My dad had made my mother a weak tea. Pete made me a coffee and dropped a Viagra into my cup. I noticed the blue tablet still undissolved as I finished my drink. He assured me he hadn't spiked my coffee. He could lie so convincingly. I thought about all the times he had kindly offered to cook or make me drinks over the years, there was nothing nice about this man. How many times had he drugged me to have sex? That Viagra, got me going alright, straight out the door.

I created my own escape plan and contacted a refuge. I took two weeks holiday from work. I filled the car with everything Pete didn't need, including the toaster and the kettle. I collected the children from school and we set off for Elizabeth House, in Stoke on Trent. I parked the car and took the children to the front door. I confirmed my name over the security system and a woman opened the door. We went into the office and after a while we were shown around the refuge. It was an old, drab and depressing building for the desolate and the desperate but I was grateful to get away from Pete. I burst into tears when we entered the communal kitchen, struggling with the idea of sharing facilities with seven other families.

Our room had three single beds, all with different duvet sets, old and worn, presumably so no-one would steal them. We had a fridge and a wardrobe. I began unpacking the clothes and settling in to our new abode. We were summoned back to the office, as a matter of urgency, to complete the claim forms for their funding. My key-worker advised me to give up my job as staying in a refuge was expensive. I listened with caution, it's easy to fall into the poverty trap when you are vulnerable but I had no intention of going there again.

I told the key-worker that I worked for Moorlands Housing and that I worked with victims of domestic abuse. She said I was still better off to claim income support as I would have little left of my earnings if I was to continue in my work. She was so very patronising as I attempted to hang on to my pride in front of my concerned children's faces. She then asked me to move my car down the road as the carpark was for staff only despite there being plenty of free spaces. The car was safer on the grounds, out of sight, but I was a victim not worthy of a privileged parking space and this certainly was not a victim centred refuge.

We slept for a few nights, crammed into one small room. The three of us chatted happily about our future. The lack of space was suffocating but we were in a place of safety whilst Pete was desperate to know where we were. This place of safety was quite strange, there were rough, intimidating women with wild foul mouthed children appearing to be ruling the roost there and quiet, petrified women and children that seemed relieved to see me.

One woman had her door kicked open and someone stole her money from her room. I explained to my children that everyone was there for a reason and to smile and be respectful, regardless of how upset or angry people appeared. We sat in the communal lounge. I introduced myself and said that I wished I didn't have to be there. It started a conversation and everyone seemed to get on. We were all in the gutter but we had all escaped abuse.

I called my cousin Tracey and she said "come down to us and we will sort something out." By the time I had got to her home, she had discussed the situation with her husband. She wanted me to sleep on her sofa and my children to stay with Carry Ann, her sister. She had worked out how much I should pay them for the convenience. Her insensitive exploitation evidenced her level of love and support for a family in crisis, she salted my wounds. We stayed in Wolverhampton for a couple of nights. I slept on Tracey's sofa thinking about how I had abandoned my children. I had shipped them off to Carry Ann's, it was like history was repeating itself but I wasn't dead as a result of leaving my husband. My children needed a home and they needed me.

I returned to the refuge, needing somewhere to live and the refuge worker advised I apply for housing. I just wanted a deposit to rent privately. I didn't need to stay in a refuge for months waiting for some horrid offer of another depressing council house. The refuge couldn't help me. I negotiated my options with my abusive husband instead and returned to live with him for a few days. He hated the idea the children were living in a refuge so he paid the deposit on a home for us to move to the following week. It was strange how he afforded me the opportunity. I guess it was a way of knowing my whereabouts and of course, he thought I wouldn't manage without him. I knew I was finally free of a controlling manipulative husband.

My cousin, Carry Ann said that she had a spare single bed and some wardrobes we could have. I asked Pete if I could borrow his Volvo estate to get them and surprisingly he agreed. Holly, Nathan and I set off for the 90 minute journey to my cousin's house and we arrived there, the car didn't break down. It was lovely to see her, we stayed for hours chatting. It was getting dark so she helped me fold down the seats and load the car. I was surprised we managed to get it all in the back of the Volvo. Pete despite all his lies had always said there was no better car than a Volvo estate. Holly and Nathan had to sit on the front seat together with panels of wood over their heads but it was only till we got home.

After a while there was black smoke coming from below the handbrake and it smelt quite toxic. I thought at first it was because I had overloaded the car and I pulled over into a lay by. I couldn't see anything wrong with the suspension on the car. I called Pete to let him know. He blamed me and gave me a load of abuse so I cut him off and burst into tears. He then called me back 'realising' it was something he had done as a short cut to save money. The heat from the exhaust had melted the wires. We waited for him to tow us back home, it turned out to be a very long night. That was the last time I would drive a car he had tampered.

I returned to work after my 2 week break and notified them of my new address. My colleagues remarked on how stressful moving house could be, it was up there with divorce, they said. It was as though my key-worker from the refuge had breached confidentiality. I laughed and joked about my stress free move and how happy I was in my new home, just with my children. I sat down with key members of staff and gave them my ideas for a much needed women's refuge for the Staffordshire Moorlands. I had found peace in my life but Stoke wasn't home. Pete sensed there was something still missing in my life. He would call round to spend time with the children, expecting me at some stage to take him back. He made my skin crawl.

Nathan moved to a new high school that was right on our doorstep. He found the transition hard, and during his first week, he took his football with him, in an effort to make friends. He was bullied on the playground by a group of Asian lads who displayed their racial hatred for "white boy ginger". They stole his ball. Nathan lay on the floor calling out for help as they kicked him in his head, face and stomach repeatedly. Some older boys intervened and saved his life. They took him to the office and went for their lunch. Nathan sat there waiting to be seen.

During afternoon registration a teacher asked why he was sat there. Nathan explained, she asked if he was OK and sent him back to class. When I saw Nathan's face, it broke my heart. He was more upset that the gang had kept his ball. I couldn't believe there was no one supervising the students during break times. There was no safeguarding check or a follow up and the poor soul was battered, bruised and hungry.

The next day, I took time off work to see the head teacher about the incident. She had no idea it had happened and apologised. After a brief conversation I realised this woman had no idea how to control her school either. She asked me to give her a second chance. I asked her if she would have considered calling the police if she had been physically attacked by a gang of racist students. Nathan never went back, he moved to a different school. Two weeks after his incident, there were police vans at the school, the racially motivated students were rioting and at war. The school was put into special measures and was eventually shut down.

On bonfire night Pete took the children to find a firework display. He followed a car that had children inside thinking they would be on route to some kind of event but they ended up on Asda's car park. My children laughed. He went inside and bought fireworks and sparklers and returned to our house. I didn't really want him around but he had manipulated the situation, I didn't want to spoil the children's fun so I allowed him into the rear garden and he set up the fireworks for lighting. I watched through the kitchen window, my children were happy and I went outside to join in their fun. Pete soon had me running back inside as he lit a torrent of fireworks that were directed at me, rather than the sky. He claimed they must have been faulty but I knew he had tried to injure me in front of my children. We had a row and it ruined their evening.

I thought back to the time when I had finished with Quilly and had an abortion, whether that had been a stupid mistake. He and his family had been so loving towards Nathan. Quilly had never hurt me or controlled me. I went for a drink and got chatting with him. So many things had happened in his life. His mom had sadly passed away due to cancer and he missed her dearly. He had been promoted to a manager position after years of service and dedication to his company. He had recently separated from his partner and took full custody of their two year old daughter. He had taken redundancy so he could look after her. He told me how he had made a fantastic profit from the sale of his house and was living with his Dad. He drove a brand new, reliable pick up truck.

We spoke about giving our relationship another try, after a while, he moved in with his daughter. Knowing he was financially secure, I didn't want him to think I was using him for his money so I made sure I paid for everything. Pete had said he would give me £500 a month maintenance but after Quilly moved in that stopped. So I sat down with Quilly and tried to talk about finances. He told me he didn't actually have any money, after his mom had died and his relationship had broke down, he had blown all the money he had, he had even given some of it away. I guess he had just been foolish during a hard time in his life.

He got a job, but he didn't like the work and the wages didn't cover the cost of his daughters childcare. He was missing his dad and his friends. We were struggling financially and I was worried. I had suffered instability with Pete for so many years, I didn't want to support Quilly and his daughter. I just couldn't afford to do it. I came home from work to find he had gone back to live with his dad, leaving some furniture and appliances as compensation, bless him. I was shocked that he had walked out so quickly. Pete found me in tears, he remarked how he knew Quilly was a parasite and he put his arms around me. I pushed him away. Knowing I was broke, he handed me £400 and left with a smug smile of hope.

I wanted to try and keep my head above water financially. I needed the maintenance money so I tried to be civil with Pete. I suggested he still came on the holiday to France. I told him I didn't have the confidence to drive all the way on my own with the children. I had my annual leave booked and I desperately needed a holiday. It was a total disaster. Pete thought it was some kind of honeymoon and we would be sleeping together. That wasn't my plan, sex wasn't on my agenda. He spent his week sulking and being obnoxious. I wanted to spend the days on the beach, sunbathing whilst the children swam in the sea. He wanted to avoid the sun and stay in the shade. He reluctantly dropped us off near a beach, wheel spun away and we found a nice spot to relax.

I watched my children enjoying themselves having fun. I lay in the sun feeling blessed, reconnected to the world around me. Nathan was free and happy floating around on his giant rubber ring, looking after his sister. I looked around at the happy families on the beach. I reflected on my marriage and my need to divorce. Holly got out of the sea and lay by my side sunbathing. We spoke about how her father and me were so different and it was impossible to be together. She agreed, he was ruining our holiday. We were getting hot in the baking sun and decided to buy ice cream. We looked for Nathan. We walked up and down the beach and looked out to sea. I felt sick inside. He was nowhere to be seen. My son was gone. I was frantic and called Pete. He pointlessly ran up and down the beach, effectively wasting more time. "Just take me back to the campsite, I need to report my son missing." I yelled.

Nathan had walked straight past us on the beach, sunburnt, lost and confused. He eventually stumbled upon a nudist beach and seeing everyone naked around him, he panicked and began to cry. A concerned French woman, covered herself with her towel and came to his rescue. She tried to find someone on the beach with a phone and then they walked for ages trying to get a reception to call the police. Nathan had no idea what they were saying. He sat with a man on a wall in silence until the police arrived. He tried to tell the police where he was staying and they sat him in the back of the police car. He was terrified because they only spoke French and he could see they were armed with guns. He thought he was going to be killed because he had seen the naked people on the beach. They dropped him back at the campsite.

As I opened the door to the caravan, my dehydrated and hungry son was eating biscuits and drinking a glass of milk. I hugged him and cried with relief, my boy was still alive, he hadn't been eaten by sharks or drowned. Pete was ranting that he had been searching for him whilst he was "Eating fucking ginger biscuits". I stared at him in disbelief. The holiday with Pete had been a disaster but losing and finding my son had been a rollercoaster of emotions on a totally different level. We headed back on the long journey to the ferry port. A Frenchman advised Pete that his tyre was flat and Pete replied "Ah Bon". It was like a scene from 'Only Fools And

Horses' when I explained to the children their dad had said " that's good" we laughed our heads off at his expense.

I had terrible sea sickness on the crossing but Holly soon cheered me up by singing the 'The tide is high' on karaoke, to a crowd of people. She was so brave and received a standing ovation at the end, bless her. We made it back to Stoke on Trent, eventually and I began exploring the cheapest way to get a divorce. £220 for an online divorce was well worth it, I ticked the "unreasonable behaviour" box, much to Pete's confusion. I spent a few minutes listing the things he had done during our marriage that was unreasonable. He wanted me to admit to adultery but our marriage hadn't ended because of an affair. I reminded him that I was paying for the divorce and this was yet another example of his unreasonable behaviour, he signed the paperwork.

Chapter 15
Love, Laughter and Livin

The taxman kindly deposited some money into my account and as it was approaching Christmas, I asked the children if they fancied a holiday for a change. I looked on line for the hottest destination, found accommodation on the beach and started to look at flights to Sri Lanka. I couldn't justify the cost of the flights which were inflated purely due to it being Christmas. We remained at home, shocked to see an earthquake in the Indian Ocean had caused a tsunami on Boxing Day, I felt blessed we hadn't gone.

My brother came to visit and I told him about my divorce. He had always thought Pete was a dodgy con man. He told me Pete took all sorts of drugs, I just hadn't got a clue. Ray was pleased to hear I was moving on. "Guess who I bumped into recently" he said and went on to tell me that Dan Clarke was also going through a divorce. That's a blast from the past, I thought, the perfect boyfriend I had dumped for a crazy delinquent. Ray said I needed a night out, he could get me a ticket for a New Years party and we could stay at his place. I hadn't been out on New Year's Eve since before Nathan had been born. Fifteen years had passed and I jumped at the offer to celebrate the year 2005 and my new life.

I had my hair and nails done and dressed up for the occasion. I bumped into an old friend when I arrived. Jayne had married and had children soon after leaving school. I had moved to Wolverhampton and we had lost touch so it was great having a catch up. I was shocked to hear she was now working in a nightclub, living it up like a teenager. She told me she had cancer but she was fighting it. Her son was living with his dad as she couldn't cope with his unruly behaviour. I knew all about unruly behaviour from my work in residential care. I had been so lucky with my own children really, they were angels. Jayne was hoping to get her son back home but for now she was glad to get some respite.

At around 10.30 the front door opened and in walked someone who had last seen me at my lowest, sitting on the floor in a disused garage, sniffing glue. "Hello, Dan, remember me?" I said. "Yes, your Rays sister" he said. After twenty three years, he still made me laugh. He hadn't forgotten me and I had been reunited with him. It felt good. He ordered himself a coke at the bar. I was impressed, he was sober, unlike everyone else around us. We were fifteen when we had been together and now we both had sons that age, Dan also had a toddler called Robbie from his second marriage. He told me how he had separated from his second wife six months previously and she had disclosed on Christmas Day that she had been having an affair. He had been staring at his New Years Eve ticket all evening deciding whether or not to go. "I am glad you came, it's fate" I said.

Dan told me he had been to prison for a freak accident, he was
if anything he was ashamed but he wanted me to know. He had
night and a guy, for no reason, had beaten him up. He was left b
few weeks later, seeing the guy again he offered him a fight on th
guy refused the offer and Dan thought he had proven his point anc
away. The guy laughed "You're a wanker". Dan spun round and thr   ..n. The
guy had raised his glass and it took his nose clean off. Luckily the doctors were
able to stitch his nose back on. He had hated every minute of prison, he missed out
on his sons early years.

There was no pretence with Dan. I knew he hated bullies and he wasn't a coward.
He didn't do drugs and was as honest as they come. I told him about my life and
what my Dad had done. He remembered the murder in Westbourne Avenue but he
had no idea that it was my mother. He was shocked that my Dad had only served
eighteen months and I had returned to live with him. "That explains why you were
glue sniffing, I guess" he said. We had both done things we were ashamed of but
they were in the past. We continued chatting and celebrated the new year with our
friends.

He invited me back to his flat and said he would rustle me something up because I
was hungry. We laughed as he concocted a liver tikka masala that turned out to be
delicious. "Happy new year Dan, this will be a good one" I said. We held each other
and kissed. I felt real love. "If we do this, can it be forever, I can't do heartache
again" I said. He wrapped his arms around me and smiled. We were naked, in each
other's arms as we drifted off to sleep but I woke feeling cold, several times in the
night and gradually put my clothes back on. The next morning we laughed about
me being fully clothed in the bed and I nicknamed his quilt "the one tog".

Pete had no idea I was back with Dan and on Nathan's birthday he turned up with a
present. I opened the door and welcomed him in. Nathan was sat on the sofa and
he walked straight passed him and handed me the gift. I was initially confused and
opened it out of curiosity. It was a gold bracelet, identical to one he had given me
before! I reminded him that we were getting divorced and that it was Nathan's
birthday. I handed him the gift back. He sat staring at the wall, speechless. I asked
him to leave. Nathan looked bewildered but he was pleased with the skateboard
and games I had given him.

The children were adapting to Stoke on Trent but I never felt at home there. On my
mothers birthday, Holly had found me crying on my bed, she asked me what was
up. She knew I called her Nan Sandra but because she was married to my Dad,
she had always assumed she was my mother. I explained what had happened to
my Mom. She gave me a hug and told me she didn't like her Nan anyway. She had
always found Sandra to be quite uninviting and now she understood why it had felt

like a fake relationship. She wanted to see a photograph of her real Nan. I hugged her and said "So do I".

After several months of commuting back and forth to see Dan, and my children loving his company, as a family we decided to rent a house together in Great Wyrley. I was worried about bumping into my Dad and Shaun Green again but knew Dan would protect me from harm. Dan's mom thought it was too soon and tried to persuade him to wait a while longer but we knew we wanted to be together so we found a nice house and we started our happy lives. "This is livin" Dan would say. I felt he had finally rescued me. I loved this man so much. Love and laughter bounced from the walls.

We contemplated having a child together and then quickly agreed that four children between us and our love for each other was enough to keep us happy. Holly loved Dan, she would share the Barbie Dolls with him and he would happily play along. He found her crying and he asked her why she was upset. She said she was worried because she didn't ever want him to leave me. He reassured her he would never do that. He just loved children and was a fun father figure. Nathan kept his distance a little, after the abuse from Pete, I thought he would eventually come to love Dan. He seemed happy making new friends and enjoyed skateboarding in the park close by.

Pete had given me £500 maintenance, the payments had been so irregular I had never depended on them. I purchased a tent and some camping equipment for a holiday in Dawlish Warren. Dan showed me the bed and breakfast property, his family had run in Torquay. We went fishing at Hope's Nose and saw a friendly sea lion. Dan caught mackerel which we fed to the sea lion and the rest we cooked on the barbecue. He paid for tickets to take us to a motor stunts show, thinking Nathan would enjoy it but he refused to go, without a reason, he stayed in the tent playing on his mobile phone. We spent the next day on the fair rides and everyone enjoyed themselves.

We had Dan's sons round at weekends and spent days out together, the family bonds were healthy and strong, everyone was happy. Pete would have Nathan and Holly for a few hours, giving them the third degree, wanting to know everything. He never gave me anymore maintenance, he used the excuse that I had bought a tent with the last money he gave me. I knew my children would make their own minds up about him and his manipulative ways, so I let it be. We had a social life and a home life now and I felt blessed to be so happy.

I did bump into my Dad and I was civil, despite knowing he had murdered my mother, destroyed my childhood and blown my chances for inheritance. I know it's hard for people to understand but we are taught to respect our parents regardless of their flaws. I always walked away feeling worthless so I kept my distance and most times, I avoided him completely. I thought I could cope but I started smoking again. Shaun heard that I was back in the village and he pulled up alongside me as I walked down the street. He had the same glint in his eye, the same smile on his face that I had always fallen for in the past. He thought he could just flick his fingers and I would be back in his life. I ignored him and told Dan how he had followed me like a kerb crawler hooking a prostitute.

Dan soon put a stop to Shaun's kerb crawling attempts when he saw it happen and went over to confront him. I knew I was safe in Dan's hands. All that time away from the village because of Shaun and my Dad, I had missed out on my old friendships. I loved being back there with so many people pleased to see me, it made me feel good. We would go out in the evenings to the local pubs and chat with others I hadn't seen for years. I realised how isolated my crazy life had been with Pete. Dan was totally the opposite, he wanted me to socialise and have a happy life. "Why would you want to stay in? We are social creatures, life is all about friends and family" he would say.

I continued to commute to Leek everyday supporting the victims of domestic abuse but after taking a 'train the trainer' course and delivering training to the Samaritans and Citizens Advice employees, I knew I wanted to train more people. I could never stop domestic abuse happening, however, I could train people on how to respond to victims and help save people's lives. The refuge was close to completion and I knew that it would bring a valuable resource for women needing a safe place to stay. I applied for a position with Sandwell Metropolitan Council as a Training Coordinator for Domestic Abuse, along with a two page cover letter to support my application as I did not have the compulsory degree. I decided to inform them about my mother, who had lost her life as a victim of domestic violence.

Dan had another opportunity to run a pub in West Bromwich, he had previously ran it with his ex-wife and had made a tidy profit there. "What do you think?" he asked. I had always fancied running a pub business. We sat and looked at the pros and cons. We were about to buy the property we were renting but we decided to spend the cash on the Forrester's instead and stay for a couple of years making money. I wanted to keep my career going and Dan was fully supportive. We made the move and made the place habitable. Holly and Nathan caught the bus to and fro trying to maintain their friendships and that was hard for them. They also had less time with me and became understandably resentful but I still loved them.

I set off for the Training coordinator interview accompanied by Bob Marley, telling me not to worry and everything was going to be alright. I regularly felt my mothers presence via the radio, it gave me the comfort I needed. I gave a presentation on domestic abuse awareness training for midwives to the domestic abuse coordinator, the NHS head of safeguarding children and the CEO of Sandwell Women's Aid. Coincidently, I had recently had training on this specific area, back in Stoke on Trent with the domestic violence forum, so I was confident and thorough. I sat with Alicia Keys on the way home, telling me, you and me together, everything's gonna be alright. "Yes, that went well Mom, we can do this" I said. It might sound crazy but that coincidental spiritual link with the lyrics of a song had always guided me and supported me.

After a second interview, putting forward my plans to complete a needs analysis and a training strategy, I was offered the job. I served my notice at Moorlands Housing. I ensured the vulnerable women I had been supporting were all in safe hands. They were all full of praise and best wishes, bless them all. We had a meal out with my manager, and all the team. I tried my best to give a speech in floods of tears, laden with flowers and gifts. It had been Moorlands housing that had found me and opened doors for me and it was such a wonderful company to work for.

I had my dream job and all my efforts were placed there. I was working along side others, setting up Sandwell's Organisation Against Domestic Abuse;SOADA. I was writing strategies, policies and training professionals on responses to victims of abuse. I was proud to deliver bespoke training to West Midlands Police, Teachers, NHS workers, social workers, housing officers and staff from many different support agencies who may have come into contact with victims.

I was invited to be a speaker at a local Soroptimist group to talk about SOADA. I had never heard of Soroptimist International, who were all women in professions and businesses that worked together at local, national and international levels to educate, empower and enable women and girls to improve their lives. Preventing domestic violence was high on their agenda. They made me feel very welcome, what a beautiful group of women, I thought.

I passionately, delivered the children's Stay Safe programme to year six pupils in several schools. It was a subtle way to talk about domestic abuse and who was available to support them. Ironically, at that age my mother had lost her life, so it was so important for these children to know where the support was and I made sure they knew who to contact. Many openly spoke about witnessing abuse prior to their dads or step dads leaving and how happy their mothers were now. They were relieved to speak about the subject in school, and said they wanted more lessons on 'things like this', It was interesting that none of these children had told their teachers about the abuse at the time. I made a big thing of that. "If you think the teacher could make things worse, then that's a sign that you need support. Did you know all your teachers have had special training and know how to keep you safe and support you?" It was the children who said nothing but listened with intent, that I was really there for.

I was also proud to be a facilitator of a therapeutic boys group, set up to work with young boys who had been exposed to domestic abuse and were now displaying perpetrator behaviours or were traumatised by the abuse they had lived with. We piloted the group first and the boys named their group the Breakaway Challengers, our work was evaluated and the results were outstanding. The diverse team I worked with had different skills, backgrounds and approaches. We offered an holistic approach and a big part of our work was the analysing and debriefing after each session, our own welfare was as important as the boys that we worked with and as a result we were the closest and strongest team, I had ever been privileged to work with.

Pete's contact with my children was dwindling away but when he heard we had a pub, he conveniently decided to take them out for the day. He arrived an hour early and Nathan and Holly had only just woke up. Dan invited him in for a coffee while they got ready. Pete hurled abuse at him "You stole my wife, you f...ing c...t" and shocked by his response, Dan chased him up the road. He locked himself in his car. After a day with Pete, my children believed I no longer cared about them and they were disrespectful towards Dan. Pete was playing his games again, he refused to pay maintenance, despite being chased by the authorities. We didn't let him bother us. Dan and I weren't a fragile commodity he could destroy.

Running a pub business in a working class area was very profitable but unlike public sector work, you have to ignore prejudice. Most regular drinkers have their own issues and strong right wing opinions. If I had challenged every sexist, racist or homophobic comment my customer base would have dwindled down to no-one. To be a successful landlady, I needed to be able to have banter with the regulars and I did throw back plenty of sarcastic comments to counteract their ignorance. I used humour to educate them rather than empower them by remaining silent. As a business woman, I sold them alcohol regardless of whether it was to celebrate or drown their sorrows. They came to the pub to socialise and to escape their mundane lives. They disclosed their private issues and I counselled them. I was their social worker, teacher and friend.

We welcomed everyone regardless of creed, colour or faith. Old Mr. Singh, a taxi driver, would call in twice a day for a swift double Jack Daniels. He would always finish his drink before I could hand him his change. "You haven't seen me" he would say. He was a gentle, kind man although my aichmophobia always kicked in as he casually walked around with his kirpan, a ceremonial dagger, symbolising his need to fight oppression. I wished society prevented such weapons being worn for religious rights, when to me they just symbolised death. I would have preferred Mr. Singh to have carried an axe whilst he went about his Jack Daniels business.

One regular told me how he paid the wages to NHS staff and had twenty people unofficially on his books, working as porters in the hospital. They paid him £100 per week each. This man conned money from desperate unemployed immigrants. He also advised me on the ways to rip off the benefit system. He boasted about how his buy to let mortgages were all funded by housing benefit. He told me his fathers generation had come to England believing the money was too good to be true and the abundance wouldn't last. Their mentality was to send money back home and build mansions. He didn't return for a few months and I thought perhaps he had gone to prison for fraud. He had started working for Cadbury's and several weeks later a lorry load of Easter eggs disappeared.

Virtually every man that entered our pub was involved with some sort of criminal activity. There were men outside selling bottles of alcohol, weapons and other confiscated items they were supposed to destroy or dispose of at work. We had shop lifters selling products to customers. We had drug dealers trying their luck. We had drug users smoking joints outside. We had people selling copyright films they had burned onto DVD's. We had millionaires holding toolbox meetings. It reminded me of the Red, White and Blue in Featherstone. You see it all in a rough and ready, back street boozer.

A group of married men formed a pool team and would meet at our pub every Wednesday night, armed with their pool cues. They would leave their cues in the pub and go to the strip club for the evening. I was working in a male dominated industry and was sworn to secrecy. It's very empowering to be 'a woman in the know' in a mans world. Dan went along with them just to get out of the pub for a few hours. It didn't worry me, I knew I could trust Dan. He only went for a laugh and told the women who approached him that he was gay. I wanted to know if anyone was being exploited there and I was surprised to hear that there was a 'no touch policy'. The men all enjoyed there 'innocent bit of fun and fantasy'. They would return to our pub to collect their cues and have a drink for the road.

One night, when all their wives were out, I got the women all together and told them I was forming a Tuesday night ladies pool team. Their husbands jaws dropped, one man shook his head, another started praying. I winked at the women and said "You just need to turn up at 7.30 with your pool cues and we can go out and play a few games." I winked at them again. None of them had cues so I said they could borrow their husbands and winked twice. Two of the wives said they couldn't play pool. So I explained it wasn't about the winning, it was an excuse to get out of the house. I winked twice again. One wife said "I like to watch Eastenders on a Tuesday" and another said "Oh yes, so do I". I was wasting my time, they hadn't got a clue about equality and must have assumed I had some sort of nervous tic or an issue with my mascara.

It was a little awkward running a back street pub and being part of the serious crime group. At times the two businesses were in conflict.The controversial BNP hosted a party at our pub on the day of the St. George's parade. The serious crime group had spoken about racial hatred and vigilance on the day. I had, along with 10,000 others, taken part in the St. George's parade, the previous year. I had witnessed a massive gathering of happy, proud to be "English" people, who were oblivious that St George wasn't actually English, nor had he ever visited England or drank a pint of beer. It was strange to see only "white" people there, but the atmosphere was of a togetherness, not of a hatred of others.

I had seen the BNP publications and spoken to members about the poor press they felt they received claiming they were a racist group. Ironically, BNP's racial superiority attempted to evidence racism was something that was equally perpetrated. Their literature gave reports of white people experiencing prejudice. I understood such things happened but I argued there was no balance on racism. Nick Griffin, the leader of the BNP had never been my friend but he hadn't offended me any more than the average customer I served, this was business.

The pub was packed and the cash drawer was constantly opening for another contribution to our profits. I was happy to sell them drinks, there were no racist comments, or any trouble as they had promised. However, I did decline their request to hold their monthly meetings at our pub, purely on the basis of not wanting to jeopardise my career or have any political links with any far right groups. Being a parent, working full time in the public sector and running a pub was enough to keep me going. And to be honest, I liked all my customers to feel welcome, regardless of race or skin colour. That day some of my regulars had stayed at home. They were back in the pub the next day. We joked about the irony of St. George, the ignorance of supremacy and how the profits made courtesy of the BNP allowed them to enjoy their 'drinks on me'. It's just nice to be nice.

My busy life was extraordinary and I felt happy, stable and in control, yet I had bizarre dream that I was on the roof of a sky scraper building and I was about to kill myself. Dan, my children and my close friends were all there, huddled around in a circle, talking about my mental health and planning how they were going to save me. I left them exploring their strategies, ran for the edge and jumped. As I plummeted towards the ground, I had all the sensations of free falling as the wind resistance dragged the skin on my face and struck my body. I then did a perfect dive into water. I swam to the surface and got out. Well that had been a waste of time, I thought. I woke from my dream. I had accomplished something impressive, I hadn't belly flopped on a dive and I could knock free falling off my bucket list.

We got ourselves a family dog. Boozer had ended up in the dogs home as a stray. We hadn't seen a dog we liked the day we visited, they were all sadly howling, yapping or trembling with fear. It was a horrible traumatising atmosphere for any dog to be there. We walked passed the kennels for a second time. Boozer sat quietly and proudly near the gate of his kennel waiting to leave. It was as though he was saying "I'm not fazed by this place, I am well behaved, I am also very intelligent, I can't believe you walked passed and never noticed me the first time round". He showed us his ball and tossed it across the floor, and invited us into his life. We were all smitten that he had chosen us.

Boozer was the best pub dog you could ever wish for. He was friends with everyone and bothered no-one. "Please keep your eye on him, he will wonder where we are, when we go to Ireland" I said to the children as we left to go away for a week. I knew my children were responsible and could look after themselves and our friends were there to run the pub, so they weren't really alone but I worried about Boozer. We had decided to tour Southern Ireland by motorbike to see how the smoking ban had affected the pubs there. It was soon to be introduced in England.

It felt great to be on the back of a motorbike having an exciting backpacking adventure with Dan but on the second day away, our friend called to say Boozer had wandered out of the pub and had been found across the main road with a head injury. The vet said the injury was a likely result of being hit by a bus or a lorry and he would possibly lose his eye. We were devastated by the news. I couldn't believe he had been run over as he had excellent road sense and would never leave the pavement without direction to do so.

When we returned home, although he was pleased to see us, Boozer looked like an alien. His eye was twice the size and blue with blood. He wore a hard plastic collar that resembled a lampshade. Each time he knocked into something he howled in pain. He hadn't been for a walk since the accident so I took it off and hugged him. " I wished you could tell me what has happened to you" I said. I got his lead and took him out for a walk. He was walking in zigzags trying to adapt to his new one eyed vision. As we walked behind the pub he started to growl at the employees in the entrance of the bucket factory. They all had beards and wore turbans, he wasn't sure which one had hurt him but I knew one of them had.

As we strolled along the canal tow path, he began to walk in a straight line, his tail was wagging and he was happy to be out on a walk. We turned round to head back home, he put his paw up to his injured eye and it burst. He ran to me, like a child wanting his mother. There was nothing I could do but take him back home and get him to the vets. I noticed as soon as he burst his eye, his pain had stopped.

A customer told me he had seen a blood stained iron bar behind the pub the day Boozer had got injured. He thought it was a murder weapon. The next day he heard about Boozer and looked behind the pub, the iron bar had gone. It ended up costing us £1000 in vet bills, but he was worth it and everyone loved him. The one eyed Boozer, had never been a racist, but now he growled at men with beards and turbans, traumatised by someone that had tried to kill him.

Apart from the attack on the dog, the worst part about having a pub was that most weeks a fight would occur. It was always alcohol fuelled violence, usually over a woman or a discussion about politics or religion. Dan would always efficiently manage the situation and throw people out. They would return the next day to apologise, shake Dan's hand and it would be business as usual. Most of our customers worked on the near by industrial estate and they would call in for a few pints during their lunch breaks. Times were changing. Employers introduced a zero tolerance on alcohol use during working hours and the government brought in the smoking ban, we decided it was time we left the Forresters before we lost our savings.

Chapter 16
Home Turf

The Woodman Inn was up for lease, back in Cheslyn Hay, the place where I was born. I was drawn back there, perhaps I had a need to be close to my old home, or close to my mother. I drove my car along Westbourne Avenue and sneaked a peak over at our house. The garden wasn't manicured, the house seemed neglected, small and insignificant. I reflected on how all three of us had lost our home that day. The murderer had evicted us without notice and benefitted financially. I should have been able to park the car and visit my mother but instead I visited the lady next door. Aunty Barbara held her arms out for a hug, she still recognised me after almost thirty years. She was delighted to see me and invited me in. "Look who's here!" she said to her husband.

We sat for over an hour talking about my parents, the events of that night and how it had impacted on all of us, even the community. Their daughters were traumatised and they had lost their friends. I told them how, on several occasions, I had drove past the house, curious but always worried that someone would see me. I had faced my fears of returning there and felt comforted by the love from my supportive former neighbours. I sensed my mother was pleased that I had settled a worry that Barbara had harboured for years, she now knew I was OK.

The Woodman Inn, had been a thriving business in years gone by. However, the last decade had seen landlords come and go under the ownership of Scottish & Newcastle. It was sad to see such a memorable place look so deserted. I negotiated down to a £10,000 deposit and refused to pay for the outdated fixtures and fittings. The property needed some TLC, the business desperately needed customers and with the smoking ban, we knew we needed to invest in a heated smoking shelter. The management agreed to initially charge us £150 per week for rent.

Whilst Scottish & Newcastle set about transferring the licences into our name, we set about developing the business. We installed our TVs and entertainment system and advertised the business. We cleaned, painted and put everything in place, including the bulbs to light up the car park. Word got round to friends and family and soon the place was buzzing. We ran the bar and Dan's sister, Ange helped us out running the kitchen, cooking up beautiful Sunday Dinners and popular steak nights.

I gained new friends in my life, one of them being Nicki. She lived round the corner and loved her real ale pints. She was the older sister to a former school friend. She had served in the police force and now was an academic, teaching at university. I loved our conversations and we would chat till closing most nights. Our neighbour made a complaint that she could hear Nicki's loud laughter from the smoking shelter. We laughed about her getting us into trouble and she agreed to only laugh indoors.

Amanda Pugh came in with her husband and I reminded her of the day my daughter was born and how chuffed I had been to see her. Amanda didn't know what I was talking about, she had never been a midwife, she owned a sweet shop. She went on to tell me "I am tickled stomached and I can't stand the sight of blood." Those were the exact words my mother used. I had a weird feeling but it explained why 'Amanda' never returned back into the labour ward after Holly was born. I was high on gas, perhaps she was there in a vision or in reality her double must have thought I was a crazy woman!

John, Graham and Tim also became good friends. They helped us out, anyway they could, restoring the pub. I still had to tolerate the prejudices from our customers and have the banter with them. When I came close to pouring a pint over a perpetrators head, I decided my night life needed some balance so I joined the Soroptimist group in Cannock. Most of the members were wealthy and elderly and I really enjoyed their company. I did what I could to help the causes. We had interesting and enlightening speaker evenings, structured business meetings and wonderful conferences that brought together women from all around the world. There were rituals of toasting the queen and an initiation process, I was proudly part of something very special in society.

We visited the Houses of Parliament and walked on the stone floors that monarchs and leaders had walked before us. I was intrigued by the gold and the glamour of the ceremonial rooms, the magnificent historical pictures that surrounded me and the strange statue of Margaret Thatcher with an extra long pointed finger. I was surprised at how small the House of Commons Chamber was as I watched the MP's debate. We had tea on the terrace with our local MP and I sampled a snapshot of bureaucratic life.

I stood drinking in the crowded Strangers Bar looking at the price list whilst everyone else rubbed shoulders. Despite the wealth that surrounded me, this was the cheapest bar I had known, it was a tax free haven. I felt my blood boil, this was a place where laws were made and you could get pissed for under £10. It wasn't down to hard work that so many of the back benchers were snoring during debates. There was no zero tolerance on alcohol use at work in this mighty establishment.

To the rear of the Strangers Bar was a large snug where people sat oblivious to a national smoking ban. There were no signs on the wall prohibiting smoking. I headed over with my cigarette in hand to join the other addicts that were puffing away. I was not permitted to enter the snug. The privilege was only for the residents of the house, residents that didn't actually reside there. It was bureaucratic hypocrisy. The smoking ban had been enforced and ignored by the law makers. My pub was smoke free, I had my house in order.

The pub brought the community together and like a charity, all the profits were reinvested into the business to serve our community. We had a scuba diving club, a fishing club and a motorbike club, hosting their meetings each week. We sponsored the Woodman Inns football team and had teams playing pool, dominoes, poker and darts. Then there were popular evenings with live bands, Karaoke, bingo and quizzes. Even the elderly residents from the local care home, enjoyed a few hours out singing a-cappella during the day time. Whilst most of the men didn't need an excuse to come, I was always busy planning events that encouraged everyone to come together and socialise. For me, having people around felt like having a huge family and I loved it.

We were a family friendly pub, that especially welcomed children, with free 'kiddy cocktails' and snacks, so they never needed to hassle their parents. There was a child safe enclosed garden, with a climbing frame, trampoline and an area to play football. We had barbecues in the summer with bouncing castles and a swimming pool. With children's themed parties, Halloween and Bonfire nights, there was always something for them to enjoy. Christmas Day was fantastic, we had fifty two for dinner and a pub full of guests until closing, New Years Eve was even better and our weekly takings just continued to grow.

There were successful "Posh Frocks" nights, giving the women an excuse to dress up to the nines accompanied by their sophisticated husbands dressed for a black tie event. I liked our charity nights, raising money for different worthy causes. The ladies evening was my favourite, with hilarious drag artists, comedians and an appearance from a delusional Elvis, the room was packed with happy women, enjoying themselves. My mother would have been proud of my efforts to improve the lives of women.The money raised went to Women's Aid and of course, I was able to introduce myself and raise awareness of domestic abuse to all who attended.

I continued to deliver domestic abuse training in Sandwell. I also delivered training on safeguarding children and became an active member of the Sandwell's Local Safeguarding Children's Board. I was offered a secondment to study for a postgraduate Diploma in Leadership and Management for Social Work. I was delighted to have the opportunity to finally get a worthy qualification but not having a degree, I worried whether I would be accepted on to the course. I was asked to evidence my academic ability with a critical analysis of my own work and after seeking some guidance from Nicki, my academic friend, I earned my place on the course.

It was wonderful to be back in education. Half the students dropped off the course due to the work involved and their other commitments. It was difficult but I spent hours collecting my research. I gave a presentation on forced marriages and child protection. I ensured it was relevant and covered a range of perspectives, one being the historical shot gun weddings, forced marriages wasn't just an issue for those from an ethnic minority. It existed in all cultures where shame fuelled a need. I also discussed different facilitators and groups, power and values. I linked the theory to the policy, and then reflected on my work, my delivery and the material I had used. Their feedback was music to my ears.

I went on to complete an assignment investigating "The tensions and dilemmas associated with delivering safeguarding training to multi-agency groups specifically related to domestic abuse." This work discussed how abuse was a socially defined construct that changed over time. My mind drifted as I read notable academic papers, reflecting on my fathers trial, being a crime of passion back in 1978. The more I researched the more links there were to my own life. The research supported my beliefs. Children were not silent witnesses of domestic abuse but drawn into the abuse and pressured to conceal it. I could feel my heart bleeding as I wrote. I had called my mother 'thick' and taunted her when she cried, saying 'daddy was the strongest' I had added to her misery. He had manipulated me and I had been oblivious to that fact.

I questioned the validity of risk assessments and our ability to effectively safeguard children based on the victims disclosures. I thought about the children who had been killed along with their mothers and how lucky I had been not to have been there that day. I researched papers on the victims impaired parenting capacities and their minimisation of the impact of abuse on their children. I thought about how my mother had hidden her abuse and how we as children thought our home life had been normal. Then, I thought how I had done the same, impacting on my own children, the cycle of abuse passed through the generations. I explored power, transference and learning theories. Every aspect dissected my life experiences. I handed in my assignment. Their feedback made me realise how valuable and important my work was and it encouraged me to further develop my knowledge.

I was a speaker at SOADA's conferences discussing the impact of the training sessions and the aims of the organisation. I was a nervous wreck at first, standing in front of so many people. I was still the daughter of a murderer, and aware my mother had been a victim of domestic violence and yet I never spoke about it. I felt ashamed of my silence. I needed to tell my story. I went to London to speak at a community care conference for social workers, and spoke about uxoricide, the impact on children, and my own anecdotal experiences. My training on leadership and management for social work was put into practice. I received a standing ovation and social workers queued to congratulate me, very few had covered the topic in their training and they now felt confident to help children bereaved by a domestic homicide.

I had also been to London, accompanied by my daughter, to meet Pat Craven, a social worker and probation officer, hosting her own event. I wanted to learn about her Freedom Programme for women in abusive relationships. We were both given her new book "Living with the dominator" I browsed through and found it fascinating linking her text to my experiences. My daughter thought everyone her age should read it. Pat had a fascinating way of presenting and I knew her work was going to help many people realise they were being dominated. We also watched a powerful play, starring Claire Moore as the 'Lady in Red' it delivered awareness on all the types of domestic abuse and the stages the victim goes through. Claire's performance unearthed the memory of my mothers misery. My daughter was captivated again.

I wanted Holly to have this awareness so she never ended up in an abusive relationship. We spent the evening in London watching Billy Elliot at the Grand theatre, another inspiring story. It was important for me to spend time with her and prepare her for adulthood. We spent a week in Barcelona, exploring the city together, it felt special to have that mother and daughter time. Working full time and running the pub, Holly missed spending time with me. I had missed out with my mother, I didn't want my daughter to miss out too.

After the holiday, I received a hand delivered birthday card, posted through the letterbox. I recognised my father's hand writing on the envelope. I opened the card. He had wrote "Love from Dad and Sandra" I read the words of a beautiful verse. It was the type of card that was full of sentiment. The type that proud parents send to their successful, much loved and treasured daughter. The card brought a tear to my eye. I went to his house and rang the door bell. I could hear my step mother calling out to my father. "She's at the door Ron, she's not coming in, I don't want her in here Ron". I was confused by her words but not surprised, she had never wanted me in her home.

I took my Dad for a drive in my car so we could talk. I thanked him for the beautiful card. I explained how the words had upset me because he couldn't realistically say he was proud of me. "You don't even know what job I do Dad, you know nothing about me" I said. He was still under the impression that I worked with children in children's homes. I gave him an update and explained I had been working in the field of domestic violence for the past five years. "I was never violent to your mother" he responded. "I know Dad, you were only 'play fighting' I do remember but you still hurt her and made her cry, domestic violence isn't all about black eyes and split lips Dad." He was still in denial and always would be. I dropped him off at his house and left.

A simple nice thought had brought us together and his lack of understanding had magnified the distance between us. I delivered basic awareness training the next day and handed out the case study which emphasised how some perpetrators didn't recognise their own abusive behaviours. I was emotionally drained when I got home. I confided in Holly but she too seemed distant. I had no idea she had rebelliously got herself a secret boyfriend. She stayed out all night. Dan and I were worried when she didn't return home. I knocked on doors trying to track down where she was. She returned home the following evening and I grounded her. I was serving customers in the pub at the time.

She thought she had got one over us and was chatting on her computer upstairs. Dan told her to switch the computer off. She started shouting abuse at Dan. I ran upstairs and witnessed Holly charging towards Dan, she slipped and they both ended on the floor. She accused Dan of hitting her, I knew he hadn't. She left the pub with some clothes and tried to convince Ange, that Dan had beaten her up, she didn't believe her either. She went to my brothers flat and called her Dad. Ray said, she could stay at his for the night to calm the situation down. The next day she went to school and told them her step father had hit her.

Pete drove down from Scotland to rescue his battered and abused daughter and smugly called me to let me know " You've lost your daughter." he said. He was a fool, convinced I knew nothing about her. I tried to explain the situation and how he was being manipulated, because I had grounded her. I knew she had dug herself into a hole assuming the grass might be greener living with her wonderful attentive father. He took her back to Scotland with him.

I called her each day, she was 'fine' and I knew the meaning of that word. Her dad had taken her clothes shopping and bought her a device to play music. Within a couple of days he had also bought her a new school uniform and she started a new school. She told me about the disrespectful and immature behaviour of the students. She wasn't pleased to know the term times differed in Scotland which meant she would have to do an extra year. On the Saturday, Holly rang me from Matalan. Her father was buying her some more new clothes. She said she wanted to come home, but was frightened of how her dad would react. I told her to wait until her dad had paid for the clothes and then to call me and I would speak to him.

Pete drove Holly with all her new belongings back to Great Wyrley. He arranged to meet me away from the pub as he didn't want to see Dan. His gas lighting efforts were wasted. "If you believed he was a child batterer, you wouldn't bring her back" I said. As Holly got out of his vehicle, I told her to put her things in the boot of my car. Pete was shocked that I hadn't swung my arms around my daughter in floods of tears, pleased to have her back. He said I was 'cold'. I explained the situation to him. Holly was still grounded for staying out all night. The week with him had just been a diversion from facing up to what she had done. Holly had used the situation to her advantage by uncovering the mystery of her absent fathers life in Scotland, where the CSA couldn't chase him for maintenance. It had been an expensive lesson for him, he had driven from Scotland to rescue her and failed to impress, he had lost his daughter. Holly was just relieved to be back home, she apologised for acting irresponsibly and our bond was stronger than ever.

I was asked to report on the domestic violence training I had delivered in Sandwell. I looked at the finalised document with pride. I had accomplished more than I had initially planned which meant more people had awareness training and everyone knew about the coordinated community approach to offer the best support to victims in high risk situations. Hundreds of professionals had also had training on the associated issues such as the impact on children, on mental health and forced marriages. I had limited the chances of another family going through the trauma of a homicide. As a result of my dedicated effort, victims were gaining the support they needed. Training was no longer a priority, my post was halved and the funding went into emergency accommodation.

I became an independent consultant and trainer, working mainly with Sure Start initiatives, volunteers and unemployed women. I facilitated a positive parenting programme to women in refuges, so they could become better parents and improve their children's lives. I also took on another role, on home turf, as the domestic violence coordinator for Cannock District Council. I had big plans for Cannock but I wasn't prepared for the difference in going from a metropolitan council to district council. When I spoke about ring fencing budgets, they looked surprised. I later discovered there was no budget in Cannock for domestic violence! My wages were paid by the Government to the Chase Voluntary Service and I was aware that the strap cashed council were unlikely to fund my position long term. I still gave the post my full attention and managed some worthwhile projects.

I was accustomed to a professional working environment at Sandwell. I thought my new manager at Cannock council seemed to bring fun to the office initially, then as I got to know him, he revealed all the signs of being a narcissist himself. He employed an attractive young woman to take on the role of the anti-social behaviour coordinator. She naively had no idea how she had got the job and struggled to cope with the role and his sexual advances. She confided in me, she found another job and moved on, sexual harassment was still a difficult thing to prove.

My manager told me how his "bitch of a wife" had left him and how he had refused to let his son go with her. He spent time drinking in his local into the early hours of the morning, driving his car back home. He was still over the limit, the next day, when he would struggle to show his face before 10am. He boasted he was earning £43k a year, almost double my wages as he plucked ideas from everyone and passed them off as his own. Ironically, I was trying to bring about a coordinated community approach in Cannock, where everyone worked together efficiently like we had done in Sandwell when I moved to my private office, working solo above Women's Aid. I just couldn't work with a perpetrator who drove me to despair.

It was during a serious crime meeting, when he questioned if spending money on a campaign on domestic abuse was even effective, that he really annoyed me. He didn't care about the victims of domestic abuse. I responded "Drink driving had been acceptable in the 1980's but following many media campaigns, our culture has changed and drink drivers were now deemed to be very irresponsible people putting other people's lives at risk". He knew exactly what I was getting at. Several police officers also hung their heads in shame. I went on "Domestic abuse is no different, perpetrators think it is acceptable to abuse their partners, regardless of the impact on their children, we need to change the culture by raising awareness, we need to educate people."

After researching what works with changing behaviours of perpetrators, I designed a poster with the media team, that showed shadows of a man, towering over his powerless wife, pointing the finger at her and in the background were two frightened young children, witnessing the abuse. This poster had a clear message of accountability. It was aimed at the perpetrator and was displayed on prominent billboards around my district. If the campaign got abusive men to think about their children's lives more then domestic homicides should reduce, along with domestic violence.

Unfortunately, most of my colleagues weren't happy about the campaign. They thought highlighting the impact on children would result in too many referrals to children's services and the support for these children was not available. I noticed how everyone wanted their own agency or department to shine, whilst knocking down the capability of others and ignoring the rights of children. It was a competitive and under resourced industry. However, from the child's perspective, they just wanted the abuse to stop, they didn't know of or expect to get any support. Indirectly, my colleagues criticised how the campaign should have involved them, they had declined my invites for discussion, busy with their own solo affairs and I wanted to get the campaign going before Christmas, when perpetrators always try their best to ruin things.

It's peculiar to see in the field of domestic abuse the professionals struggling with power and control, so many intimidating female characters, going behind your back, stuck in their own clan, firing at anyone that wants to bring a coordinated response to safeguard children and victims. Surely we were all on the same path, preventing deaths, violence and abuse. They made me feel like a dangerous lose cannon, an outsider not worthy of praise. There were fewer incidences of domestic violence reported during that campaign, analysing the statistics, put a smile on my face, and coincidence or not, there was no recognition from my critics.

I left Sandwell with its efficient ways of working and took on the role of domestic violence co-ordinator full time. I managed a project with Birmingham Royal ballet for young girls exposed to domestic abuse to take part in a dance production at the Hippodrome. Expressing their feelings through dance developed their confidence and understanding of healthy relationships, something I knew would have benefitted me at their age. I didn't want them to be vulnerable, I wanted them to be empowered and they were. The project evaluation highlighted the positive changes in their lives.

I also worked alongside youth workers and young women to run their own campaign aimed at raising awareness for teenage girls. I knew youth club was the place to find young girls like me. It was a privilege to run such a project. The girls were soon spreading the word themselves, I was so proud of them. I provided training to school teachers, emphasising their opportunities to notice the signs and intervene, "It's OK to ask them if they are OK" I said whilst I thought back to my school days. I had to ensure children received the support they required. I helped to get a sanctuary scheme up and running to help victims. My passion to do more lived on.

It was time to put my efforts into supporting children affected by uxoricide. I had done my research, there were no services specifically set up to help those forgotten children. I needed to raise awareness nationally. Julie Blindell, from the Guardian newspaper published a report based on my accounts, highlighting the lack of support. It was emotionally draining telling her about my life but that wasn't the only cost. Despite being a reputable feminist writer she had a distorted twist on my story, there were half a dozen errors in the report and I was portrayed as a stereotypical victim, not a woman set on a mission.

An editor from a popular women's magazine read the article and offered me £200 to feature my story on a double page spread. This captured a different audience to the Guardian so I was happy to regurgitate my emotional baggage again. The magazine had sold out locally and I had to ask around to find someone who had a copy, that I could look at. The publishers could have sent me a copy but didn't think to. I found that humiliating, exploitation of the press goes hand in hand as anyone impacted by a homicide will tell you. It's not ethical that writers do not show you a copy of an article before it goes to print, it can be so damaging to people's lives. I wasn't happy with the way it focussed on my life rather than my mission but that's what readers like.

I was asked if I would take part in a documentary series called 'Living with Murder' to be shown on Sky's Crime and Investigation channel. Hearing my story, from the horses mouth, there could be no distortion, I thought. I can finally focus on the children I want to support. The film crew were with me for three harrowing days. Then they filmed my brother, Aunt Linda and Aunt June. I didn't see the film until it was on TV, many of my accounts had been edited out, I had even made a mistake saying Pete had been a category C prisoner instead of an A, and my opportunities to communicate to those suffering or perpetrating abuse were omitted for the entertainment value. The film was out there and there was no going back. A good ethical producer would ensure you were happy with the final film before airing.

I received a lot of positive feedback from the documentary as I tried to repair my mental state of being, destroyed by reflecting on the past, in order to help others in the future. Tom contacted me and told me his story, he was comforted that I had highlighted the issue he too had faced. Jean, congratulated me for my strength and told me she had ended up in foster care. The film was shown in Australia and seemed to have more of an impact there. I had people tracking me down and telling me how there was no support in Australia either. At last, I had people in my life who knew what it was like, peer support is so empowering, it made me feel less isolated and more determined to set up a service.

I was delighted to see my Aunty Joan turn up at the pub, she had never visited me before so it was a pleasant surprise. She had seen the documentary and was fuming, she raised her hand to slap my face and seeing the happiness in my eyes, she stroked my cheek. "Oh Diane, did you forget about me" she said. Aunty Joan was relieved to hear that it was the film crew that had edited out her involvement in my life. She told me my Aunt Hilda was angry that I had spoken out, the truth hurt.

We sat for a couple of hours chatting in the corner of the pub. She told me about how happy she was when we lived with her. She spoke about her own abusive relationship with her own husband, how she had hidden it from us and how difficult it was making ends meet. Having the foster care money had improved her life financially, given her the freedom to buy what she needed for the family. She had never in her life had a family holiday, she had never had the funds to do such a thing, and she spoke about the wonderful memory she had.

I had totally forgotten about that holiday. It had been around the time of my Dads release, we had all gone to Prestatyn Sands. I remembered Hilda's children, Joans children and Ray and myself on a beach writing our names in the sand, doing what children do. I guessed it had been a time of celebration for my Dad's family, hence a wonderful memory for Aunt Joan. The documentary had brought us back together, it had reunited us. I hadn't thought about the impact this film would have on my Dad or his family, how he might feel ashamed. Here we go again, I can't cut off the ties to the man who killed my mother because I am his daughter. I remembered how happy my family was on that holiday. I was happy because we were reunited with him, guilt surfaced.

The next day my Dad was stood at the bar and I poured him a beer. Dan didn't greet the man who had killed my mother. He protectively stood by my side instead. I explained my reason for participating in the documentary and explained about the editing that had occurred outside of my control. Like my mothers murder, he had little to say on the matter but seemed very understanding about children needing support and my mission to save lives. He treated me with kid gloves but commented on how Sandra thought the whole thing was a pack of lies. I had shamed her, not him. A vision of those scratches on my face appeared and I heard her voice bellowing " You're a spoilt little bitch. You think the world revolves around you!" The truth was out and my Dad knew I had broken my silence.

The local newspaper, the Chase Post published an article, which highlighted my wishes to set up a charity to help children bereaved by domestic homicide. Again I received positive responses from strangers and support from my friends and colleagues at work. I felt so empowered by their words of encouragement but at the same time I felt an emotional wreck. I took time out to look after myself, I had developed strategies over the years and knew what worked. I went swimming and relaxed in the sauna. I took the dog out for walks and spent hours in the garden at peace with nature.

The lovely, Mr. Hooper sent me a beautiful letter, he was aged 83 and was delighted to read about me in the newspaper. He offered to support me in the setting up of a charity. Dan picked up the phone and dialled his number. "I have a lady here who wants to speak to you" he said as he handed me the phone. I was in floods of tears but it was wonderful to speak to him. After thirty years of worrying about me, he was reassured and pleased to hear I was back in the village.

I did go to visit him and we proudly watched some old films of the Gingham Girls doing their displays. I stayed with him for a couple of hours. We talked about the calculator he had bought me and how I had treasured it. He told me he had wanted to give it to me himself. He thought I would have been at my Moms funeral. He had attended that day, just to give me a hug and a present. We both had a little cry. Then he said he wanted to give me some money to set up my charity. I politely and appreciatively refused to take his money. He was an old man and I didn't want to take advantage of his kind generosity. This was something that society should pay for, it should be routine safeguarding practice. I had looked a gift horse in the mouth based on my principles and walked away. One day, it will happen, I thought.

I came across a video on YouTube of a lecture presented by Barbara Parker and Richard Steeves regarding a study they did with adults, like myself, who had experienced Uxoricide as a child. There were common themes, many of the children had no support, had turned to drugs, been involved in risky behaviours and the criminal justice system. The cycle of domestic abuse had continued and most had also felt the need to forgive their fathers as they were still a part of themselves. I contacted Barbara to thank her, the long term effects had never been studied and it made me feel quite normal. She put me in touch with Carol, one of the participants of the study. Carol was a serving police officer and we had several conversations over time. We would laugh about our similar struggles and support each other. We were both outwardly strong women trying to change the world for the better.

I looked at another study from the Netherlands. Immigrant children were over represented, the majority had experienced domestic violence prior to Uxoricide, more than half of them had witnessed the murder and over half didn't know if they had received any support. I collected all the research I could find, to help me to set up a charity. I was emotionally exhausted, I needed to rest my passion and concentrate on my business and my day job for a while.

I was trying to move forward but as a consequence of breaking my silence, our pub business was threatened. An old friend of my father's, a perpetrator, who had once held a shotgun to his wife's head, decided to cause trouble, along with a few women married to men of a certain clan, those who believe women should do as they're told. Their local club, had suffered financial hardship as most of their customers had flocked to the Woodman Inn. The shotgun hero, a reputable, untouchable member of the Parish Council, enjoyed the opportunity to inform us that Scottish & Newcastle had not actually applied for an entertainment licence.

Scottish & Newcastle, had the technology to see how much beer we were selling, and had increased our rent for the third time to £800 a week, so we knew without entertainment, we would lose customers and we wouldn't make ends meet. On top of that we had a group of drug fuelled hooligans turn up and cause a fight inside our pub and then a riot erupted outside. I was told they had come from Featherstone, say no more. I called the police terrified Dan would get hurt as he tried to restore order.

The county council advised us that it was not just our entertainment that had to stop, it was any form of sport that was watched or heard by our customers. They weren't happy when I laid out the temporary changes. What the council expected from the customers was ridiculous and they went to the press. ITV news took advantage of a humorous situation and televised the customers wearing blindfolds whilst people played darts, dominoes and pool and they had shots of the customers miming to the words on a silent Karaoke. The news footage was hilarious but it made a laughing stock of the Licensing Department at the county council. Scottish & Newcastle refused to comment but admitted to me that the oversight was their fault and told us not to worry about the rent. I applied for the licence.

I sent invites to all the households in the vicinity and set up a meeting, with council officials and police presence. I had nothing to hide and was willing and able to keep everyone happy. The room was packed as we discussed the benefits of a thriving pub business to the community. The majority were fully supportive of our licence application. Many praised our efforts to rejuvenate a desolate pub and raise money for local projects. A couple complained about not getting any sleep due to the lights on the car park being on until closing time. Our regulars mocked them. I retained order, empathised and suggested they purchased some black out curtains.

Our nearest neighbour, and friend of the Parish councillor, had bought her house because she used the pub, but now she drank at the club. She claimed her garage door rattled from the vibrations from the loud music and she couldn't hear her TV in her own house. She didn't want us to get an entertainment licence because of the noise. Her comments were absurd. She went on, people had left their empty bottles of Magner's cider on her wall. Her intentions were clear, she just wanted to see the pub shut.

The smoking ban had also impacted on two neighbours, who said they could hear people talking in the beer garden when they lay in bed before we closed at 11pm. Our other neighbours said they didn't have an issue with noise. They preferred to see customers coming and going, rather than looking at a depressing empty car park. I offered to monitor the noise levels and to put up notices, to encourage people to respect the neighbours and keep their voices down.

After the meeting, I invited the environmental health official to do a sound test. We turned the system up full blast, it was obvious it was impossible to work in such a loud environment, we opened the windows and doors and stood by the neighbours property. You could hear a faint bass beat. I adjusted the volume to its usual setting and nothing could be heard outside. I had clearly proven my point of victimisation and harassment that day.

In the kangaroo court at the council, the Parish councillor and the woman who complained about the car park lights, accompanied my neighbour. She put her complaint forward, adding another comical account of her witnessing heroin addicts shooting up in the doorway. I remained calm and professional. I asked the police if any syringes had been found, there were no reports of syringes. I informed the council that with the training I had done on drug addiction, it was very unlikely that heroin addicts would stand in a doorway injecting themselves. I assured them, I had zero tolerance on drug use, which was why the pub was so popular with families.

I highlighted the fact that I did not sell Magner"s Cider and they probably belonged to the young teenagers who were seen drinking alcohol on the field nearby on Friday evenings. The environmental officer gave her evidence on the sound test she had done. I was dumbfounded when she said there had been no wind on the day of the test, which in her opinion could impact on carrying noise to my neighbours property. I shook my head in disbelief, perhaps the wind rattled her garage doors then as it was not my music. I was on my own, it was their word against mine.

I had clearly been set up. The chair of the meeting, officially refused to give us an entertainment licence in light of her complaints. He offered us the opportunity to 'prove ourselves' over the next year, having a maximum of ten events and each one involving a fee to the council. With the cost of running a commercial business dependent on regular entertainment, I was faced with a lose, lose situation. I looked the chairman in the eye, there was sympathy. He had assumed I had the finance to survive, having no idea of commercial costs and how much the business relied on entertainment.

When I got back home, my neighbour looked over at me with a victorious smirk. I asked her if she had any guilt for lying to the council. She ignored my question and fired one back, "What is this telling you?" I couldn't believe the woman's lack of awareness ."That your vindictive actions have not only cost me my business and my home but other people's sense of place and belonging." I said as my blood began to boil. She didn't care and went on "It's telling you, it's time you left" she wasn't worth my energy, I walked away.

We could sell food but Ange had long left unable to commit her time and despite Nathan completing his catering course he refused to work for us. He had the opportunity to be his own boss and make a name for himself but he resented the idea. He went to work for JD Wetherspoon's instead. We offered a Thai lady, nicknamed Guy, the same opportunity we had offered my son. She jumped at the chance and it got off to a good start.

We got to know all the local Thai community, as Guy had friends helping her in the kitchen. Others would visit on occasions and we hosted a couple of Thai evenings, where we all dressed in Thai clothing. They were all beautiful souls, including the ladyboys and the former prostitutes that saw England as a rich place to live, enabling them to escape the sex industry and send money back home to care for their parents. When they realised I worked in the field of domestic violence, they began to tell me their stories.

Each women had been bought by an English man. They spoke of their love for their husband yet each one had suffered abuse. Even Guy, who considered herself lucky, was in a difficult relationship, with two children and a mortgage and no right to remain in the UK. I supported them and gave them all advice. Some went into refuges and safe houses to escape their husbands. Guy's family didn't appreciate my involvement in her life, allowing her the opportunity to gain financial independence. They eventually made her leave. We had no further contact but she had all the information she needed on the support services if her relationship got any worse.

Within a few months our customers dwindled away. I had received two letters about investors owning the property going into administration, a third investor came on board. I realised that Scottish & Newcastle just made their money from the beer we bought. Having free rent helped but the bills and the business rates were so high. We had to pay for our beer order in advance and some weeks we struggled to find the funds, there was never enough beer to get through the week which, for us, was an extremely embarrassing way to run a business.

We were forced, like many struggling pub businesses, to buy from the 'white van man' so we had beer to sell to our remaining customers. The local beer supplier, delivered every day and was half the price. Whilst those that were freehold, doubled their profits, leaseholders, like ourselves were on a slippery slope. Scottish & Newcastle would fine us for every barrel bought else where, which meant buying beer to sell, often cost us more than we could sell it for but a pub with no beer couldn't function either. This was a win win situation for them. It spiralled and no bank in the land would help us.

Our supportive area manager was replaced, the new one, reminded me of a bailiff. He said there had been no written contract for free rent, we had to pay all the rent arrears, which now stood at £13K or leave. As we filed for bankruptcy, a fictitious report was delivered from Scottish and Newcastle: highlighting the 'damages' to the property, this debt had been inflated to £53K. I was outraged, there had been no report when we took over the business. We had put all the profits back into the business, and by this time I had added a further £16K of my own earnings. We added value to the property, we didn't damage it. "You're going bankrupt, you won't be paying anyway" the area manager advised. It was a national scam, backed by solicitors, all legal and above board. Two pubs were closing every week. The general consensus across the nation was that the Government's smoking ban and the sale of alcohol in supermarkets had impacted on pub businesses, I and many other leaseholders, knew different.

Chapter 17
The Penthouse

Luckily, Scottish & Newcastle couldn't legally evict us, my daughter was only fifteen so we were entitled to be rehoused and the council said for us to stay put. I looked at the private rental market, no-one would take us on as a tenant with £13K in commercial rent arrears, despite having sufficient income to pay their rents. I was still attending the Soroptimist meetings and surrounded by so many wealthy people, I felt such a failure. South Staffordshire housing came to our rescue, there was a three bedroom flat in Great Wyrley becoming available. We sold off all the stock and equipment we couldn't take with us and waited for a viewing.

The idea of moving to a council flat, signified a return to the land of poverty. I hated the idea, but we needed a roof over our heads. I counted how many times I had moved since 15th of April 1978, including living in a car and a refuge, this would be my 16th move. I thought about every council house I had lived in, they had all needed work, and I anticipated the top floor flat would need some work and by gosh, it did. I could see my brothers flat from my kitchen window, he had been there for years.

We had no choice, we had to accept it. The housing association gave us £250 in B&Q vouchers to spend on paint. We had it completely plastered, decorated and carpeted throughout. We bought new furniture, doors, skirting boards and curtains. Once we had climbed the communal stairs, we had a pleasant peaceful place to call home. We nicknamed it "The Penthouse".

Dan and I, lay on our bed watching TV. "Isn't this bliss" I said and he agreed. Working full time and running busy pub businesses for four years, we had forgotten what normal home life had been like. Just being able to turn the TV over and watch what we wanted was priceless. We both felt strangely liberated, as much as we had enjoyed the company of others, serving them on demand, we now appreciated our uninterrupted togetherness and Nathan and Holly seemed happier they could spend more time with us too.

Whilst Dan started a new career in engineering, my work as the domestic violence coordinator came to an end. The council said they didn't have the funds to keep my post going. I wasn't surprised, especially as they wasted so much on higher salaried employees that made very little impact on the community. I started applying for jobs in the field but it seemed I was either over qualified or I didn't have the bilingual skills needed to work with ethnic minorities. At the same time, the requests to deliver domestic violence training dwindled as companies had either already had staff training or they were making financial cut backs.

After a couple of months of getting nowhere, I started to get quite down hearted. I removed my false office nails and took on a temporary job for minimum wage, working at "Greasy Lils" a notorious truckers cafe. I had enjoyed working in the canteen in Goodyear's factory years ago. I thought working at Greasy Lils would keep me sane and working the night shift allowed me to be available for interviews. I spent most of the evening cleaning the areas most staff feared to go near and had great satisfaction making it safer, in food hygiene terms. I got to know all the regulars on first name terms. I demonstrated excellent customer service and never had a complaint. I worked my fingers to the bone, every muscle ached yet the owner gave my job to a young girl. He said, he knew I would be moving on and she was desperate for work. I walked away, with grease under my fingernails, trying to keep my dignity in tact.

I needed a new career so I applied for a job selling solar panels where I could earn an excellent salary whilst saving the planet. I thought about when I was at school and the jobs I had selling Avon and the Tote, I could sell anything if I believed in it because people trusted me. I loved the idea of being an eco warrior. The interview with Peter Hunter was based in a plush office complex near to Birmingham Airport. Peter liked me and knew I would do well.

He questioned how Dan would feel if I was suddenly earning £80k or more a year, "this sort of money can end relationships" he said. I reassured him that Dan would only be delighted if I was earning that amount of money. "He would be planning a trip to Mugello to watch the Moto GP and deciding which new motorbike to buy" I explained. I told him how we had just lost our business and we were living in a council flat. He stated that the job was "commission only because we only employ high flyers." We needed to earn some serious money, we were struggling to survive on Dan's wage alone.

I spent a week away from my family, in a Manchester hotel, completing their sales course. It was quite a treat, the food and accommodation was all paid for and I made new friends. The presentations were excellent. The directors were serious and professional and we were reassured that all the leads were from people who wanted solar panels. I learned everything I needed to know about the product, how to calculate the savings for the customer and how to measure the size of their roof to determine the number of panels they could have. My new career was going to be so exciting and I couldn't wait to start.

Having leads around Worcester and South Birmingham areas, I was running up a debt on my credit card paying for petrol everyday but I followed the sales pitch and people were signing contracts left, right and centre. The full commission was paid after installation and my first payment took five weeks. I was still out of pocket. Peter told me not to panic, we were selling more than the fitters could cope with and they were taking on new staff to cope with the demand. He had graphs on his wall, highlighting how much I had coming.

I had sold £300,000 worth of solar panels before I realised the company was a scam. They owed me over £3000 in commission when I refused to take another lead. I had customers calling me up for advice, some even accused me of ripping them off. I called my colleagues I had met on the course, we were all out of pocket. Despite working for virtually nothing and having a credit card debt myself, people had lost significant amounts of money.The company went into administration.

I was embarrassed I'd been conned and now had to find credit card repayments too. On top of this I was worried about our dog. He seemed fine in the flat but by the time we had got to the bottom of the stairs he would sit down to rest. I had been tugging him on the lead, not understanding why he didn't want to go for a walk. I visited the vets and discovered he had cancer of the spleen, any excitement or activity made him anaemic. The vet felt it wasn't worth putting him through an operation as the success rates were quite low. I didn't want to see him suffer.

Boozer went for a short last walk. He sat by the school gates, a tear run from his eye as he looked at me, saying his goodbyes. I patted his head, the old boy had never hurt anyone, he had been through so much losing his eye and now he just wanted to rest. I thought about my Gramps 'ready for the knackers yard'. I had a sense of deja vu, as I stood in the place my mother had stood in my dream. The dog she had was Boozer, I felt reassured she would look after him. Dan and I stroked him as he peacefully died at the vets. We were both heartbroken. We went to a pub and drowned our sorrows together. He had been the most loved dog either of us had ever had and we knew our lives would never be the same without him. He was special.

A few weeks later, my brother was remanded in custody for drug dealing. I had lectured him for years but he had never listened to me. He wasn't your stereotypical dealer. He didn't go round with guns or knives in a fast car. He had an old estate car and a loopy Dalmatian dog called Poker, who he adored. People weren't intimidated by him, he was 'safe'. His 'friends' all loved him but so did everyone else in the village. He couldn't hold down a real job, he wasn't able to sleep without Sambuca and Cannabis. He had a terrible short term memory and an auditory processing disorder just like me. He had no luck finding the right women in his life. He was only happy if he snorted white powder and only slept if he smoked cannabis so he dealt to feed his habit.

I didn't want to look after his dog when he went to prison, not so soon after losing Boozer. The 'dotty dog' had known me all her life and gained my sympathy shivering, with her tail between her legs. She was nothing like Boozer but we took her in. I knew what it felt like to be abandoned. She had no road sense and dragged me around on her suicidal walks. She drove us crazy jumping over the furniture and covering us in her white hairs. She would bark if someone opened the communal door, probably worried that our front door was going to be knocked down and we were going to be taken away too. We received a letter from the council complaining about her barking. I sent an email back advising them, that I had spoken to the dog and she had assured me she wouldn't bark again. It probably put a smile on their faces, but what else could I do, she was a crazy neurotic dog.

I attended both court dates for my brothers trial. They spoke about his addiction to cocaine and cannabis use as self medication for his childhood trauma. He had told his probation officer he was having to sell drugs to pay for the drugs that the police had originally confiscated, he was in a vicious circle, he owed the main drug dealers and many of his regular customers owed him. Like me, he liked to do his bit for the community, helping others in their times of need. There were a lot of needy drug addicts willing to exploit him. He had to be one of the poorest drug dealers on the planet. He was sentenced to four years and given anti-depressants.

Being out of work, living in a council flat and having a brother serving time for drug dealing impacted on my self worth and I became quite depressed. Going through the bankruptcy took a huge weight off my shoulders but I was still broke. I couldn't afford to spend money on meals or contribute to the Soroptimist's fundraising events. Being around so many wealthy and successful women made me feel even more of a failure so I wrote them a letter and resigned. I continued to apply for jobs but I just couldn't get an interview.

A former colleague gave me a call, regarding another sales job. I was pessimistic at first but he assured me it was nothing like the solar company. There was a decent basic salary for a start. I had an interview in central Birmingham and began working for publicservice.co.uk selling advertising space in a magazine called Public Servant that was distributed to the public sector. I enjoyed the work, chatting to interesting CEO's from relevant companies about different feature stories we were publishing. These often included interviews with ministers, civil servants and specialists. We brought the public and private sectors together and I became very knowledgeable on current affairs and developed good networking skills.

Holly was seventeen when she shocked me with the news that she was pregnant, she had been with her boyfriend, Harley since she was fifteen, not long after she had come back from her week in Scotland. I liked Harley, he had nice qualities but he was younger than Holly and was yet to find a job. I worried how they would survive financially with a baby. She applied to the council for a flat.

My Aunt Linda discovered my Uncle Malcolm was having an affair. It didn't surprise me, knowing what he was like. My cousin said they didn't know what to do or say and asked me to visit her. I went down to see her and helped her to put things in a skip. She was hurt with her husbands betrayal but she was clearing her house and moving forward. I knew she would be OK. She divorced him, sold the house and bought a small bungalow. She started seeing a man called Jack so I knew at least she had found love and wasn't lonely.

I had walked around Birmingham after work. The window displays were reminding everyone that Mother's Day was approaching. I had purchased a card and a gift for Dan's mom. Every year I would struggle on Mother's Day. I sat on the train journey home, watching the world flash me by. When I got back to my car I broke down in tears. I had no sense of belonging, just empty loneliness. I called my Aunt Linda, having lost her own mother, I thought somehow she would understand what I went through every year. She listened as I poured my heart out.

I had worked at publicservice.co.uk for a year when the company went into administration. The employees were entitled to a redundancy payment of one weeks wage for every year they had worked there. My colleagues had been there for years and were chuffed with their payouts. They had already planned to join another similar company. I received my one weeks wage and decided sales was not for me.

I started applying for higher quality local jobs within my skill set and landed a job as a business development manager for a mortgage company. This was a great job that I had managed to get just by sending a speculative email. I had absolutely no experience and they liked that, they could train me their way. My role was to visit new build sites and chat to the girls in the sales office and keep them happy. I also learned all I needed to know about about mortgage applications.

Earning a fantastic salary, I was able to support my daughter, when she moved into her flat. I bought her bed, a cooker and a washing machine. When Eli was born, I was the proudest Nanny in the world. I joked that she should have a DNA test as he looked like his father and I wasn't sure if she was the mother. He was a golden baby, who loved to sleep. She had no problems breast feeding him. She was a happy new mother, besotted with her son. Eli bought me happiness. I was so pleased history hadn't repeated itself. I thought about my mother, she should now be a great grandmother.

Psychic programmes on TV fascinated me and I often wondered if my mother could communicate with me via them. I paid to see Psychic Sally and Lisa Williams but neither of them spoke to me. I went to see a local woman. I told her nothing and wrote down everything she said. She claimed my Nan wanted to thank me for nursing her at the end of her life. My mother wanted me to forgive my father and said it wasn't his fault.....That was typical victim mentality mother, it was not your fault....She mentioned lots of interesting things that had a ring of truth. She mentioned a terraced house and St. Michaels church which confused me. I spoke to my Aunt Linda who confirmed they had lived in a terrace house as children and my mother had got married in St. Michaels church. I couldn't spend my life relying on psychic communication even though it fascinated me. I had to remain in the present time.

I kept pinching myself at work, I was getting paid for chatting and giving out champagne and bottles of wine. I joked in one sales office about the nice wine I had bought being on a buy two get one free offer and how I had the free bottle. Our office was getting plenty of referrals and my boss had not had one complaint from the notoriously bitchy sales women earning high commission rates on every mortgage we arranged. He gave me a boxed bottle of champagne to thank me for developing the business and doing so well. This was the first time in my working years, that I had been personally thanked and handed a gift. I was overwhelmed, John was the best boss ever. My time in the public sector, with policies laying out restrictions on the acceptance of gifts was behind me. I was now being rewarded for my effects. John went off to Italy for a couple of weeks and then Dan and I went to France on holiday. My life had never been so normal, it was easy work and going so well.

When I returned to work, I was called into the office. The boss of Taylor Wimpey had complained to my boss about his girls not getting champagne anymore and only getting the buy one get one free offer from Sainsbury's. He said I had embarrassed him and I lost my job. I left the office in tears. His business partner told me John hadn't slept for a week, knowing he had sacked me for a stupid reason, it had been one of those days and he had taken it out on me. I had been excellent for business and they wanted me back. I had arranged to meet him and discuss my return to work. I declined on principle, I couldn't work for a man like that. I started a law degree, I was fed up with injustice.

I visited my brother each month, taking his daughter or my children along for company. I would persistently lecture him about the day he gets out, inspiring him to create a better life for himself. My Dad never visited him in prison. It's funny how we visited him after killing our mother but he didn't want to visit his son. He would turn up at my flat on odd occasions and always say "I can't stay long." It felt as though he was sneaking about behind Sandra's back and she was timing him. He would ask how Ray was getting on and I would update him. He would talk about the times he had tried to guide Ray and how Ray would never listen. He blamed the people he associated with. "Ray has issues" I would add. He wasn't interested in me, my children or Eli. He would leave me feeling empty and worthless, like he had done all my life. I just hoped he wouldn't come again.

On his final visit he said "You might as well have these" as he handed me three photograph albums he had rescued from his garage, whilst having a clear out. I thanked him and told him, how nice it would be, after all these years to have a photograph of my mother. My anger inside was bubbling to the surface as I realised I was ironically, expressing gratitude to the man who had murdered my mother.

"You didn't just steal her from me and Ray, you ruined our lives Dad, are you surprised Ray has a drug addiction? He sold drugs to feed his habit because he can't cope with it Dad. You wrecked my family, and destroyed their lives" He said he knew that. "No, you don't know Dad, it was me who was there trying to support them, you were in prison remember, working out in the gym, making matchstick models and doing a business course. It was me who witnessed their grief, not you!" He was silent. Whilst prison may have been a challenge, it provided no justice to the broken souls in my family.

"It was down to you that my Nan had cut me out of her will." He thought that was wrong and reassured me that we should have been entitled to our inheritance. He said it was wrong that Linda and June had not passed my mothers share onto us. "What's wrong Dad is that you didn't think about passing my mothers share of the house onto us either. Why didn't we have bonds? I can't believe you were allowed to benefit financially from her murder." He told me he hadn't thought about it, yet he had thought about having bonds in his own name. He was selfish, through and through. "And Dad, it doesn't end there, you stole the grandmother from our children, they never had a Nan in their lives. My Mom missed out on our lives, she should be a proud great grandmother now" I had finally said my piece and he left.

I sat on the sofa and opened their wedding album, I noticed my mothers handwriting and her spelling corrections of the words Saturday and St. Michael, her husband's name had remained as Ronnal not Ronald and that made me smile. In almost fourteen years of marriage she had never amended the spelling of his name. It was in 1964, when they married and I calculated she was eighteen years old. I studied the photographs, ignoring my fathers sanctimonious smile, fixated on my innocent mother. I copied a picture onto my mobile phone, and zoomed in on her beautiful face, it was as close as I could get to her.

I noticed another spelling correction of my name inside my Christening Album. I knew she had lost her first born Julie and thought about how my mother must have worried throughout her pregnancy and been relieved that I had survived. Perhaps the baby in my dream was Julie and they were now reunited. I was shocked to learn I had weighed in at 9lb 5oz. Mom would have been twenty-one and looked a proud, gentle mother in the photographs. There were no pictures of my father holding me. I browsed through the family album, containing exclusive snapshots of our happy lives. I put the albums in a drawer and retreated to the local pub.

Dovegate Prison were advertising for prison officers. It was in Uttoxeter which was a far drive from home and it was far from my ideal career choice but it was a field that was unlikely to make you redundant or go into administration. I needed a secure career. I had hopes of training domestic abuse perpetrators there eventually. The fact that many were released back in to society to reoffend, I thought I could attempt to educate them and bring about change in their behaviours. I took part in the group interview process and was wise enough to realise its objectives. One young lad was clearly a racist and had prejudiced views about prisoners, no way will they take you on, I thought.

I began my seven week training to be a prison officer, alongside around fifteen men and four women. I was surprised to see the same young lad on the course, insignificantly, his dad already worked at the prison. He had a lot to learn, and with his attitude I knew he would learn the hard way. The training was thorough and intense but I enjoyed most of it. One woman left, realising she couldn't cope with the academic side. She had assumed being a prison officer just involved walking around locking and unlocking doors.

There was circuit training twice a week, where I managed to shed two stone and feel as fit as I was in my school days. My biggest fear, as a smoker, was the bleep test. I defeatedly stopped running when I came close to death. I had actually past the test but they let me run on, curious to see how far I would go. Being on the wings of the prison was like walking around a council estate but there were less women, no children or pets. I did notice there was a disproportionate number of black prisoners reflective of the inequalities in society. I didn't feel intimidated by any of the inmates. I was mentally and physically fit. I felt proud wearing my uniform, realising what an important role I had to play in society.

I had restraint training experience working with young people in care and although prisoner restraints were a little different, I found them easier to do as you worked in three's. I pulled two young and inexperienced trainers up, when they were doing a demonstration of how to securely escort a prisoner. Their hold was correct but it was back to front, so they were walking backwards, which in my opinion wasn't the ideal way to move a prisoner. I wondered if their dad's worked in the prison too. They frowned on my advice and made me look the fool. When their lead returned, he took them to one side. They looked over at me as he whispered. Power goes to the heads of some people and they think 'trainees' won't notice their mistakes. The lead took over and demonstrated the correct way to escort a prisoner, the way I had suggested. I said nothing and joined my partners to practice the correct manoeuvre.

By the seventh week, I had passed every exam and had just the practical restraint of a prisoner to do in full riot gear. We were called out at different times to do a restraint of a prisoner in a mock cell. The young trainers role played a prisoner, having weapons and using force, this experience was as real as it got. There was a code word the 'prisoner' could use which meant we were to release them on the grounds of health and safety. Being in riot gear and restraints lasting a while, it was exhausting work. My fellow females were struggling. One was crying after doing her second restraint, I sat in the corridor giving her support. The second one was sick after her second attempt and didn't have to continue. The third one managed to do three attempts and wet herself. I was the oldest woman, I had survived the experience but I was totally ready to drop.

The main trainer came in and called my name again along with two other men. We had to do yet another restraint, this time with him as the 'prisoner'. He smiled as if this was some sort of threat. He didn't worry me, it was three against one. During this restraint, the 'prisoner' was aggressively swearing, spitting and playing hard to get as they do. I made the arm lock and signified to my colleagues. Now I confess, my mother taught me honesty was always the best policy, you are not supposed to speak to the prisoner and I did. He looked into my eyes and snarled "You haven't got the bollocks!" I was on my fourth restraint of the morning, I was knackered and this wasn't a real prisoner. I sarcastically responded "Nope, I haven't because I'm a woman." and I laughed. He called out the code word and accused me of trying to break his arm.

It was a ridiculous accusation, I had never hurt anyone doing a restraint, I never would. I was totally baffled why he was pretending I had hurt him. He didn't even mention the comment I had made. There were no marks on his arm. I went into the governors office, to be told I had failed the restraint aspect and due to this factor, I could not be employed. The trainer claimed I had lost my temper, which made me laugh, I am probably the most patient person you will ever meet, but it was his word against mine and the governor fully backed him.

Everyone else had passed the course, except one of the guys I had done the fourth restraint with, he was also outed. I gave him a lift home and we chatted about what had really happened. I knew it had taken them seven weeks to do the background checks, no one had asked me about my Dad, Dan or my brother, but I hoped their criminal backgrounds wouldn't prejudice my career. "It's funny you should say that" he said and he told me about his grandad who was serving a life sentence for a serious crime. Prejudice, the daughter of a murderer, the partner of an aggressive man and the sister of a drug dealer, I had to be high risk.

The following week, I returned my uniform and said goodbye to yet another career, knowing something better would come up. I signed on for unemployment benefit after looking at the jobs I had no experience or qualifications to do. It was embarrassing after all these years, I had landed back in the same building. Dan's wages were only covering the bills and food. I had reached the point where I didn't care what I did, I just needed money to buy my alcohol and cigarettes again. My self esteem had again hit rock bottom.

Dan forced me to see the funny side, he made me laugh whilst I attempted to find work. I signed up with a job agency who pretended they had plenty of temporary jobs available. I worked nights in a factory for a week on quality control, my quality of life was out of control. I was then offered a few hours cleaning, here and there, and gave the agency the brush off. I joined another agency who were recruiting for Amazon, and along with hundreds of other hopefuls, I completed forms, answered simple aptitude questions and passed a drugs test. My application simply got lost in their disorganised office. I called to find out what was happening, they said they would get back to me. They must have lost my number or quit their job as I was never contacted again. Just finding a basic, unskilled job seemed impossible.

The benefit advisor suggested I attended a 'back to work' course for a week, oh the humiliation! I parked on the car park and was greeted at the door and shown into the room. I received a nice free pen to sign the register and helped myself to coffee and biscuits. We were given badges to write our names on and were encouraged to get to know each other. The trainer wanted us to support each other through the 'process'. I stood chatting to a few women and commented on how civil we were being treated. I made my way around the room getting to know everyone.The caterers turned up with our buffet food for lunch and I reflected on my negative preconceived expectations of the course. This wasn't so bad, I thought.

We sat down and the trainer introduced himself. He told us about his career and asked us all to speak about the work we had done in our lives. A woman in a wheelchair went first and told us she had never officially worked because of her disability but she had raised her own children and looked after others. Her house had always been like a crèche. We laughed as she stated children saw her as an asset, they exploited her for having a permanent lap to sit on. I thought about how difficult her life must have been and admired her positivity trying to find employment in a prejudiced world.

I went next and told everyone about my work with preschool children and being a nanny, then working with challenging children in care and then with care leavers. I spoke about my passion working in the field of domestic violence and how I was now unemployed, struggling to find a new career. The other women talked about their similar careers. There were some who had been social workers and had now retired. Others had been teachers or worked with children in care, and quite a few mentioned their involvement with cases of domestic violence. We all had so much in common, I felt totally at home.

The trainer went on to explain that today's session would probably change our futures for ever. I cheekily commented "Do we all get a job at the end of this then?" We all laughed. He said it was the best job in the world becoming a 'foster parent'. I had been in the wrong room for over an hour, I gave my apologies, asked if I could keep my pen and left.

Further down the hall was another room, with a piece of paper taped to the door, STEPS 2 WORK it said. I knocked the door, entered and apologised for being late. Sat in a semi circle were five desolate people, facing a smartly dressed black man, who appeared to be out of his comfort zone. You could cut the atmosphere with a knife. None of them wanted to be there and a couple appeared to be hard faced racists.

I signed in using a secondhand pen that some desolate person had already chewed, and replaced it back into a recycled margarine tub. I looked around the room, there was no coffee and biscuits, no buffet, not even a jug of water to share. I sat down with them and broke the ice " Can I tell you all a funny story I said?" Within a few minutes, everyone was laughing about my experience in the other room and talking about their lives, how they felt and what made them feel more confident. As human beings on a course we all deserved a new pen and at least a cup of 'council pop' to drink.

One of the hard faced guys, was last to speak. He said he was dyslexic and hated being in a classroom, he hated school and was only there because he would lose his benefits if he didn't attend. I said there were lots of labouring jobs being advertised in the job centre and if he didn't want to do the course why didn't he ask the job centre to help him to apply for them. Just because he couldn't read or write didn't mean he was no use in society. I boosted his self esteem. "You won't be bothered about that poxy benefit money then, you'll have loads of money and you'll be proud of yourself because you'll have earned it." He agreed "Fuck this shit, I'm going to get a job" he stood with his shoulders back and proudly left the room.

The trainer was pleased I had changed the dynamics of the group and he knew I was on his side. He began the session with a quiz but was unaware he was showing the answers to the questions on the PowerPoint. I pointed it out but he didn't know how to remove them. It was obvious, this man had received no training for his role and I became his mentor. Having training experience myself, I was able to help him with simple little things that made his job easier and the course more professional. On the last day I asked him if his company had any vacancies. He told me I could do better, his employer was subcontracting, his pay was extremely low, he was being used. He thanked me for my support and said he had learned so much. I had also reminded him that he could easily be in my shoes looking for work.

I returned to the job centre the following week and updated my advisor on what I had learned from the experience because I had learned something. I needed to help others, starting out in life to make good career choices and set their paths towards a solid future, I needed to inspire others. After another month of applying for jobs and not getting anywhere, I started to feel my hopes for the future were delusional. I was on a slippery slope, I had no petrol in my car and it seemed more likely that I would become an alcoholic before I found work. I thought about the words of Margaret Thatcher, I got on my new bike, Dan had bought me for my birthday and headed for the careers office.

I had a nostalgic bike, similar to the one I had shared with my mother as a child. It had a bell, a basket and a comfy saddle. In my head riding a bike was effortless but after so many years of smoking, I had only cycled for a few minutes when I dismounted to get my breath. My heart was pumping faster than it had ever known, I thought I was going to die. I walked to the next lamppost trying to disguise my red faced embarrassment. I had lost my ability to ride up a small incline. I was off and on the bike like a yo yo on a two mile journey but I finally made it up the hill to Cannock.

The careers officer looked at my CV and said " Can I be honest with you Diane. You have some fabulous work experience but this is a very intimating CV, you're unlikely to get an interview when you are more experienced than those that will be interviewing you, we need to strip this back." I thanked her for her valuable advice and spent my journey home, free wheeling down hill with the wind in my face, overtaking the traffic. The first job I applied for, using my new CV, got me an interview with a training provider.

I gave an interesting presentation on Equal Opportunities, dressed in a new suit I had bought on my credit card. I had invested money on creating a positive first impression and hoped it wasn't wasted. They gave me positive feedback and said they would like me to return again to deliver a micro lesson on first impressions. I also needed to have a police check and knowing that could take over six weeks, I took the night shift at the Screwfix factory, cooking and cleaning in the works canteen just to improve my financial situation.

I hated my time washing pans and scraping oil from the griddles every night. Trying to sleep during the day was impossible, council workers mowed the lawns, the water board seemed to be drilling for oil, people had their garden strimmers going, cars were coming and going, doors were being slammed and Poker would bark. I was praying to God that I wouldn't be at Screwfix forever. I prepared my micro lesson, I stole someone's idea, improved it and made it fit for purpose. That's what all good teachers do. I headed off to Nova Training with my unforgettable resources, a packet of interesting mince pies.

Chapter 18
Teacher Time

My micro lesson to three young people was observed by three centre managers this time. I firstly explained what a CEO was and told the young people to imagine they were now a CEO, this raised their spirits and engaged them. Each young person was presented with a photograph and information of a CEO from different supermarkets and asked to introduce themselves.

The CEO of Tesco, introduced himself first, he boasted he earned £6M last year and told the group he had started his career working in Tesco's as a sixteen year old, stocking the shelves every Saturday. The Morrison's CEO went next and declared a £4M salary. He mentioned he was from a working class background and believed apprenticeships were important to help young people get their career going in retail. The third CEO, from Sainsbury's had a £8M salary, he was born in Birmingham, went to university and had worked for Mars, Galaxy and Pepsi. We had a brief discussion about what they wore for work, what they had in common with these people and why the CEO's were all men.

I presented the CEO's with six mince pies, they were to choose the best one to be a supplier for their supermarket, and complete a simple tally chart answering three sets of criteria; Does it look good? Does it smell right?and Will it sell? Now this presentation was supposed to be about first impressions at an interview and the managers looked confused. I winked and smiled to them. The comments the CEO's made during the presentation were all recorded on the whiteboard and after they had decided on the winning mince pie, I went through how this all connected to first impressions at an interview.

The first mince pie, had looked good but it "smelled funny" it was covered in eucalyptus oil. No-one wants the employer to think we smell funny. We shouldn't go for an interview smelling of body odour, cigarettes, cannabis or cat pee on our clothing or wear overpowering perfume. All they will remember about us is that we smelled disgusting. The second mince pie had been smeared in mud "it was filthy". We shouldn't go wearing dirty clothes or looking like we haven't washed. We don't want an employer to think we are filthy people who don't care about cleanliness.

The third mince pie, I had crushed "that's wrecked" we need to iron our clothes, comb our hair and look pristine, not wrecked. We want the employer to know we care about presentation. The fourth mince pie was covered in different colour icing, candles and silver balls. "I actually like this one" one said but another CEO said "it's a bit OTT" we discussed Tattoos, makeup, piercings, hair styles and clothes that would not be appropriate for an interview. The fifth was "soggy" soaked in water.

We should allow enough time to prepare for the interview, not turn up with wet hair because we have got up late and rushed out. We want the employer to know we will be punctual and organised. The last mince pie hadn't been tampered with, it smelled "fine" looked "perfect" and "was definitely the winner". The employer will always choose the one that is well prepared, well presented and most appropriate for the job.

The young people had made judgements based on appearance and now had a new perception. They thought the presentation was unforgettable. I had made my mark and started a new career, developing my own teaching resources as I engaged many young people in education. These were children, who for whatever reason had dropped out of mainstream education. Like me, some had learning disabilities and found it hard to concentrate. Some had not had the best upbringing whilst others were looking for love and praise and most of them were challenging as they had slipped through the net, let down by society. I got the job and started a new career.

Ray had a chance to start a new life too, he was released from prison and moved in with me. Robbie had to sleep on the sofa on Saturday nights but he didn't mind. I thought, living with me would give Ray a drug free environment to make his fresh start. I wanted to teach him a new way of living. He got himself a job but shortly after starting he had taken Poker out for a walk and was reading a text on his phone, he stepped backwards and fell down into the brook and broke his leg. He lost his job and spent the next few weeks cooped up in the flat recovering.

We were invited to my Aunt Linda's wedding. She married the man called Jack, who seemed to want to welcome me as part of the family. I enjoyed the day but my Aunt Linda looked unhappy, she seemed exhausted with life. I kept glancing over at her. I could see she had lost her sparkle and I was concerned about her health. None of my cousins seemed concerned. They said she had a new set of false teeth and that was the issue. I hadn't seen her for so long but I was shocked to see her deteriorate so quickly. It was her wedding day so I didn't want to make her feel worse about herself by voicing my concerns. It was nice to spend time with them all that day.

Ray enjoyed being with the family too but at home he was hard to live with, he had mood swings and we suspected he was using drugs again. We found him difficult to support. He spent a lot of his time out with his friends or cooped up in his bedroom as though he was still in prison. The room was a mess, the curtains permanently closed, Rizla's and ashtrays were here and there. All this confirmed our suspicions that he was back on drugs. Dan bottled things up for my sake but one night, they had a row and Ray took his dog and left the flat. I gave up on supporting my brother, it had been a second failed experiment to intervene in his life. At least Robbie had a bed to sleep in again on Saturday nights.

Holly and Eli would meet me from work and I would drop them off at home or they would come into my flat for a while and eat dinner with us. Whilst I was now managing financially, Holly was struggling on benefits and getting into debt. Her boyfriend Harley had still not found work, she had had enough. I asked her how I could support her. I offered to give her £1000, or help Harley to find employment or she could move back home. She chose the latter giving up on her flat and Harley.

We went out and bought bunk beds for the single room she shared with Eli. Nathan had a double bed in his room and his girlfriend Sammi often stayed over so it was the only option. Robbie was back on the sofa on Saturday nights but again he didn't complain. Eli was happy on top bunk and Holly was just glad to be back living with her mom. Dan had his motorbike stolen and complained that living in a flat meant you couldn't have anywhere safe to keep a motorbike. He wanted a garage or at least a man cave.

Having all Eli's belongings soon filled the flat and a few things were stored in Dan's father's shed, along with my redundant bike and Dan's new motorbike. I asked the council if we could move to a house after a few weeks of overcrowding. They said we could only move to a four bedroom property and they were like gold dust. They told us to try to exchange but after six months we realised we were unlikely to ever get someone who was willing to swap a house for a flat.

I looked at private rental but there was nothing we could afford. A brand new four bedroom property sat empty a few streets away but it was £1500 a month. If we had been on benefits we could have claimed housing benefit for that property but I didn't want to waste that much on rent every month, it seemed crazy. We couldn't get a mortgage because of the bankruptcy. I asked a builder if we could rent a derelict bungalow and we would pay to make it habitable. He declined, he said it wouldn't be 'fair' to rent it out in that condition. I'd lived in far worse properties.

Although Nathan and Sammi had started saving for a deposit for a house, neither of them earned a fortune and that dream was still a good few years away. I suggested we save together and bought a house we could all live in for a couple of years. We could pay the mortgage for them and any profit could have been used to buy a second property. It was a win win situation. I would much rather pay rent to my son than a landlord but Nathan wasn't keen on the idea. He didn't want to complicate things and just wanted his own little love nest like most young couples do.

I didn't think it was fair on Eli not having any outdoor space to play. Dan and I missed gardening and we all missed our barbecue's. We felt depressed not being able to sit out in the sunshine to get our essential vitamin D. We would go on holidays, visit parks and sit in beer gardens to compensate. We even bought a camper van so we could get out at weekends. We just needed a house with a garden really but we were trapped in the overcrowded 'Penthouse'.

Dan's parents told us about a friend who was giving up her council house to move into a bungalow. It was a house with a redundant coal house. She had said many tenants had converted theirs into a fourth bedroom or a utility room. Holly, Dan and myself went to view the property. It had a drive and a pretty welcoming front garden. We looked around, it felt so spacious compared to our flat. It was very clean, tidy and full of sunlight. There was a conservatory and a decent sized back garden, with a shed. We looked at the old coal house, there was ample room to convert it and we were happy to fund the conversion ourselves but the housing association wouldn't allow us to move there because it was classed as a three bed property. A couple moved in, they had two children and plenty of space.

A few months passed and I received a phone call that a four bedroom property was becoming available and we were second on the list. The property was in Cheslyn Hay. I tried my hardest to keep my composure knowing four bedroom properties were like gold dust, the people on the top of the list were likely to accept it. We were told the property would be ready for viewing the following week. I couldn't sleep, I prayed to God that we got it and after asking around the only four bed that the locals knew of had been the home of a notorious family. The children had all grown up and moved out. Their mother had lived alone there for years and had died in the property.

We pulled up outside the property, it didn't have a drive or a dropped curb like the other properties, it had an overgrown, neglected garden, surrounded by a tall hedge. There was an ugly concrete slope to the front door and scaffolding poles utilised as makeshift disability hand rails. "I have a good feeling about this neglected hovel" I said to Dan and he agreed. The more we looked the worse it got, we peeped through the window, surely the ones above us on the list wouldn't want it, not unless they were as desperate as us.

I got emotional on the phone when the housing officer told us we would be viewing the property with the other family. They were dangling a carrot in front of my face, I was hungry but someone else had the opportunity to eat it first. I knew this carrot would be soft and smelly, it would have white fluffy fungal growth, be partially chewed by rodents and plastered with parasites but we were starving. After eight years living in the 'penthouse', I just hoped this family were fussy eaters and we finally stood a chance of moving out.

On the viewing day, Dan and myself pulled up outside the property early to check out our competition. A couple pulled up in an old car, accompanied by a girl around ten years old. I could tell they preferred cakes to carrots. We stood chatting to them. The woman told me she had two sons, one had behavioural problems and a learning difficulty and because of this they needed a bigger house. Their eldest son didn't like sharing a room. They had already paid for a dropped curb and a block paved driveway, where they lived.

Her husband was a plasterer so if it needed plastering 'here and there', that wasn't an issue. I asked for his number, just in case we needed a plasterer in the future but to be honest, I just wanted it so I could contact them if need be. I felt my blood boiling when I told her about our living arrangements. We didn't live in a house, Eli had nowhere to play, there was seven of us at weekends and poor Robbie had to sleep on the sofa.

The housing officer arrived and apologised for being late and led us to the front door. I followed Dan and the others "You guys are alright, you all have trousers on, I'm the one going to get bit here" I said as she unlocked the front door. The housing officer stepped inside and said she was sorry but the house needed to be fumigated before we could go in. We all peeped through the door. You could smell an awful odour and see the illegal polystyrene tiles had been knocked off the ceiling onto the floor, they had perfectly illuminated the fleas. It was just as I had expected.

On our second visit, Dan told me to forget it but I couldn't. I visited the property the following week without him. The girl excitedly picked out her bedroom and told me she had the smallest room at her house. I told her how lucky she was not having to share it with her mother, like my grandson had to. She said "my mum wouldn't fit in my bedroom" I explained we had bunk beds. I was trying my best to get their sympathy vote. We were definitely more needy than they were but the carrot was out of my reach.

I rang the housing office three days on the trot as they waited for the couple to get back to them. I texted the plasterer to find out what was happening. I had no response but the next day we got the best news ever, we were offered the worst house I had ever had the opportunity to live in. We waited another three weeks for the maintenance team to empty the rubbish from the property and strip the walls. Holly wanted to be a joint tenant, she had the idea after we had renovated the property she could buy it and we could put half to the mortgage.

The housing officer handed us the keys and said she was embarrassed that as a housing association they rented properties in such a poor state. I told her not to worry we were just happy to get the space we needed and having gardens was a luxury. We soon discovered the house was riddled with woodworm, wood louse and mice and that required a few weekly visits from environmental health. Just like our flat we had it completely re-plastered and replaced all the doors and skirting boards. Gradually the horrid smell of the house eased, and with fresh paint on the walls it started to feel like home.

The housing association refused to provide any skips for the rubbish. We had to get rid of that ourselves. They charged us full rent on both properties and said it was our choice not to move in to the property, despite the rodent issue and having no heating. They did fit a new bathroom, removed the old gas fire and installed a combination boiler so we didn't complain. We got the upstairs carpeted and moved in. Dan continued to laminate the lounge, dining room and utility room. Then he tiled the kitchen floor and walls. Every spare hour we had was spent working on the house. We were all exhausted. We had again spent a fortune on someone else's property. From hovel to home, it had taken six weeks of hard labour.

It hadn't taken long for me to progress at work either. I had become a qualified assessor and gained a teaching qualification, teaching a range of courses for Nova Training. I moved to a larger centre back in Bilston and I jumped through hoops to reach 'grade one' teaching status, embedding so many elements to each lesson. Our company had an Ofsted inspection for outstanding excellence, the hard work paid off. However being a fantastic teacher, for a profit making company had its drawbacks, attendance rates were high, more young people wanted to join and my work load continued to increase. I regularly requested a pay rise and eventually I was given one.

Dan's mom organised a combined party for Dan's 50th, his sisters 40th and his Dads 80th which was a very memorable day. I felt a little envious of the Clarke family bond but it was nice to see everyone together. I still had contact with my Aunt Linda but it was only the odd message on Facebook. I knew she had sold her house and moved to Tenerife with Jack, so the family could enjoy quality time together. By this time, I didn't think she referred to me as being part of her family. I had hoped she would invite me. I wanted to spend some quality time with her, to catch up on so many things. I wanted to tell her all about my life and how special she had always been but I could only do that if she asked me to visit her. It was crazy that even as an adult I still feared family rejection. Holly reminded me how she had never visited us and questioned why I was bothered.

Two weeks after Dan's birthday it was my 50th birthday. I went out for a meal with my work 'family' and they decorated the room and made me feel very special. We had become very close as a team and I adored every one of them. I felt grateful to be loved at work and at home. Every year, I thought about the tape recording of my mother's voice and how she was missing another birthday but my 50th was different. I had her photograph enlarged and admiring her face, sat on my sideboard, I felt she was part of my life again. It's funny how a simple photograph can change your life. My children made a fuss and spoiled me with new plants, flowers and jewellery. Dan and I treated ourselves to matching watches.

Facebook became popular and it was an irritant at times, a reminder of my mothers family having their get togethers and my exclusion. I was still connected but it was a fragmented connection. I used social media to raise awareness of domestic violence. Victims would message me for advice and I would give them support. I received comforting words from friends when I uploaded pictures of my mother on her birthday and Mother's Day. I would post things about my life and it was my friends that commented most of the time. I was in touch with lots of people who had lost a loved one through murder. I wasn't alone, the peer support was empowering. Facebook made living with murder easier to handle and it felt good to offer words of support to others.

Jackie had lost her daughter to murder and had, like me, taken part in the 'Living with Murder' series. We had become good friends over the years and often supported each other on Facebook. She called me to ask if I would be interested in raising awareness of knife crime by taking part in a special episode of Eastenders, a prominent soap on TV. I had a conversation with the producer and he explained the storyline. Shaki, had been stabbed to death and we were all to attend his funeral, with photographs of our lost relatives, turning the audiences attention to a real issue in society that tragically impacted on people's lives. I knew it would be an excellent way to raise awareness and if it saved just one life, participating would have been worth it.

The day before filming, I headed down to London on the train, accompanied with my daughter, Holly, who also wanted to take part. We stayed at Jackie's home for the night, along with three other women, who had all lost a son to knife crime. The six of us chatted until four in the morning about our lost relatives, the court cases, the perpetrator, and the impact on our lives. There is a strange bond between us, we all know what it's like and being together helps us feel normal and understood. We got a few hours sleep and then headed off to Elstree studios.

There were around fifty people taking part in the episode, we travelled on a coach to the venue. The cast were all respectful and friendly people. It was an overwhelming day for everyone but we were all there to help save lives and that made it a proactive experience. We could wear what we wanted. I wore something warm and comfortable, it was a bright blue top, everyone else wore clothes more appropriate for a funeral. I felt different, not just for my attire but for another reason. The majority had lost sons to knife crime, a couple had lost a daughter, sister or brother. I was the only one who had lost a mother and the only one who was the daughter of the murderer. I held the photograph of my mother, in her memory, acknowledging all the mothers who were killed as a result of knife crime and their silent children left handling uxoricide.

After a long day filming, photographs were taken with cast members and we returned to Elstree Studios. We were given unsupervised access to the Eastenders set, which Holly and myself made the most of. I had photographs of me serving in the shop, drinking champagne in the cellar of the Queen Victoria pub and digging on the allotment. Holly sat in Phil Mitchell's chair in his garage and had a go on the swings in the park. We had so much fun, it compensated us all for the funeral experience.

Viewers that watched Shaki's funeral said it was a powerful episode that brought them to tears. Friends and colleagues congratulated me and admired my strength and courage to highlight the issue and help save lives. We needed to do something as knife crime was causing so much misery to people's lives. I felt proud to have been involved in the fight against knife crime. My Aunt Linda disapproved, she called and told me how my involvement had undone her 'twenty years' worth of counselling. It was still easier for her if I remained silent.

Once the decorating was finished in our house, we spent all our spare time working in the back garden, landscaping, fencing and erecting a summerhouse. We were growing fruit and vegetables, being back in touch with nature, made me feel alive. Dan had his man cave at last. Eli had a trampoline and outdoor activities to keep him entertained. We lay on the lawn in the sun and cooled off in a swimming pool. We all enjoyed sitting out in the garden and having friends and Dan's family round for barbecues. Holly started working for my cousin Scott. He was the only family member that visited. It was still heaven.

Things were going so well in our lives, when one of our close friends suddenly died from pancreatitis. Graham was a few years younger than us, he had gone to hospital with stomach pains and he passed away the next day. It stunned both of us. We had been out with him the day before and he had been his usually happy self. The funeral was a tribute, he had so many friends all mourning their loss together. I felt for his wife Vicki. I didn't know how I would ever cope if I was to lose Dan.

Just a week after Graham's funeral, Holly called to tell me the devastating news that my Aunt Linda had been rushed into hospital with a stroke. As distant as our relationship had become it broke my heart that I had no idea whether she was alive or dead. I had been so close to her in the past. My cousins went to visit her but didn't let me know how she was. I had noticed my cousin had checked 'in Tenerife' on Facebook. I sat in the garden crying, pointlessly sending messages to my aunt, trying to make contact. Apologising for not being there and explaining how I had felt since my Nan's death. I felt powerless and alone, I was missing that Barlow bond. Dan was oblivious, in his own world, at the top of the garden, tending to his runner beans. I text her again and said when he comes back with his runner beans, I'm going to ask him to marry me. I thought if she survived that would at least cheer her up. Dan said "Yes!" He disappeared to the shops and returned with a celebratory box of chocolates.

Linda's daughter, Melanie called the next day to air her opinions of me. She let me know that her mom had read all my messages and shown them to her. She told me never to send anymore. That really didn't bother me. I only wanted to know how she was. I cried with relief when she said she was OK. Melanie became irate and asked where I had been for the last fifteen years. She gave me the impression that her mother had suffered because of my absence from her life. She explained that her mom had to have counselling, and insinuated that I was somehow to blame. Perhaps the Eastenders episode had impacted on my aunt's mental health but I couldn't be blamed for the death of her sister. Melanie started bawling down the phone that I was a crazy woman that needed counselling.

I reflected on our relationship. Melanie had always liked me when I bought her presents at Christmas or took her to the park as a child. We had a sisterly relationship but she was a lazy unappreciative child. It was me that always helped her mother out with the house work. She may have been jealous of that special relationship. She knew that I had supported the family bakery and the bouncing castles businesses. Melanie had no idea how difficult my life had been. I had never asked her for support. As cousins we had never fallen out. In the past fifteen years, she had never shown an interest in my life, called or visited me yet she resented the fact that I no longer supported her mother and couldn't believe that I even cared for my aunt. I hung up the phone and thought 'what a bitch'.

I called my Aunt June, I knew she was petrified of flying and she would need some support. They were very close as sisters and not being able to see her would have made her feel worse. June told me, she was in a state and that Linda wasn't out of the woods, she had actually had two more mini strokes. Melanie had not told me this. Nathan offered to take me to her house so I could support her. To be honest, after the call from my cousin, I needed a 'Barlow' hug myself and thought June would want the same. She told me not to visit because her son was coming round. I couldn't understand why that made a difference and she couldn't explain. I said "Do you know what June, I give up, it's obvious no one in this family cares about my feelings, all I've every wanted was love and all I get is rejection" I hung up.

It turned out that the reason Aunt June didn't want me around was because her daughter was ill. She was masking an eating disorder and didn't want me to see her. I had training in eating disorders and could have supported her too. June later called me, possibly under the influence and shouted down the phone "You're that murderers daughter, you're a bastard just like him, I don't want anything to do with you ever again". All I had done was offered to be with her and give her a hug. I couldn't believe she was being so abusive. I felt no guilt and hung up.

I broke down in tears at work the next morning and had a chat with my manager, Mick. He reminded me, that I was one of the strongest women he had met. He said I was an inspiration and he quoted a line from the bible known as the Serenity Prayer. 'To accept the things I cannot change; Courage to change the things I can; And the wisdom to know the difference.' Mick was right, I couldn't change what had happened in the past. I had to accept they didn't care that I loved them and wanted them in my life. My time was better spent teaching the young people of Bilston, and that took courage. I thanked Mick for his kind words and went to my classroom knowing I had the chance to change their lives, so they had healthy relationships and protected themselves from exploitation.

As a teacher, I had the freedom to cover topics relevant to the learners personal development. I wanted to deliver lessons that would engage and inspire them to be successful and well balanced individuals. My life and work experience helped me forge a balanced curriculum that was interesting and fun. Many of my learners had low self worth. They lived in social housing with unemployed parents trapped in poverty. We looked at inspirational people who had succeeded in life. We looked at the housing market, mortgages and deposits. We discussed the long term benefits of buying a property compared to renting. We calculated the costs of furnishing and decorating a property. They soon became experts on budgeting for household bills simply playing a game and even investigated the set up and operation costs of running their own commercial businesses.

As eco warriors, they went outside, measured the building and calculated the number of solar panels they would need. They researched manufacturing costs and shipping costs to complete the project. We walked along canal paths, counting steps and calories burnt whilst we completed a clean up project. Every lesson included equality and diversity, to eliminate discrimination, harassment, victimisation and any other conduct that was prohibited by or under the Equality Act 2010. This advanced equality of opportunity between those that shared a relevant protected characteristic and those who did not share one, and it was all about establishing and maintaining good relationships. I had them risk assessing the buildings accessibility from a wheel chair users perspective, scooting around on computer chairs and creating accurate floor plans to show improvements they would make. There was always a reason for my lessons and I would get a buzz at the end of the day as my learners reflected on their learning.

We often used the town centre to explore real life learning. We investigated accessibility everywhere we went. I gave them challenges, "Take photographs of the clothing items you would purchase for an interview, look for the cheapest and smartest outfit, and meet me back here in 30 minutes." We would analyse and record their findings on their return. The winning outfit cost £4 and included a pair of shoes, a skirt, a blouse and a jacket all discovered on a buy one get one free, sale rail in a charity shop.

We had discussions on human rights and issues such as how to recognise when a relationship was unsafe, what constitutes sexual harassment and sexual violence and why these were unacceptable. They learned about their legal rights and responsibilities regarding equality, online rights, as well as how to report abuse or get advice. They understood how to access support for any issue in life. We looked at citizenship and acts of kindness. Everyday there was something new and useful to empower them with the confidence to voice their concerns in cases where their rights were not respected.

There were lessons on how to improve their mental health. We looked at the suicide rates and discussed reasons why so many young men were at high risk of suicide. We had interesting visitors presenting information on topics such as sickle cell, hate crime, driver safety, drug addiction and gambling. We took a group of learners into Featherstone prison to talk to three men, who had all made a poor decision in their life and as a consequence were all serving sentences for murder. Being a teacher had been my childhood ambition but watching the young people develop into respectful and confident learners willing to make a positive impact on society, melted my heart. I didn't just teach, I would build trust, listen, guide, motivate and praise. And every morning, without exception, I would ask each and every one of them, how they were feeling.

I cut off the contact via Facebook with my family and started planning our wedding. It was something positive to look forward to. Neither of us wanted anything flash, we just wanted to be married. I sent text invites out to everyone we wanted there. My mother's family didn't respond to their invites but that was their choice and I wasn't going to let their absence at my second wedding upset me again. I booked the venue and arranged the catering. Nathan created a beautiful unique wedding cake, with the bride and groom sat outside a campervan, complete with Mr. & Mrs. bunting, which perfectly reflected our lives.

Dan's mom, Joyce, insisted that she bought me a wedding dress, knowing I had no mother she wanted to make the wedding easier for me. I was blessed to have a women in my life that understood my needs. We spent a couple of days looking for the right dress and we found one. Accompanied by my daughter and her student discount card, it cost £52 and it was perfect. Holly had a bridesmaid's dress. Our son's, Dan's Dad, his brother, my brother and Dan all had matching suits and cravats. I wanted my Mom to be with me on the day so I had a special ornate framed photograph, of her on her wedding day, hanging from my bouquet. A silver heart hung from her photo, inscribed with the words 'Always in my heart, forever in my thoughts'.

On our wedding day, I had my hair, make up and nails done at Angie's new hair salon, we drank a glass of wine, I put on my wedding dress and I felt great. I was about to marry my best friend, the man I loved most in the world and I had no nerves, no worries and no regrets. I arrived at the registry office full of excitement. My brother was suited and booted, nervously waiting to give me away. I reassured him there was nothing to worry about. "I will hold on to you, we just walk in together and then you sit down, come on Ray, you can do this" I laughed.

I had chosen 'War of the Worlds, Forever Autumn' track to be played whilst Dan, family and friends waited for my arrival. Dan, his brother and myself were obsessed with the War of the Worlds Album and this track was about a man not having his woman around, so it was perfect. I kissed my mothers photograph and took my brothers arm. We walked in as Feargal Sharky was singing 'a good heart these days is hard to find, please be careful with this heart of mine.' Feargal reminded us both of Dan's hairstyle when we were fifteen, the song made us both smile. I found it funny when Dan said, "All that I have, I give to you", he had nothing but his love to give, every penny we earned had been spent on our home and garden. By this time, all our guests were in stitches of laughter. Along with the registrar, we uncontrollably laughed our way through the rest of the service, it was the best wedding ever.

We went to our venue and were surrounded by so many people we loved and cared about in our lives. A superb live sixteen piece band was playing which added to the atmosphere and got everyone dancing. It was a wonderful, joyful celebration of our togetherness. It really was the best day of my life. As the new Mrs.Clarke returned to work, my classroom was full of congratulations confetti and balloons, even my work family and my students shared in the celebration, I felt blessed.

Chapter 19
Work Life Synergy

During my fiftieth year, the golden anniversary of my life, I looked at what I had achieved. I was happily married, my children were grown up and settled and I had fulfilled my childhood ambition to be a teacher. I had cut off all the negativity from my life and now I just wanted to enjoy it. We travelled the country, meeting up with family and friends at festivals and different camper van events. We enjoyed socialising and relaxing with likeminded people. My work life balance required burning the candle at both ends and gradually it caught up with me. I needed a couple of weeks away to recharge my batteries.

We took a belated honeymoon to Gozo. Dan's sister and brother in law, had emigrated and taken over a bar bistro and a bike hire business. Ange booked us a seafront apartment and it was idyllic. We travelled the island on a motorbike sightseeing, swam in the warm clear ocean and sunbathed on the beach. Gozo was more than a holiday destination. My soul found peace in the warmth and love of a spiritual presence which manifested a sense of belonging. When it was time to leave, I looked out of the car window and the tears ran down my face. I wanted to stay there forever. We flew back home, back to reality, teaching and burning the candles. I knew I wanted something more in life, I just couldn't figure out what it was. I needed to progress, so I began a management course. The trainer asked us where we would like to be in five years time. My colleagues talked about their future aspirations and I said "I would like to be on a beach, on an island, in the Mediterranean!" I wanted to be back in Gozo.

I was a dedicated teacher. Every student needed my help and support and I couldn't let any of them down. It was difficult to manage at times so I looked at ways to improve their experiences. I split my class into three groups that rotated throughout the day. Everyone had some individual attention from me, everyone had access to a computer to develop their skills and they could work in a team supporting each other to consolidate their learning. In the teaching world, this is known as 'blended learning' and it worked well with my mixed ability learners. It's ·was what got me my 'grade one' teacher status.

As more learners started, my work load increased. I had an overcrowded classroom and an incident occurred, tempers were frayed. Some learners felt intimidated, terrified to be in the room, whilst others became argumentative, complaining about a lack of space, it became impossible to do blended learning. I had to focus more on behaviour management for a while. The following week, I had an extra eight new students and agreed with my learning support colleague to split the learners into two classrooms. She was a highly experienced teacher for learners with special needs and had around ten students in a smaller classroom. I still had a full classroom but everyone had their own space to work.

I felt like a miracle worker managing two classrooms at the same time. An IQA visited to do an annual observation on me, she was accompanied by a young trainee IQA, everyone was settled and working well. These were challenging and needy children and I now had them settled and doing maths all day. I deserved a medal for behaviour management and engaging them in learning. The IQA spoke to a couple of the new students and as a consequence I lost my grade one status. She suggested that I tried 'blended learning'. I did my best as a teacher to deliver the best results. I could have requested another observation but that straw broke the camels back. I was jumping through hoops trying to prove myself to people who couldn't actually do my job. The pressure from senior management was immense, ridiculous and soul destroying.

I returned home deflated. I smiled as I observed my daughter. Holly was in a happy stable and healthy relationship with Jason, he had pretty much moved in with us. He played his guitar and had such a relaxed outlook on life. His daughter, Jade was the same age as Eli and they played happily together in the garden like siblings do. She would sleep over and our house was full of love and laughter. I visited Nathan and could see how content he was with Sammi and his two cats in his new little cottage. He loved his car and his work. He cooked mouthwatering meals to encourage children with anorexia to eat at a residential unit. I was proud of the way he had turned out. I visited Daniel and Kate, they were happily married, and had Connor our second Grandson. Robbie still stayed with us every Saturday. We were all very close and happy. There was just something missing in my life, perhaps I just needed a less demanding job, I thought.

I was enjoying completing the management course, and learning about coaching and NLP. I didn't really see myself becoming a manager for Nova Training. That role was as stressful as teaching. Instead, I applied for a recruitment post within the same company. It was closer to home so I could recoup six hours a week on less travel to work. I could deliver the same induction each time so there would be no planning to do. I could still support the needs of the students and earn the same salary. I had worked with recruitment officers for years so I had a good understanding of their role and having the teaching experience, I could better prepare the young people for the classroom and provide an informative handover to the teachers. It seemed a no brainier so I gave up teaching for an easier life. Several colleagues and the former recruitment officer had warned me it was a bad move but I didn't listen.

My new manager was a woman I had previously worked with, when she, herself, had been a recruitment officer. She had an addiction to McDonald's food and a weight problem which I assumed masked some deeper issue. I hadn't been a threat to her back then and I started my new post full of competence, excitement and positivity. She inspected and changed every plan I made and micromanaged every thing I did. I was oblivious to the fact that I was now working under the management of a corporate psychopath.

In the Bilston centre our morning buzz meetings had always been a motivating start for the day. We would share our plans and discuss any strategies for managing certain students to ensure the team worked efficiently together. Her morning buzz meetings were just bizarre. She demonstrated the effectiveness of her NoNo shaver, on removing her facial hair, whilst she boasted about her personal affairs, talked about her sex life and her relationship with her subordinate partner. She appeared quite narcissistic. The others would laugh in disbelief. I tried to laugh with them but what she said was often offensive, inappropriate and totally unprofessional.

My previous managers had regularly checked the students files for compliance and because of their high standards I had become an expert in file maintenance. Her files were the worst I had seen in any centre. She blamed the previous staff and I set about rectifying her countless mistakes. She claimed I was an idiot, as she swore black was blue and manipulated everyone to agree with her. She had no conscience and enjoyed being cruel to certain staff and students.

Whilst I spent time getting to know the new learners during their week of induction, my manager would make them feel unwelcome. One young man had been out of education and living in care for six months. He had disclosed to me that he had been brought up with domestic violence and his mother had now rejected him for being disruptive towards his new step father, that was attempting to 'fix' his issues. He felt abandoned by his mother, had difficulty sleeping and struggled to get out of bed. The first day in class, he was very nervous and had difficulty concentrating. The teacher said she didn't like his attitude during our lunch break. I told her to be patient, he would settle, I'd seen it so often before. My manager believed she knew how to handle his type. She laid the law down, when he returned after lunch and he walked out.

Unsurprisingly, he was off sick for the rest of the week and she claimed I wasn't doing a very good job of retaining the learners. This was becoming a very sick situation, she was playing power games with people's lives. I engaged him again and suggested he attended just the afternoon sessions for a couple of weeks, to help him settle in and he agreed. My manager didn't support the idea and said he had to do mornings, she wanted to see his 'commitment'. So when he arrived on time, I spent twenty minutes praising him, assessing his mood and preparing him for making his next big step, entering the classroom once more. I could see he had tried to style his overgrown hair, he had made an effort to look his best. In an ideal world, I would have taken him to the barbers and had a nice walk and talk to put him in a better place before he had entered the building. He was an exhausted, traumatised and vulnerable young man.

Within half an hour he had been punched in the head by another challenging learner, the teacher disliked. My manager had watched the incident on CCTV and told me to "Deal with him." I took him into a room and we sat down. We looked at the reasons behind the incident and how he could move forward. He didn't want to be in the classroom but he knew his education was important. The teacher had told him off but he acknowledged he could have spoken more politely and agreed to apologise to her.

We talked about what had happened. The other student had been staring at him, making grunting noises. I explained that this student hated being in the classroom too, he had anxiety and special needs. He told me he had tried to ignore him and then he had told him to stop. The teacher told him off, the other student had laughed at him getting into trouble. He had stood up in frustration and received two punches in the head. He hadn't hit him back and felt such a coward. There are times when humans can't take anymore, he had hit rock bottom, he wanted love, acceptance and praise and all he was getting was rejection, complaints and punishment.

I understood how he felt and practiced a NLP technique on him to help guide him. He looked me in the eye as I spoke and he exhaled with relief. He had tears in his eyes as I reassured him that I was there to support him, he wasn't alone and that things were going to get better. My manager was watching us on CCTV, sensing progress she came in to intervene. She delivered a triple threat "This, Mr.xxx is my centre, I say who comes here. I don't tolerate anyone who thinks they are Mr. Big. Violence is not acceptable in my centre!" He looked at me, shook his head in disbelief and punched the door in frustration. As he walked out of the centre she told him if he returned she would call the police. He called me the next day to ask if he could come back to centre as he hadn't hit anyone. I had to say no because my manager thought he was a safety risk to all students and staff. I advised him to contact the Cannock centre as the staff were more welcoming there. She reminded me of my evil step mother, with her insensitive approach to traumatised children, and her need to have control.

Of course she didn't want the centre to be a place of excellence. She wanted as few learners as possible and constantly reminded me this wasn't 'Bilston'. She had total control and refused to delegate any responsibility to me, other than making her a coffee. I reluctantly did what she wanted and then she ridiculed me for poor performance. "You're a recruitment officer, why are you on a management course?"

she said as she tried to make me feel worthless, discouraging my personal development. I was returning home every day saying "Do you know what she said today?" Dan had heard so much in such a short time that he said "She is a bully, smack her in the face!"

I was set up to fail in a perfectly calculated way. I had never known a predatory person like her in the workplace. I rode her bulling wave, I wasn't frightened of her but she under-minded me, humiliated me and criticised me in front of my new silent work colleagues. I felt isolated. I hadn't documented anything of what she had said or done over the six months I worked with her. I had no evidence but her treatment started to seriously impact on my health. I would go home trying to forget her and she would be a topic of our conversation. I couldn't sleep. I dreaded going to work and she literally made my blood boil and my skin crawl. The palms of my hands were itching and blistering, she thought I had some sort of contagious disease and warned me not to contaminate the office.

I went to see my doctor about the blisters that were appearing on my hands. For the first time in my life, I broke down in tears as I told the doctor how I was feeling. She said my symptoms were all stress related and caused by my manager, the corporate psychopath. She advised I speak to HR and signed me off on the sick. I discovered I wasn't her first victim, there had been several before me and that's why my colleagues had advised me not to apply for the position. I took another relaxing holiday to Gozo, with Dan and Robbie. It was almost a week before I was sleeping normally and my hands had stopped itching. HR called and offered me a teaching role back in Cannock. I did not have to work under her 'management again'. My colleagues encouraged me to put in a complaint but like most victims I didn't have the energy and as she manipulated those at the top, I feared they wouldn't believe me.

I had a gradual return to work, there was no pressure at the Cannock centre and Sue, my manager was very supportive. She tried her best to boost my self esteem. She said my 'first impressions' lesson was the best she had ever seen and I was a dammed good teacher. I helped out with the planning for the new curriculum but I still felt broken. I didn't feel strong enough to return to teaching. Sue begged me to stay when I handed in my notice. Everything happens for a reason and I thank the corporate psychopath for breaking me. It was down to her management style that I had revisited Gozo and realised that life was really about living not working. My life was going to change.

I had plans in my mind. Firstly, I needed to sit in the sun and recuperate. I had started to write this book ten years ago and needed the time and emotional strength to complete it. I also needed to follow my dream and set up a charity for children who were bereaved by domestic homicide. CICA had finally changed the 'under the same roof rule' so I was now entitled to apply for compensation. With this money, I could afford to set up a service, work for myself and run things my way to improve children's lives. I definitely wouldn't be employing psychopaths, or bullies, only genuine passionate people that know how to bring about positive change for vulnerable and traumatised children. Realistically, I still needed a little job to pay my way. Dan's brother in law said I would easily get temporary work and he offered Dan a salaried position working alongside him, in his bike hire business. Dan loved working on motorbikes, so we were certain the move would be the best idea for both of us.

I wasn't worried about leaving behind our children, they were all happy and settled in their lives. Even Ray had established a long term relationship and moved in with Donna and her two children. I was told some sad news that his ex-partner had been found dead. I wondered how my niece, Amber would cope without her mother. Her death reminded me that life was short and precious, we had to follow the right path to make the most of it. I knew we could stay in touch with everyone with Facebook and WhatsApp and with free holidays for the family on offer our decision was fully supported. We had our home to return to if things didn't work out. It was worth taking a risk on living the dream.

The week before we left Ange called and said that Dan's job working with her husband wasn't going to happen, his partner hadn't yet left the business and it was a 'difficult' situation. She said he could do some construction work with a friend instead. Dan was a little disappointed but as long as he had work, it wasn't going to be an issue.

I planned a road trip to last two weeks. I found the quickest and cheapest routes, having different places to visit and stay every day. We bought a box trailer to pack up our belongings and we equipped the campervan with everything we needed. We even had a bottle of champagne for our wedding anniversary. I wanted our trip to Gozo to be a relaxing holiday and a memorable journey.

Chapter 20
Road Trip

After much stress, faff and hassle we were almost ready to leave. Dan was anxious and impatient, so I took the damp washing from the tumble dryer, put them in a long life bag and placed them in the box trailer with the rest of our belongings. We drove round the corner onto the high street. I looked in the wing mirror and watched a wheel trim from the trailer bounce it's way to freedom. I started laughing and wanted to go back and retrieve it, Dan refused to stop and continued to drive regardless. We made a quick visit to Dan's mom and dad, said our goodbyes and set off for Portsmouth. Google claimed the drive would take three hours so we had plenty of time to stop off at a shopping complex before reaching the port. However, Dan drove straight past the junction, resisting the opportunity to buy his necessities. I laughed again "Please relax Dan, there is no rush, just enjoy this experience" I said.

We arrived at the port, embarked without a search and went straight to the cafe as we were both famished. After our meal we found a windy deck to have a cigarette and waved goodbye to the grey skies of England. We looked for our reclining seats, numbers 8101 and 8102, we passed hundreds of empty seats laughing in confusion. When we realised the numbers were on the front of the seats, not the backs, we gave up and headed for the bar.

Dan ordered a couple of drinks and was impressed with the prices, in comparison with the Colliers, which was one of the most expensive pubs in our village. We sat down and listened to two young girls on the stage trying to sing, I would have left the room but Dan said a comedian was on next, so I was happy to stay. The next act was actually a magician. He was OK, the usual magic tricks, nothing special but he was a little funny. He sang a cheesy song to Dan, asking him to guess what was in his sandwich. Dan said it was 'bacon', it turned out to be chicken so his trick didn't work. The entertainment was so atrocious we couldn't help but laugh.

The next act was the headliner, who reminded me of Nathan's girlfriend Sammi. Her facial expressions and her hair was so similar it was uncanny. The show then finished, there was no comedian but by this time, we had found a smoking deck and had a few alcoholic drinks so the evening didn't seem so bad after all. We went to find our reclining seats but the place was deserted and in darkness so we just sat on the front two seats. I woke up every couple of hours, cold and uncomfortable wishing I hadn't listened to a friends advice about not booking a cabin.

As soon as the breakfast bar opened, I bought hot coffee and croissants, trying to thaw out. We left the ferry and set off from St. Malo to Mouzillon. We stopped at an aire and I hung the wet washing over the bungee straps to dry inside the trailer. We picked up some Mouzillon biscuits and a kind of tortilla type of quiche and headed for the Roche's establishment. Madame Roche welcomed us to her beautiful vineyard and invited us for wine tasting that evening. We had a look around and then sat in the van to eat our food. Having not stopped to buy beer, Dan drank my vodka and the bottle of Champagne and was asleep by 3.30pm. I sat updating my road trip diary. Madame Roche spoke very little English. She thought Dan worked for the Bureau, we thought that sounded impressive so we left it that way. She gave us food and we sampled lots of her wine. We purchased four bottles of our favourite and had drank two of them before bedtime.

We showered in the morning and skipped breakfast because Dan had packed the can opener 'somewhere in the trailer' and I wasn't going to get everything out to find it. We said our goodbyes to Madame Roche and set off for a goat farm in Eslonnes. Dominic, the proprietor was hard to track down and when we finally found him, he asked us to come back in three hours, when the farm would be open. We didn't want to hang around so we set off for Jean-Fredericks goat farm instead. On route we found a supermarket and stocked up with Dan's necessities. We realised that our left rear indicator wasn't working on the trailer. Dan was passed caring, he had investigated the problem, the bulb was working. He reassured me we would be ok as most of the turnings seemed to be to the right!

We had a tour around the farm. There were hundreds of female goats, in separate pens, being fed by a robotic feeder. They all seemed at home, happy and friendly, apart from the three bucks. I guessed they were concerned all their male friends had been sacrificed for penile dysfunction. There is no joy in being a minority, segregated, sexually exploited and outnumbered by the opposite sex. I bought, goat liver, goat cheese and goat soap. I had to buy the soap just to compare it with my usual 'Dove' soap. I also bought a bottle of red wine, which I do say, I liked very much. We made friends with the farm cat and hundreds of flies decided to join us in our camper as I cooked dinner. Dan was convinced they would be gone by the morning so we put our heads under the covers and got an early night.

I had a weird dream, I was back in Cheslyn Hay, driving a red soft top car. My Gramps had indoctrinated me with his superstitions and told me, red cars were dangerous. I landed it into someone's front garden and was concerned I would lose my license and couldn't go on my trip to Gozo. I wondered where our campervan was and realised I was dreaming. I guessed my subconscious was telling me to be careful with the red wine and not to drink and drive, obviously.

I went back to sleep and had another dream, this one was more bizarre. We were all on the Star field, where everyone went for carnivals. Dan had passed out and the young people around him were laughing because he had taken a 'lucky E'. I spent time addressing each and everyone of them, lecturing them about the risks of taking drugs and how they could kill you. I turned around and Dan had gone. His old time friend, Stoney told me to go after him.

I searched for hours and ended up in a pub, in Cannock, I couldn't find Dan and had lost my phone. Bindia, a work colleague from Nova Training, called me on my key fob and said she had a call for me from Stoney. She put me through to him and he explained to me that Dan had left me because I always wanted too much, the best of everything, the most expensive, I just couldn't make do. He went on to tell me I was dressed in my 'slims'. I looked down and noticed I was wearing my Pyjamas. I realised, I was an old lady with dementia, Stoney had become my guardian and he was jealous, I was still looking for the love of my life. I woke up pleased to see Dan's face. I decided to keep my eye on Dan's medication and not to expect too much from him.

The next morning we were woken by 'The Hounds of the Baskervilles' barking from a pound near by. The van was still full of flies so we skipped breakfast again. Dan checked the wires to the trailer and fixed the indicator much to my relief. He didn't fancy trying to back out from where we had parked so he drove slowly and carefully, down a narrow muddy and bumpy lane instead, eventually we made it back to 'The Hounds of the Baskervilles' and got onto the main road, the indicator by this time, had again stopped working. I spent the next two hours swatting flies with no sign of the mission completing. We laughed, they were obviously emigrating with us.

I visited my first hole in the floor at the next aire. Dan decided to wait for a more familiar looking toilet. He thought if we left the doors and windows open on the van, the flies would leave of their own accord, whilst we stood outside, stretching our legs. Dan was impressed with an outdoor washing machine facility that was next to the car wash. I suggested he took the trailer over and washed all the farm muck off, which was splattered all up the sides. Dan looked anxious, it was out of his comfort zone. "No, it's French" he said. I didn't make a fuss.

We stopped and bought more supplies, which now included a can opener and a can of Raid. After fumigating the van, we continued our fly free journey to Nadine's and George's fruit farm in Correze. We camped in their chestnut orchard and I was in my element foraging. Dan didn't fancy doing the wonderful 5K walk around their lake, the other campers were more enthusiastic. I sat with Dan basking in the hot sun waiting for the farm shop to open instead. I bought some home made jam and liqueurs. Nadine gave us a bag of apples and invited us for morning coffee when we heard her bell toll. We played boules with the exhausted campers when they returned. They found us quite amusing. We had no idea of the rules but enjoyed the competition. The raspberry liqueur went beautifully with some white wine and saw us off to bed.

The next morning I went for a shower and found there was no lock on the door. With so many people on site, I opted to wash my hair, face and armpits instead of risking being seen naked. Nadine rang her bell and we all assembled in the back of the shop around a large table. It was all very French, with a kiss on both cheeks and a 'bonjour' from everyone, an overwhelming but welcoming experience. Nadine passed around sponge cake and asked us if we wanted some homemade liqueur adding to our coffee, we were sensible but most of the others indulged. We had no idea what everyone was chatting about but it was a very civilised start to the day. We said our goodbyes and continued on our journey.

The weather had turned from overcast, to a misty rain as we travelled through Montvalent, which had to be the best scenery on our route. There were so many stone walls and cottages, it seemed similar to Wales but on a much grander scale. We laughed as we went into 'Pouppoup Road' but then we ended up on a single track road going up and down a mountain through the clouds, with ninety degree bends, visible only by our satellite navigation. Dan began to get extremely stressed with the driving conditions.

The Aubrac mountains in Aveyon were renamed "The Ball Ache" mountains by my husband who spent his time swearing and complaining at the slow progress we made on a rainy washout day. We finally arrived at the duck farm, there wasn't a duck in sight, the place was deserted. We continued our journey and parked up at a nice beauty spot. Aveyon is a walkers paradise but Dan didn't want to walk in the rain. We sat in the van eating snacks, soup and wine and camped down for the night. Dan's brother in law woke us with a call from Gozo. He said his marriage was over, he was crying. We knew they had a volatile relationship and we assumed they had just fallen out.

We were minding our own business, continuing our journey, when the police pulled us over into a lay-by. We were in a strange country and although we were doing nothing wrong, we were both petrified. We sat nervously waiting to be arrested. Around 8 police motorcyclists and several police cars surrounded a black stretched limousine and passed us by. They were obviously escorting someone very important. As we passed through Figeac there were security people everywhere. "That will be me, one day, filthy rich and looked after" I said. Dan laughed in hysterics, we were a million miles away from such a privileged lifestyle.

Dan started driving up another mountain. He complained this one was worse as it was a clearer day and he could see how high we were, 850 metre's above sea level and just a metre away from a nice drop. "Just be careful Dan" I nervously said. We stopped at another aire and admired the views whilst Dan regained his composure. We weren't far away from Domaine Jordy, our next vineyard in Montpelier.

Frederic Jordy's landscape was truly beautiful, we parked on some hard standing. Dan popped the roof on the van and we sat out in the sun. He started to get a bit anxious, he was about to run out of beer and had hardly any cigarettes. I tried to calm him down, we could have survived until the next day, with the alcohol we had and my nicotine lozenges. He looked over at the terraces and then noticed a church and a graveyard next door. "I don't fancy sleeping next to them tonight" he nervously said. He made me laugh, my protector was scared of the dead. "They're at peace, this is a perfect peaceful place, let's just soak it up" I said.

He continued to moan and groan until I did a Google search to find the nearest shop and off we walked. We couldn't find the shop and Dan grumbled all the way back to the van. "How do people survive, they can't just live on grapes!" he said. I asked him again to calm down and relax. "If you think I'm angry now, wait until I run out of fags!" he said. We knocked on Frederic's door and he came to our rescue. We went down into to his magnificent cellar and purchased twelve litres of red wine. After a couple of glasses and a classic pot noodle, Dan started to appreciate just what he had, plenty of snacks and plenty of good quality wine, ooh la la! By 4 pm he was fast asleep.

The next day Dan decided to take an easier right turn from the vineyard signposted 'cirque du vallies' it looked like a tourist sign. In hind sight it was ideal for walkers. The dirt track got as wide as the trailer and the verges dropped into a stream. It was impossible to turn around. We continued with visions of losing the trailer. We passed a man holding a shot gun, he gave us an evil eye. I didn't want to be his next shot of the day. "Just keep driving" I urged Dan. He was probably confused as to why we were suspiciously driving round a footpath in a van, towing a trailer but we weren't taking any chances. We had travelled for about two miles in two hours before we eventually got back onto the road. We shared the last cigarette and laughed as we drove passed Domaine Jordy vineyard again.

Dan pulled up outside a supermarket in Montpellier. I bought some bread and beer and returned to the van. I went on the hunt for a tobacconist. "Ou est le tabac, s'il vous plait?" I asked everyone, each one, headed me off in different directions. I couldn't find a tobacconists anywhere. I started to head back to the van but I couldn't remember my way. I didn't have my phone on me so I couldn't even ring Dan or do a Google map search. I'd always liked the song 'Lost in France' but this was no joke. I was terrified and nearly brought to tears by the situation when I spotted a car sales I had passed and managed to figure my way back. I was so glad to see our muddy trailer was still there. I had been lost for around an hour. Dan told me off for not having my phone, asked if I had bought cigarettes and said "Come on let's get out of here."

We pulled onto the next petrol station and I bought five packets of cigarettes to keep us going. The ride to Saintes-Maries-de-la-Mer was much better but both of us were recovering from shattered nerves. We walked around the grounds of Manade des Baumelles, admiring the cowboys white horses and their black bulls, bred for a nice steak and the odd traditional bull fight expedition. We watched a coach party of people taking tours on the back of tractor trailers. We looked in at the restaurant, it was packed. We decided to return for a meal after everyone had left, both of us keen to sample their steak. The restaurant closed after the coach party left. We cosied up in the campervan with snacks and wine and had another early night.

I wished Dan a happy wedding anniversary the next day. My mobile data had run out so we stopped off at a McDonalds to contact our family and update my status on social media. We arrived at the Domaine des la Tullieres and were interested to see their varied glamping choices, wigwams, a converted bus, a transparent igloo, a boat and other luxury chambre's to stay in. It really was a unique place. We asked to book a table for a nice romantic meal to celebrate our anniversary but the restaurant was closed and only operated for booked parties. So we took a walk into the nearest town, had a few beers, bought more cigarettes and returned to the van for a ham sandwich. I finished off the goats cheese that Dan had lost the love for.

Dan chatted to his mom and his brother on the phone. I thought about Amber attending her moms funeral and how she would be feeling. I sent her a message and spoke to Holly who had been with her at the funeral. It was sad day for them. I was a million miles away from reality. I had escaped but it was still difficult to get to sleep. I could hear a young fox cub calling out for it's mother. Perhaps his mother had been killed and he was all alone in the world. Mother's are so important to us all, I thought.

We were both in need of a shower so we decided not to visit the tulip farm and book a night on a campsite. After missing the entrance four times, we finally pulled on to the site and parked up at the reception. We were told the facilities were closed and then spent a stressful half hour trying to leave the carpark without hitting a tree, a kerb or a gate post. It was a nightmare trying to manoeuvre a van and a trailer back onto the road. We stopped off at an Aldi store and stocked up on supplies. We sat in the van eating an ice cream watching three people emptying the commercial bins, they filled two cars with fruit and veg that all looked fresh. It's crazy what supermarkets throw away.

We parked at an aire and had a warm baguette and paid for showers. Dan was intoxicated by late afternoon and settled down to sleep it off. I sat in the passenger seat reading my book for hours. A lorry driver pulled alongside me and continually blasted his horn. The driver didn't speak English and I had no idea what his issue was. Another truck driver pulled up behind him and came over to explain, we had parked in a bay for lorries, the overnight parking was further down. The noise disturbed Dan's sleep, he woke wanting to fight every lorry driver on the planet. I was so embarrassed.

Dan drove a few metres to the overnight parking bay for campervans. He parked behind a lorry and started ranting at the innocent lorry driver for parking in a campervan bay. Then he went "to sort out the bullies who think they are big, just because they have a big truck and a horn." I closed my eyes, thinking there was going to be a mass brawl, the police would arrest Dan and lock him up and we had a ferry to catch the next day. He returned still irate and went straight back to sleep. I continued to read my book for another couple of hours.

The next day we sat in the van watching around fifty single men walking down a particular track into the woods and returning ten minutes later. It must have been some sort of alfresco rendezvous for gay sex. One lad took the path three times and we suspected he was for rent. Another man turned up in a kinky cowboy outfit. Midway through our observations we noticed a female dressed in ranger attire, attacking a new arrival with a baseball bat. Dan visited the toilet and then this woman started on him, thinking he too was part of the troupe. She was ok when she realised we were English and together. She told us they were having "interactions behind the trees". I gave her the thumbs up and she smiled. She was a woman on a mission.

We caught the ferry from Toulon and said goodbye to our tour de France. Dan managed to watch half of a football match before someone switched the TV off. I asked him not to start a fight. I slept on the floor for a few hours here and there. We had breakfast and sat out on the decks. It was a beautiful sunny day at sea, the crew shut off the sunny side of the ferry so they could enjoy the rays and clean the decks for hours. We were supposed to dock in Sicily at 1pm but frustratingly, the hours passed by and Sicily was nowhere in sight. The receptionist said it was "due to traffic on the motorway" she was either on drugs or something was lost in translation, we disembarked at 5.30pm.

Again we were desperate for nicotine and every shop we visited refused to take card, eventually we found one and bought six packets. Sicily was all hustle and bustle and it was getting dark. We parked up in a rundown area where there was plenty of traffic. We were both hungry but felt nervous about walking back down the road to a Mc.Donald's and finding our van and trailer gone on our return. It was a hot night in the van, we ate what we had and the mosquitoes ate me.

I used Google maps to take us to the nearest ATM the next day, it was out of order so we waited for the bank to open at a cafe across the road. I noticed a security guy with a gun guarding the bank. There were three people in the queue before me so I observed the security procedure to individually gain access via a camera snapping your mugshot. This wasn't a bank you could easily rob, I thought. Unlike UK banks where we foolishly stand in a queue, I took a seat and waited my turn, the bank teller said he couldn't give me cash, I would need to return in the afternoon, when the cash machine had money. I had wasted my time but I had enjoyed a pleasant cultural banking experience.

We received a warm welcome at Sanfilippo campsite. It was immaculate, there was a private sandy beach, showers, a shop and a bar but they too didn't accept card payments. We caught a bus into Cefalu and got some cash and cigarettes and looked around the beautiful town, it was stunning. We devoured a Sicilian meat feast meal at a beach restaurant, the first real meal we had eaten on our road trip.

After a restful sleep, I asked Dan to call at the shop and see if there was any fresh bread or croissants. He returned empty handed but said they had some. What is it with men? I went to the shop and asked the assistant what flavour filling was the "mtea" croissant, thinking it was something Sicilian. He couldn't really explain so I got a cream one for myself and an "mtea" one for Dan to try. I thought it was hilarious when he moaned there was no filling in his croissant it was 'empty' I suggested he add some homemade jam, he just tucked in with a hard done by face, that was karma!

We sat on the beach sun bathing and making pebble towers all day. A metal detectorist with a snorkel searched under the sea for treasure. Dan had his metal detector in the trailer. He said he had an idea, it was a secret but it could make us millions. I had seen a similar episode on 'Only Fools and Horses'. We enjoyed a couple of days staying put, relaxing. When it was time to leave, we needed two other campers to help us get the trailer out of our pitch. We set off for Catania way too early and pulled up outside a block of flats, a few minutes drive from the docks.

A smart looking man was talking to us in Sicilian from the pavement and then he came round to my side of the van. I hadn't got a clue what he was saying but thought it was something to do with pulling out away from the bins in front of us. He waved the traffic in front of us and put his hand up telling us to wait. He opened my door and tried to snatch my bag, that was between my legs in the footwell. I held onto my bag with my legs and he pulled so hard, the handle came off the bag and he fell backwards into the road and ran off. Dan chased him down the street. He came back to check I was OK. I was in shock but the robber had got away with nothing.

We waited by the docks for the ferry. The ferry office was closed and a random man appeared and said there was a shuttle bus coming to take us to check in. I was confused, still recovering from an attempted mugging, Dan said he would remain with the van and trailer so no one could steal them, whilst I got in an old car with four strangers to check in. I was anxious and suspected I was possibly being kidnapped. I was relieved to get back to him and get on the ferry. I couldn't help counting the people on board, there were more staff than paying customers. Around ten of us ate the evening meal, which was cold meat balls, beans and chips.

We got to Malta just after midnight and wanting to be in familiar surroundings, we continued our journey to Gozo. We arrived in Marsalforn at two in the morning to find another dodgy looking man hanging around the car park. Dan stayed awake all night and saw him five times, convinced he was up to no good. The next day we emptied all our belongings out of the trailer and stored them in a room at the back of Jacks bar.

We had met some lovely people on our road trip, drank plenty of wonderful wine and seen the beauty of France and Sicily. We had also experienced new firsts; being pulled over by the police; being separated and lost; surviving an armed psychopath; an attempted mugging and a dodgy man of the night. We had shared these wonderful experiences with a swarm of flies, driven in stressful conditions towing a large trailer and rested at a rendezvous for gay men, and those with big trucks and horns, yes it was a very memorable journey we could never forget.

Chapter 21
Living the Dream

I sent off my application to the Criminal Injuries Compensation Scheme (CICA) and advised my brother to do the same. I began working on the deli counter in the local supermarket. I had no intentions of staying there long, it was just to keep my mind active, I was living in a new country so I had plenty to learn. My employer was a small flirtatious man, who had a case of strabismus, bless him. I tried my best to ignore his disability but I was never quite sure if he was talking to me or someone else. The windows to his soul were not aligned. His cost cutting practices were also inefficient. To flush the toilet I had to use a bucket of water, the hand basin behind the deli counter was just for show and the fresh meat arrived frozen so the fridges would overheat and constantly leak.

There was a change of plan for Dan, he proudly became the bar manager at Jacks bar. My brother-in-law was keen to make alternative arrangements, whilst I was at work. In return for Dan's labour, we were offered free food and lodging. This was difficult to back out of, without causing offence, Ange thought this was helping us. We hadn't crossed two oceans to live in someone's spare room, we needed our own space. Dan was happy to support his sister and enjoyed running the bar. He felt part of the family business but he had no financial reward for his efforts and his self worth soon disintegrated. It was 'difficult' because my earnings barely covered our expenses but lying on a beach in the Mediterranean, still felt like I was living the dream.

My job on the deli, enabled me to learn about the Maltese culture and observe people's shopping habits, baskets filled with sun dried tomatoes, olives, white vinegar and cake baking ingredients. I noticed the men appeared to have control of the finances and many of them did the shopping. It felt like I was in a time warp, back in the 1970's, when I was a carefree child. I finished work at 1pm and would walk home in the sun with my goats cheese and stuffed olives, smiling uncontrollably, at the simple, happy life I had. I absolutely loved it.

I asked my employer for a job contract because I wanted to pay tax and national insurance and have holiday entitlement, like everyone else. I also needed a contract to obtain my Maltese ID card so I could open a bank account, insure a car and get health care. He knew I needed a contract but I was an immigrant and all he gave me was excuses. My landlady told me, to be careful with him. He was paying me less than a legal wage and he was known on the island for 'liking the girls'. I applied for numerous jobs and finally got an interview for a refuge worker position in Malta.

I set off the day before, catching a ferry and a taxi to a nice seafront hotel in Sliema. There was lots of hustle and bustle as I ventured out alone and looked for somewhere to eat. I found a wonderful restaurant and relaxed. The next morning I booked a taxi to take me to my interview. The taxi driver dropped me off at a garage door, took my money and left. It took me half an hour to find the correct location.

The interview seemed to go well. I told them that my mother had been killed and I had a genuine passion to help victims of domestic abuse and save lives. It's always difficult to assess whether this fact will totally ruin your chances of employment. Being the daughter of a murderer isn't a protected characteristic and the prejudice is rife. I discussed my previous roles and responsibilities working in the field. I was asked how I would manage to communicate with people who didn't speak English and why I wanted to work with victims in a refuge when the salary was so low. They also thought the travel to work was too far. None of these were an issue for me, I could use a translator, the salary was much higher than I was being paid at the supermarket and I was happy to travel to help victims of domestic violence.

They decided to offer me a casual position, I didn't care, I had my foot in the door. This English woman from Gozo, had a chance to work in the field of domestic violence once more. They would soon realise how dedicated I am to saving lives, I thought. I continued to work on the delicatessen knowing I would soon be moving on to make a difference to victims of domestic abuse in Malta. I wanted to know everyone who worked in the field, before I established my own charity.

Accompanied with my friend, Kay, I travelled to Malta again for an event hosted by the Soroptimists. We were all wearing orange scarves as part of the 16 days of activism to eliminate violence against women. There was a screening of the film 'Sold' which was based on a true story of a girl from a rural village in Nepal who was sold by her family and taken to a grotty brothel in Kolkata called 'Happiness House'. The film evidenced the horrific brutality of sex trafficking. There followed a panel discussion on related issues which highlighted the need to build resilience amongst young women. It was an enjoyable evening being surrounded by like minded people.

Covid-19 struck, things at the refuge were 'put on hold' and I began working seven days a week, stocking shelves as the locals panicked and rushed to buy supplies for lockdown. I was on my feet so much at work, I developed plantar fasciitis which caused intense pain but as the only wage earner, I had to continue working. I built a good relationship with Mary, my manager, and we felt proud to be doing our bit, as a valued, essential workers. We were stifled in the heat, struggling to breath wearing masks but together we kept the shop well stocked, immaculate and germ free. Our customers were anxious about the pandemic, some were in tears, talking about lockdown loneliness. I would give them support and try to ease their fears.

My employer was impressed to see my posts on Facebook reassuring local people our shop was clean, Covid safe and well stocked. He knew I supported his business but he still wouldn't give me a job contract. I contacted the refuge, several times, aware that domestic violence cases were increasing but I heard nothing back. Perhaps they didn't want to work with the 'murderers daughter' after all, or was it because I was English? I felt worthless. Dan was no longer needed in Jacks Bar and because the tourist industry had been impacted by Covid it was difficult for either of us to find another job.

I was asked to train the new staff, my boss thought I was 'good at my job', bless him, it wasn't really rocket science. My teaching experience came in handy. The new staff would stay with me for a few days and then move to another one of his supermarkets. My feet were killing during one eight hour shift and I sat outside to have a cigarette, whilst the shop was quiet. My employer opened the door and looked down at me as I stretched my poor painful feet. I reassured him I was just having a quick cigarette, he said nothing and walked away. He didn't have an issue with me smoking but he did have an issue that I was sat down. What a slave driver this man was, no contract, no holiday, and no breaks.

A couple of weeks later I heard, his wife had found out he was having an affair with one of the young cashiers. I wasn't surprised to hear this. He had always been cheerful and a little flirtatious towards me but suddenly, he switched and became quite rude and arrogant. He sent me a text, saying he had to let me go as I was "too slow" for his business. I forwarded the message to my manager, we were both stunned, after seven months of being 'good at my job', I had been sacked.

Perhaps he had seen my Facebook posts about exploitation and violence against women, I know perpetrators hate that stuff. Or maybe he thought I was the one that had told his wife about his deception. I text him back "You're crazy for saying I'm slow, not sure what your issue is but you should speak to people face to face". My job was given to a young attractive single mom, she was Maltese and I had just trained her. I had been used, abused and dropped by yet another exploitive man. I was furious and although I tried my best to find another job, not speaking Maltese was a barrier and my qualifications weren't recognised. So, to survive, I rolled my sleeves up and found some cleaning jobs.

Forty years had passed by when CICA made their award for compensation. Finally society had recognised me as a victim of crime. HMRC didn't have the evidence that my Mom had worked back in 1978 so I had no entitlement for my financial dependency on her as a child. Neither was I entitled to compensation for the impact on my health as I hadn't used anti depressants to mask my pain, or received years of counselling to try to fix something that could never be fixed. I had researched my way through PTSD and that could not be counted as evidence. Dr Peter Levine said 'Trauma is perhaps the most avoided, ignored, belittled, denied, untreated, and misunderstood cause of human suffering.' CICA needed medical evidence to understand the impact this crime had on my life. I was still grateful for their basic offer of compensation.

Ray, on the other hand, had all the medical evidence, he had been given anti depressants in prison and had counselling, neither had been of any use to him but it meant he was entitled to significantly more than the basic offer as he could prove he had PTSD. His childhood trauma had been ignored, in a world that didn't care about his long term outcomes. Like many others effected by uxoricide, he had developed a drug addiction and had sold them to feed his habit because he couldn't hold down a job. He'd paid the price and ironically served double the sentence than my father had served for killing our mother. CICA punished him again, and told him he wasn't entitled to any compensation because he had served a sentence. His unresolved trauma continues to reverberate long after the original offence.

During the epidemic domestic violence continued to rise, along with child abuse, suicide, poverty and unemployment. People were depressed, traumatised by loss and fear. Doctors were giving advice on how to improve people's mental health and reduce the feelings of isolation. I was no longer alone, as I witnessed society go into PTSD meltdown. The tourist industry terminated, along with my cleaning jobs. CICA, became my Coping In Covid Award, with hardly any other income, the compensation was slowly dwindling away with my hopes to set up the charity. I found a virtual friend 'Stock Moe' and did some due diligence. The richest man on the planet said "People should be nicer to each other, it wouldn't hurt to have more love in the world". Elon Musk was a man with morals, someone who valued human life, so I invested a small amount in Tesla as part of a diversified portfolio.

I had never invested money before and I watched the money grow each day and then plummet. I felt my time on earth was never going to be a rich experience. There would always be winners and losers. I tried my best to be positive. I then received a call to say my Aunt June was in hospital, she had cancer. I reflected on our last conversation, just like my Nan, it had been all about my father. She had never known what my life had been like. I'd never burdened her with my troubles, I had always turned up smiling and from her perspective she had resented that.

There were no flights back to England because of the Covid restrictions so I couldn't visit her one last time. I messaged my Aunt Linda, I wanted her to know that I still loved her. She never responded. June passed away the next day. I sent my condolences to my cousins. I wrote a poem in her memory and Holly offered to read it on my behalf if she had an invite to her funeral.

My Aunt June

I remember my Aunt, sat on our settee, putting on lipstick, as happy as can be
She would paint her nails a flashy pink and ask me "Diane, what do you think?"
My carefree Aunt, was full of delight, dancing with Mom and staying the night
Her boyfriend was nice, his name was Rusty. He had ginger hair, his jokes were crusty
Then she got married, Wilf was his name. I was her bridesmaid but it wasn't the same
She moved to Telford and we lost touch. My Aunt June was missed so much

Shandy, her dog, was her only friend. Wilf had left her, that marriage did end
So back she came, sat on our settee, putting on lipstick, as happy as can be
My carefree Aunt, was full of delight, going out with Mom and staying the night
Sad times came, when she lost her sister, I tried to help but she really missed her
We would lie in bed and start to chat. We'd talk for hours about this and that
"There's a nice man at work" one night she said. She told me about him, as I lay in bed

She asked my advice "What do you think? He wants to take me out for a drink"
By this time I knew all about Mick. I hadn't met him, but I got to pick!
He made her laugh, she liked him so, I told her "Yes, you should go"
She put on her lipstick, she bleached her hair and wore her high heels without a care
Off she went on her first date. "How did it go?" She'd come home late
My carefree Aunt was full of delight, "Oh he's lovely" she'd had a good night

He brought her happiness, but I got to pick! The man she married, my uncle Mick
He made her laugh, he made her smile and I went out of her life, for a while
The next time I saw her, she had Suzanne. She was still happy, with her happy man
Along came Stephen, the family of four. That was enough, she didn't want more
We'd sit on her settee and have a chat. We'd talk for hours about this and that
Mick made her laugh, he made her smile and I was gone again for a while

Years passed by, I missed her so. I hoped she'd call to say hello
Or visit me to have a chat, to talk for hours about this and that
My carefree Aunt, I loved so dear, has left us now, or so I hear

An angel in heaven, on a fancy settee, putting on lipstick, as happy as can be,
She's painted her nails, she's bleached her hair and wearing high heels without a care
My carefree Aunt is full of delight, she's dancing with my Mom tonight
And let's not forget, she's pleased to see, my Nan and Gramps, and Shandy
She has no pain, she means no wrong, so don't be sad or cry for long
She is back with the man, I got to pick! She's smiling now, with uncle Mick

A few weeks later, I had spent an hour in solitude, sat on the beach looking at a beautiful blue sky. It was a day of nostalgia. I thought about my mother's funeral and felt her presence. Later that day, my cousin Scott, uploaded a video on Facebook of 'my family' releasing balloons, after my Aunt June's funeral. I sent a GIF with balloons as a tribute. My family hadn't told me and Holly and Nathan had not been invited.

I'd had my fair share of losses so I wanted to withdraw every penny as the stock markets continued to crash. Stock Moe assured everyone to ride the wave, this was the best time to invest so I bought more shares. I was still in the red. We went into a second Covid lockdown and I couldn't find any employment. I had a meeting with the CEO of an organisation that supported victims of domestic abuse in Malta, she was keen for me to expand the business and offer the service in Gozo. Nothing on the Maltese islands happened over night so I focused on my book and decided I would teach myself everything I needed to know to set up a charity for children bereaved by uxoricide.

My biological clock was on permanent standby and the day of the week became irrelevant. I had a mindful of thoughts and at times I was overwhelmed. Would my book sell, would it make any money? How can I fund raise for the set up costs? How do other charities operate? Should I be a CIC? The dilemmas and questions were endless and of course Google had all the answers, many had pros and cons and opposing opinions. It had taken months of research, working day and night, building up contacts and hosting zoom meetings. I finally had trustees on board, a draft strategy, policies and a constitution and yet there was still so much to do.

I had been up all night researching and I went to bed exhausted, with a head full of ideas. The next thing I knew I was on route to my subconscious, heading to a venue, I was late and I was the main speaker. I entered the dimly lit auditorium from a back door and looked down to see it was full of people, taking their seats. I headed for the stage which ironically was in a different room. I wasn't happy, how could I speak at such an important event, without the audience seeing me. The trustees, along with people I had never seen before were all sat, centre stage, around an oval table, with their laptops, paper and pens. I had forgotten to bring both and there was no room at the table for me.

I was handed a microphone and as I tested the sound, I walked back to the auditorium to begin my talk. There were five men, pouring water over the audience, the soaked women were standing and leaving in disgrace. The men dragged me away and took me to another room. Their intent was to use me as some form of brutal entertainment before they silenced me forever. They began to torture me. I managed to get to the door to escape. I took a step to freedom and felt the door hit my back. I was wedged between the doorframe and the door, unable to move, I screamed for help. I wasn't taken seriously by the first man that came to me, his female colleague could see I was suffering and she laughed. I woke up in tears. There were children out there in pain and I was "tortured" not being able to help them.

I continued to connect with professionals and build a network of people who I believed could give me the best advice and support. I organised a strategy meeting with stakeholders that highlighted their hopes that the service would cater for children bereaved by a domestic homicide or suicide in the context of domestic violence. I spoke to adults who had been bereaved in this way and current carers of children to help shape the service. The CEO's of notable organisations from the fields of domestic violence, restorative justice, bereavement support and child trauma services were very supportive. The NSPCC was keen to know about the charities future development and stated how they could support us once everything was in place. Victim Support has been the hardest organisation to get on board and is still work in progress. They already offer a service for all victims of crime. The head of services offered me support, bless her, that wasn't quite the support I had in mind.

I reflected on my findings and thoughts for the charity and what these children needed; at least one framed photograph of their loved one and a memory box of important items to connect them, their belongings, letters and cards from their old school friends and teachers so they could stay in contact, the opportunity to attend the funeral, someone unrelated to act as an advocate and a guide, spiritual religious support to suit, specialised complex needs counselling, training on healthy relationships, self belief and life-skills, someone to help organise compensation and look into their financial interests so they can invest for their future, positive past times, activities and holidays, a restorative justice approach to initially see their parent if they wanted to and if required prison visits explained, monitored and supervised, school mentors ensuring there are no cases of bullying, support with learning and achievements, healthy living advice to ensure they sleep and eat, and close to my heart, someone who would be there throughout their life to wish them happy birthday each year, motivate them, praise them and support their mental well-being during any difficult days or milestones.

During my research, I had tremendous respect for Dr. Bessel Van Der Volk. He understood me!! Bessel did his own research in a domestic violence clinic. After years of studying trauma he said the people who were the most hurt and the hardest to treat were the people who were getting traumatised at home. And whilst I have done my best to educate others, I had always come across people who thought children were all different, some were fine and some just needed counselling. This naivety is a public health issue. Bessel claims this type of trauma is more expensive than heart disease or cancer. As many children are bereaved by uxoricide as children suffering from Leukaemia but there is very little research and no specialist support. The consequences of this childhood trauma has more long term consequences than any medical disease. Adverse Childhood Experiences (ACE's) are only just starting to be acknowledged.

There is physical evidence, for these traumatised children, brain scans have proven this. When you get really traumatised as a child, your frontal lobe shuts down, you can see on a brain scan that is has completely disappeared. This is the part of your brain that concerns your Self, controls your working memory, helps you concentrate, make good judgements and is responsible for movement, social and sexual behaviours. When your frontal lobe shuts down, you are left in a state of confusion. Another part of the brain instead gets activated, it's where trauma lives and secretes stress hormones. It's known as the sympathetic nervous system, it's basically our animal brain.

With PTSD the trauma keeps reactivating. It's in constant protection mode, on hyper alert ready for the next traumatic battle. Your body goes into flight, fight, or freeze. The only thing that seems to work is to do sympathetic nervous system therapy to calm the animal brain down. When I think about my good times singing in the choir, playing a musical instrument, relaxing in the sauna, swimming, country walks, treasure hunting on the beach, dancing, yoga, role plays, all these activities have calmed my animal brain and helped me to live with PTSD.

To feel safe, the traumatised brain needs to learn how to relax, so activities like yoga, allow you to relax and allow you to breathe normally. Acting helps you to feel what it's like to be powerful. As I left the house for work, I went into work mode, I was acting, be it professionally, but work helped me to survive. My child sympathetic nervous system said 'I'm confused, this is all my fault, I am a bad person and don't deserve love'. Therapists may try to intervene with traumatised children but nothing changes because the brain cannot rest or relax to reactivate the frontal lobe, the Self. You are left in a land of confusion on hyper alert, hence so many traumatised children become addicted to anything that helps them escape, be it drugs, alcohol, bingo, gambling or gaming.

Instead, what Bessel recommends therapist should do is focus on movement or balance therapies to induce calm. Clarity, I call it, when you are not confused, you know who you are and what to do. Some therapists, who are brave enough to take on a child bereaved by domestic homicide sadly add to their confusion. They might have qualified as a therapist, but they still need to learn what works for their patients. Therapists can't treat childhood PTSD, they can work with the child to help them heal and find their safe place. You see, I was on my way home, to that place of safety. My parents had, to best of their ability, protected me and kept me safe, it was my place of safety that I lost. Yoga, swimming, walking, dancing and singing all gave me that safe feeling back.

Another aspect, which is vitally important is the social support the child receives. Mother Teresa once said, "We can cure physical diseases with medicine, but the only cure for loneliness, despair, and hopelessness is love. There are many in the world who are dying for a piece of bread, but there are many more dying for a little love." Friends, acquaintances, co-workers, relatives, spouses and companions can all provide a life enhancing social network. The issues with children bereaved by uxoricide, domestic homicide or suicide in the context of domestic abuse is that their social network can be in conflict with each other. They can be totally ostracised, left in the care system or moved between different carers. Children need emotional support that indirectly helps them during times of crisis and chronic stress. This charity shall connect children, support their carers and develop their social support.

Whilst things have changed for victims of crime, children are still believed to be resilient. My family had no-one to support them, GP's, Valium, Cigarettes, Alcohol, nothing cured them. I gave my grandparents a reason to get up for a whole year after my mother's murder. I continued to support them and my mothers sisters. My Barlow bond was eventually broken so I could look after myself. In their eyes, I had always been 'too young' to understand. They had suffered a traumatic death but they didn't understand the long term impact of living with domestic abuse, or what it felt like to be the daughter of a murderer, and they didn't live with a man and a step mom that couldn't offer security, love or support.

My father recently suffered a bereavement himself. His wife died and I sent my condolences. I hadn't spoken to him since the day he handed me the photograph albums. As a named executor of her will, he needed my permission for him and my step sister to access her ISA to pay for her funeral. It wasn't an issue and I gave my permission. In his grief, he apologised for not being a good father and for not showing us any love or affection throughout our lives. He might not be comfortable with me having a voice and publishing this book but he understands my mission and supports my efforts to "do the right thing" to improve the lives of other children bereaved by Uxoricide or domestic homicide or suicide in the context of domestic abuse.

Daddy was always the strongest, in my family. He hadn't been the best father a child could wish for but he did teach me how to make egg and chips and despite that not being a healthy meal, it is still one of my favourites. As his daughter, I forgave him in his time of crisis. It was an emotional byproduct, I didn't want him to end his life. I had always hoped he would make it up to me. I matured and despised his selfish nature and his flawed humanity. I protested and confronted him but my wounds wouldn't heal. He couldn't fix what he had broken without love and affection. I was left without any support and developed a codependency on unworthy people. I had high expectations and was let down time and time again. People I trusted and loved salted my wounds and left me with more scars.

However, in my attempts to make sense of my life and survive, I have learned so much. I do know how to relax and enjoy my life; how to teach others and how people learn; how to conduct risk and needs assessments; how to manage projects and measure outcomes. I have become an expert in trauma and domestic violence and the impact on children. I manage people's negative behaviours and know how to improve people's wellbeing. I am a leader and a manager who believes in valuing staff and their personal development. I am also fully aware of my weaknesses. I still have PTSD but I handle it and I handle the 'experts' that patronise me, with their ignorance and prejudice. Some people drive me crazy with their trivial complaints but I still listen and care. If it's not a life or death situation, I know they will survive. I'm not perfect and have lots to learn about the funding mechanisms for a global charity.

Setting up a charity on this scale is a challenge and it isn't for the faint hearted. I started my research into this subject, forty three years ago, by observing my families response to their trauma. I was too young to know about emotional transference, I supported them for as long as I could and that was a difficult challenge for any child to take on. I could have been their family liaison officer but I couldn't help them as much as I had wanted to at the time. Protectionism meant I wasn't privy to news articles, court cases, inheritance law, or even a funeral. I was unable to be the voice for my mother in the trial so that justice was served. Yes, I was too young, too young to know I had rights.

I received a private message about a domestic murder and a young person that needed my support. I didn't ignore it. We started exchanging messages. That person will always be special, she gave me my first referral and of course that young person will be special for the same reason. Regardless of how big CatchU gets, I will always cherish this young person. We just chit chat most days about anything other than that! She sometimes feels 'confused' and of course I know all about that feeling. These children need to know we are here to care, they are not being ignored anymore. CatchU will be their voice, just as Refuge, Mankind, Women's Aid, Stonewall and many other organisations speak on behalf of victims of domestic abuse.

On the15th of April, 1978, I may have lost my mother but she had left me holding a medal. It was something so special, only her love could have replaced. This was a medal for a mission, in memory of all the mothers and fathers who just wanted to be loved but lost their lives. The judge, jury and journalists need to know that 'crimes of passion' do not exist. It was a crime of 'heartless, brutal, selfishness' that left me on a non stop rollercoaster but I held on to that medal.

Whilst I walk along the beautiful coastlines of Gozo, I look like a typical tourist. I feel the sun on my back. I am fascinated by the preservation of time that surrounds me, the oldest freestanding buildings in the world, are on my doorstep. The imposing Ġgantija Neolithic temples, were a place our ancestors studied Sirius, the brightest star in the sky. I'm blessed everyday by Jesus who watches over me from Tas-Salvatur Hill. I look up to the blue sky, I hear the birds sing and watch the butterflies and bees find their favourite flowers. Timeless moments of presence, where my soul has found peace and happiness.

I am Diane Clarke, CEO and founder of CatchU, the Charity for Abused & Traumatised Children Handling Uxoricide, domestic homicide or suicide in the context of domestic abuse. We may not get any funding for years but the sales of this book will help to get things going. There will be more hoops to jump through before the children can come. They will take part in a life changing therapeutic programme, here in Gozo. They will gain wonderful memories and leave knowing CatchU will always be here for them for the rest of their lives.

This book is now complete. It's been painful and emotionally draining, to say the least. I would like to thank you for your purchase and helping us on our way. If you want to help CatchU complete it's mission and become a valued Patron, you are welcome to visit www.Patreon.com/SetupCatchU You can join for just £2 per month and in return you will have an insiders perspective and witness our transparent practices. You will be able to follow our progress and give us your opinions. Every Patron will help to put the sunshine back into these children's lives.

Too young to know

I thought that they were stronger than me, but now I'm not so sure
Spell bound with sadness and cups of tea, with 'grief' they cry some more.
The sun is shining, no-one can see, the curtains are full drawn.
I hear them say "she was so happy" in the years before I was born.

They had known her full of glee. They'll miss her, so they say
There's more tears, a pot of tea and they go on their way
A chance to play, nobody can see. "So dear mother of mine
are you in heaven, possibly? We'll be good, we won't whine."

I know she's gone and won't be back, unless I have a dream
She can tell me what they lack, what does 'grieving' mean?
A new life, what a relief, I'll look after my brother
My school friends have no grief, but now I have no mother.

So should I be sad, happy or glad? I really am confused.
I would like to say "I miss my Dad" will my rudeness be excused?
Thy kingdom come, thy will be done, hallowed be thy name.
I called your name you didn't come, things are still the same.

Murder and guilt, hidden so well. This hill to climb is steep.
A blanket of shame, I cannot tell, a secret I must keep
My voice has gone, I cannot sing, my life is standing still.
I have to deal with everything, oh Dad, what did you kill?

Diane Benton, 11 years old

Printed in Great Britain
by Amazon

66520031R00119